P9-CDF-356

Finding Water

BY JULIA CAMERON

Books in *The Artist's Way* Series

The Artist's Way
Walking in This World
Finding Water

Other Books on Creativity

The Right to Write
The Sound of Paper
The Vein of Gold
The Artist's Way Morning Pages Journal
The Artist's Date Book
(illustrated by Elizabeth Cameron)
How to Avoid Making Art (or Anything Else You Enjoy)
(illustrated by Elizabeth Cameron)
Supplies: A Troubleshooting Guide for Creative Difficulties
Inspirations: Meditations from *The Artist's Way*
The Writer's Life: Insights from *The Right to Write*
The Artist's Way at Work
(with Mark Bryan and Catherine Allen)
Money Drunk, Money Sober
(with Mark Bryan)

Prayer Books

Answered Prayers
Heart Steps
Blessings
Transitions

Books on Spirituality

Prayers from a Nonbeliever
Letters to a Young Artist
God Is No Laughing Matter
God Is Dog Spelled Backwards
(illustrated by Elizabeth Cameron)

Memoir

Floor Sample: A Creative Memoir

Fiction

Popcorn: Hollywood Stories
The Dark Room

Plays

Public Lives
The Animal in the Trees
Four Roses
Love in the DMZ
Avalon *(a musical)*
The Medium at Large *(a musical)*
Magellan *(a musical)*

Poetry

Prayers for the Little Ones
Prayers for the Nature Spirits
The Quiet Animal
This Earth *(also an album with Tim Wheater)*

Feature Film

(as writer-director) God's Will

Finding Water

The Art of Perseverance

Julia Cameron

JEREMY P. TARCHER/PENGUIN

a member of Penguin Group (USA) Inc.

New York

JEREMY P. TARCHER/PENGUIN
Published by the Penguin Group
Penguin Group (USA) Inc., 375 Hudson Street, New York, New York 10014, USA •
Penguin Group (Canada), 90 Eglinton Avenue East, Suite 700, Toronto, Ontario
M4P 2Y3, Canada (a division of Pearson Penguin Canada Inc.) • Penguin Books Ltd,
80 Strand, London WC2R 0RL, England • Penguin Ireland, 25 St Stephen's Green,
Dublin 2, Ireland (a division of Penguin Books Ltd) • Penguin Group (Australia),
250 Camberwell Road, Camberwell, Victoria 3124, Australia (a division of Pearson
Australia Group Pty Ltd) • Penguin Books India Pvt Ltd, 11 Community Centre,
Panchsheel Park, New Delhi–110 017, India • Penguin Group (NZ), Cnr Airborne
and Rosedale Roads, Albany, Auckland 1310, New Zealand (a division of Pearson
New Zealand Ltd) • Penguin Books (South Africa) (Pty) Ltd, 24 Sturdee Avenue,
Rosebank, Johannesburg 2196, South Africa

Penguin Books Ltd, Registered Offices:
80 Strand, London WC2R 0RL, England

Title page: Ohara Koson (Shoson), *Egret on Willow*, Arthur M. Sackler Gallery,
Smithsonian Institution, Washington, D.C. Robert O. Muller Collection, S2003.8.1959

Most Tarcher/Penguin books are available at special quantity discounts for bulk purchase
for sales promotions, premiums, fund-raising, and educational needs. Special books or
book excerpts also can be created to fit specific needs. For details, write Penguin Group
(USA) Inc. Special Markets, 375 Hudson Street, New York, NY 10014.

Library of Congress Cataloging-in-Publication Data

Cameron, Julia.
    Finding water : the art of perseverance / Julia Cameron.
        p.   cm.
    Includes index.
    ISBN-13: 978-1-58542-463-4
    ISBN-10: 1-58542-463-3
    1. Inspiration.   2. Writer's block.   3. Creation (Literary, artistic, etc.).
    4. Perseverance (Ethics).   5. Diligence.   I. Title.
    BF410.C36   2006   2006029098
    153.3'5—dc22

Printed in the United States of America
10   9   8   7   6   5   4   3   2   1
This book is printed on acid-free paper. ∞

Book design by Marysarah Quinn

ACKNOWLEDGMENTS

Elizabeth Cameron, for her commitment
Sara Carder, for her care
Carolina Casperson, for her daring
Jane Cecil, for her grace
Sonia Choquette, for her vision
Judy Collins, for her generosity
Tim Farrington, for his fortitude
Joel Fotinos, for his faith
Natalie Goldberg, for her resilience
Bernice Hill, for her sagacity
Jack Hofsiss, for his leadership
Tracy Jamar, for her grit
Linda Kahn, for her clarity
Bill Lavallee, for his strength
Laura Leddy, for her prayers
Emma Lively, for her perseverance
Larry Lonergan, for his guidance
Julianna McCarthy, for her inspiration
Robert McDonald, for his art
Bruce Pomahac, for his belief
Susan Raihofer, for her insight
Domenica Cameron-Scorsese, for her loyalty
Jeremy Tarcher, for his wisdom
Edmund Towle, for his friendship
Claire Vaccaro, for her eye
Rosemary Welden, for her enthusiasm
Elizabeth Winick, for her shepherding

To the artists who have gone before me,
leaving a trail of hope and perseverance

CONTENTS

The Quiet Animal

Oh quiet animal, sleeping,
What dreams lie within your cells?
What ages brought you here
Through coal and ice?
Eye twitch, lip curl—
Blood dreams again.

Blood is always dreaming.
Scheming to move us forward and take us back,
Dreaming the dark places,
Caves and the backs of stars.

Your ivory bones are the tusks of time
Who eats with all our mouths.
That crescent moon? It's just a bone
Thrown beyond our reach.
The stars at night were someone's baby teeth.

The blood remembers
What the mind forgets.
The soul is a quiet animal.
Given less to thought than memory,
More to dreams than plan,
The soul owes more to half-remembered God
Than waking life as man.

—J.C.

PROLOGUE

IT IS MIDDAY, midweek, midwinter. A light snow is falling. Under its spell, Manhattan is hushed. There is a Currier and Ives aspect to the cityscape. Wreathed in scarves and bundled into coats, New Yorkers plunge through the streets, grinning like children at the weather. Snowfall always brings the city quiet—that, and a sense of expectancy.

The lightest frosting of snow and Central Park becomes a fairyland garlanded in lace. Under the soft gray sky miracles seem possible—as when an eagle suddenly appears, lifting off amid the park's pine trees with an audible beating of wings. In Native American culture, sighting the great bird signals that great good is about to happen.

I am ready for good omens. Entering a new book, I want to believe that what I write will prove to be useful, blessed. Walking in the park, when the great bird soared near me, I felt a quick sense of wonder. "That is an *eagle*," I thought. "And this is *New York*." (For many years I lived in New Mexico, where the spotting of an eagle, while rare, was still to be expected.) This is the third time in five years that I have sighted an eagle in New York. Egged on by my own skepticism that the birds really could exist in Manhattan, I have done the research and learned that eagles do live in Central Park, released there deliberately by the Forest Service. Even knowing this, they seem miraculous to me. And so, yes, I believe the bird to be a great good omen. I believe this new book to be blessed and I am grateful for the encouragement.

I am fifty-eight years old. I have been a writer since I turned eighteen. That makes forty years at my craft. I have written plays, novels, short stories, songs, poetry, reviews, and journalism. I have had lean years and fat years. With twenty books to

We never know the worth of water till the well is dry.

ENGLISH PROVERB

my credit, I have written long enough and often enough to deserve the badge "writer." I have become accustomed to the twin horsemen of a writing career: the desire to write and the fear that this time I will not be able to pull it off.

Over the years, writing has become easier, a daily routine. But there are many days when my stint at the page still takes all of the courage I can muster. "Please, God, send me ideas," I pray. Then I listen and type out what I hear. "Inspiration" is really as simple as the act of listening and being willing to trust that still, small voice. Some days I am willing to trust. Others, I am not. On those days, I must pray again. "Please, God, send me the willingness to just listen and write." And then I must listen and then I must write.

Over the years, I have learned that there is a flow of ideas that we as artists can tap into. The flow of creativity is a constant. We are the ones who are fickle or fearful. I have learned that my creative condition and my spiritual condition are one and the same. Making art is an act of faith, a movement toward expansion. When I am stymied in my work, I am stymied in my spiritual condition. When I am self-conscious as an artist, I am spiritually constricted. I need to pray to lose my self-centered fears. I need to ask for selflessness, to be a conduit, a channel for ideas to move through. At a time like this, I again post a sign at my writing station, "Okay, God, you take care of the quality. I will take care of the quantity." In other words, it is time to resign as the self-conscious author. It is time to let Something or Somebody write through me. How the ego hates this humbling proposition! And yet, great art is born of great humility.

"The music of this opera [*Madama Butterfly*] was dictated to me by God. I was merely instrumental in putting it on paper and communicating it to the public," declared Giacomo Puccini.

"Straightaway the ideas flow in upon me, directly from God," stated Johannes Brahms.

These men were not proselytizing. They were simply reporting their creative experience. Artists work with one ear cocked to the Divine, although they may call it by another name. As the

What do you know better than your own secrets?

RAYMOND CARVER

virtuoso violinist Stéphane Grappelli assured us, "Great impro-visers are like priests. They are thinking only of their god."

The grace to be an acolyte, a servant of art, is the best prayer that an artist can offer. The grace to be again—one more time—a beginner is the most useful position an artist can take. Rather than being full of ourselves and our accomplishments, we are better served by emptying ourselves of our honors. "Show me what it is you want from me," is a serviceable prayer. (And the prayer can be uttered to God, to the Muse or even to Art itself.) Every great piece of art contains a whiff of transcendence. A Pollock or a Rothko has a transparency to it. Looking at the work, we catch a glimpse of the artist's soul. "Show me what it is you want from me," they clearly prayed to *Something.* Their art is a record of the answer they received.

But very often what God wants for us is not quite what we had planned. Our egos may tug us one direction while our souls yank us in another. I remember walking one day through the New Mexican sage fields, plotting the novel that I intended to write next, when suddenly I was directed to write a small prayer book about gratitude. "Not me! Not that!" I wanted to protest. The guidance was clear and implacable. How was it possible to write such a book without seeming to be a pious poseur? And yet, how was it possible not to write such a book when it was what was asking to be written, nudging at my hands and heart like a collie dog wanting to be stroked? No, the directive was not to be ignored, and so I did write that book. The novel I planned on came later.

There is a divine plan of goodness for us and our work, but we must go along with the plan in order that it may transpire. Careers do not unfold in an orderly manner. They do not pro-ceed A to B to C. They zig and then they zag. We must tack with them. We must be willing to be made what it is God is making us. For our own comfort, we must be willing to surren-der to a power greater than ourselves. At the moment, my career as a public speaker is flourishing. I am an intensely private per-son who approaches all public engagements with dread, and yet,

I never know when I sit down, just what I am going to write. I make no plan; it just comes, and I don't know where it comes from.

D. H. LAWRENCE

The material itself dictates how it should be written.

WILLIAM FAULKNER

the invitations keep rolling in and there is rent to pay. So I am, for a while at least, a public speaker. Similarly, there have been years when I was rendered a journalist, a screenwriter, a teacher—never quite what I chose. I had to believe that something wiser than I was choosing for me. Investing too heavily in a single artistic identity—Screenwriter! Playwright! Novelist!—and insisting on living out that identity can put us into conflict with the flow of our destiny. We do better to roll with the punches and to repeat to ourselves the simple prayer, "Thy will be done." We are often rendered something better than what we might imagine.

According to Joseph Campbell, it is possible to see the tracery of destiny in a life. He believed that once a person reached middle age, it was possible to see the contours of fate, the firm nudges we had received that sent us down this life path and not that. Campbell believed that there was a plan for each of us—and I believe the same thing. I believe there is an overarching *Something* that cares for us with great tenderness. It is this *Something* that we seek to contact when we work at making conscious contact with a Higher Power. It is this *Something* that guards us and guides us, tutors us and mentors us, moving us always toward our good if we will but cooperate.

How do we cooperate? There are a few basic tools that move us into conscious contact with our Creator. The use of these tools is simple and practical. We do not need to search in obscure corners for a pathway to our Maker. The road is broad and clearly lit. God meets us more than halfway if we undertake the simplest of motions toward Him. As we work to become more of the all that we can be, we come into contact with a benevolent guiding force. Some of us will call that force "God." Others will call it "the Universe," "the Higher Power," "Spirit," "the Tao," "the Force," or even, "the Muse." It does not matter what we call it. What does matter is that we experience it—and we will.

When we move toward our own creativity, we move toward our Creator. When we seek to become more spiritual, we find

ourselves becoming more creative. Our creativity and our spirituality are so closely interconnected they are in effect one and
the same thing. Speaking of God, we often use the terms
"Maker" or "Creator" without recognizing that those are the
terms for "artist." God is the Great Artist. We are creations and
we are intended, in turn, to be creative ourselves.

The thought finds the words.

ROBERT FROST

The Basics

Being an artist means: not numbering and counting, but ripening like a tree, which doesn't force its sap, and stands confidently in the storms of spring, not afraid that afterwards summer may not come.

—Rainer Maria Rilke

I HAVE WRITTEN about creativity many times and in writing about it again I find it necessary to repeat myself. Some things are simply too important to be skipped over. I have been teaching for twenty-five years. In those years, I have discovered that certain pivotal tools *always* work to enrich and enlarge our lives. Because the tools work consistently, it is always worth reteaching them. In my own creative practice, I use many of them year in and year out. If you are already familiar with some of these concepts, I hope you will enjoy this review and use it to renew your practice. If the ideas are new to you, what follows should be sufficient to give you a firm grounding.

This book is structured as a twelve-week course with an alternating series of exploratory essays and matching tools, "Divining Rods." Their aim is to help us to discover the living waters of creativity flowing through our often busy and difficult lives. The essays will trace my daily personal process of "finding water." The tools, many of them perennial favorites of mine, function like dowsing wands to point the way to further spiritual growth.

Morning Pages

In order to find our creativity—or, for that matter, our spirituality—we must begin with where we are. The Great Creator meets us exactly where we are standing—in "the Now"—but sometimes we do not know where that is. We may have moved through our lives unconsciously for a while, perhaps for a great while, and so we must find and take up a tool that tells us where we are and how we actually feel about that. This is the beginning of honesty, and honesty is the first step toward greater creativity.

So, where exactly are we? And how do we really feel? The tool that best helps us find our spiritual bearings is called Morning Pages. I have used them myself for more than two decades. I have written about them many times and I write about them again now because they are the bedrock on which a spiritual awakening can be based.

What, exactly, are Morning Pages and why should we undertake them? Morning Pages are three pages of longhand stream of consciousness that locate us precisely in the here and now. They are written first thing upon awakening and they tell us—and the Universe—what we like, what we don't like, what we wish we had more of, what we wish we had less of, what we wish, period. Our wishes, our unspoken dreams, are the voice of our soul. By letting our soul speak first thing in the morning, we align ourselves with the Great Creator. Over the years, I have come to consider Morning Pages to be a valid form of meditation, perhaps a form uniquely suited to hyperactive Westerners.

Morning Pages catch us as close as possible to our waking mind, before all of our well-meaning defenses are in place. They catch us when we are vulnerable and open. They catch us at our most honest and fragile when we are, perhaps, a bit discouraged, a bit daunted by the day ahead. Pages seldom sound polished or positive. In fact, Morning Pages may seem, at first, to be nothing but a series of gripes, a list of grievances about our discomforts, both psychological and physical. For this reason I sometimes dub Morning Pages "Brain Drain." Here is how they might sound:

"I am awake and I am tired. I feel stuck but I don't know quite where, and I don't know how to get out of it, either. These sheets feel positively gritty. I need to change my bed . . ."

"I forgot to call my sister back yesterday. I wonder if her marriage is going to last. I forgot to buy kitty litter. The car has a funny knock. I need to remember to start on my receipts. I don't want it to be a big emergency like last year. Dear Lord, I hate the IRS."

Griping, whining, kvetching, complaining—Morning Pages help us to siphon off our negativity. We see the cloud of resentment that hangs over us as we begin our day. We learn exactly what we resent. We learn exactly what strikes us as unpleasant or undoable. Without Morning Pages, we may only notice such things on a subliminal level. We don't like something but we don't quite register that fact. It may strike us as too petty, as somehow beneath our dignity. "Toughen up," we might tell ourselves. We may urge ourselves to be more grown up. But such urgings seldom work. Instead, we go through our day accompanied by a constant drip, drip, drip of subtle negativity. This dispiriting sound track is so omnipresent we may not even realize that it is there.

When we first undertake Morning Pages, we are often astounded by the number of things we feel bad about. We may worry that by admitting our negative feelings we are encouraging them. This is far from the case. Jungians call it "meeting the Shadow." I call it meeting the Shadow and asking it for a cup of coffee. When we ventilate the negative, we make room for the positive.

Writing Morning Pages, we lay our negative sound track onto the page. We get it out of our head and on its way to being out of our life. We register it with the Universe instead of just suffering through it unconsciously. For example, you may write, "I hated the way John treated me in that meeting yesterday. He stole credit for my ideas."

An ounce of action is worth a ton of theory.

FRIEDRICH ENGELS

Take care of each moment and you will take care of all time.

BUDDHA

There it is in black and white. You are facing something unpleasant that previously you may not have dared to look at squarely. Caught with our guard down first thing in the morning, there is nothing vague about our feelings. We know what is going on and we have our opinions about it. Moving the pen across the page, we discover that we are not the victim of circumstances. We have choices as to how we respond. Morning Pages show us our options. You may "get" that you are being used and that you yourself have been complicit. Just facing the facts, you may experience a substantial shift in your self-worth. When you are in a meeting with John later that same day, you may find yourself being suddenly assertive. "Thank you, John, for bringing up *my* idea about restructuring. Let me elaborate a little on what I had in mind. . . ."

Originality does not consist in saying what no one has ever said before, but in saying exactly what you think yourself.

JAMES STEPHENS

Morning Pages are like a spiritual chiropractor. They put us back on our spiritual spine. They help us to correct our course. We learn to stand up for ourselves if we are being trod upon. We learn to hold our tongue if we have been too hotheaded. Perhaps for the first time, we experience a sense of balance. This is exciting, as we sense that we are becoming more truly ourselves.

Morning Pages are simple and yet profound. To our joy, we discover there is a wisdom inherent in the process itself. We speak to God through our Pages and God speaks back to us in the form of heightened intuitions and inklings. The "still, small voice" gets amplified so that we can easily hear it. We are all adjusted in the precise direction that we need to grow. As we become more honest with God about our dissatisfactions, God is able to do something about them. God works through us to work on us. Increasingly, we take positive actions in our own behalf.

Morning Pages are tough-love friends. They single out the patterns that are defeating us. "I drank too much last night," we write. Then another day, "Drunk again last night." And another, "I am too hung over to move." The Pages urge us to take responsible actions: "I have to do something about my drinking." And then, "I wonder if I should try Alcoholics Anonymous. I could."

Morning Pages make us more graceful, but that grace is very practical. We feel the nudge to our consciousness when we are off course, and we act upon it. If we don't, the Pages will bring up that lack of action and nag us about it until we are willing to take action. Subtle and pedestrian seeming, Morning Pages actually make for radical changes. We learn where we are off kilter and just what we might want to do about it. Pages initiate change and they also walk us through that change. We do get sober. We do lose weight. We do taper off of codependent relationships.

But Morning Pages are not all bad news. Sometimes an insight comes to us as we write. We have a sudden breakthrough to clarity. "I get it! Why didn't I see that before?" We abruptly see exactly how we have been sabotaging ourselves. And we see how we can stop. Sometimes we get the glimmer of a new idea, a change in direction that we could take. We get the notion, "I could try it this way instead of that way." Sometimes Morning Pages will suggest a brand-new creative project. We will find ourselves entertaining a course of behavior that had never crossed our consciousness before. If Morning Pages put us in touch with the flow of good new ideas, they also give us the boat to rest in as we ride that flow. Morning Pages make us feel secure—secure enough to take risks.

I had been writing Morning Pages for fifteen years when suddenly the notion that I should try writing music appeared. I was forty-five years old, certain that I was not musical, and yet inclined, too, to trust the Pages after so many years writing them. "What shall I do next?" I asked in Pages. "You will be writing radiant songs," the Pages advised me. "Wouldn't it be fun to write a musical about Merlin?"

I was incredulous. "Oh, c'mon," I thought. "If I were the least bit musical, surely I would have known it by now." I had been raised as the nonmusical member of a very musical family. My piano lessons had lasted precisely six weeks—long enough for me and everyone else to get discouraged. And yet, the Pages persisted: "You will be writing radiant songs."

The typewriter separated me from a deeper intimacy with poetry, and my hand brought me closer to that intimacy again.

PABLO NERUDA

You can't sit around thinking. You have to sit around writing.

DAVID LONG

Sure enough, within a month, having shown no prior musical inclinations, I was suddenly writing songs. Conditioned to believe I was untalented musically, Pages made me open to the possibility that I could be wrong. It is now ten years since I began writing music and I have written three full-length musicals and two albums of children's songs. I now write music as easily as I write prose—and nearly as often. I think of this late blossoming of my musical talent as a fruit of Morning Pages. The lesson I take from it is that we may all be far larger and more gifted than we suspect. If we will but listen to Morning Pages and trust them, we will be led to unfold in miraculous ways.

"I was a lawyer until I began doing Morning Pages," a very successful Broadway actor recently told me. A day at a time, a step at a time, the Morning Pages led him out of his unhappiness as a lawyer and into a flourishing theatrical career. To see him onstage is to feel, "Now *there* is a born actor," but he was not a born actor. He was a "made" actor and Morning Pages are what made the making possible.

"Julia, I was drinking in the outback until I started doing Morning Pages. Now I am a sober Hollywood screenwriter," another practitioner told me. Her Pages mentored her into sobriety, and her sobriety mentored her into a new career.

A Chicagoan in her midfifties who had always dreamed of a playwriting career undertook Morning Pages with fear and trepidation. She longed to write but she feared writing. The Pages proved to be a gently greased slide into her own creativity. She is now an award-winning playwright.

Of course, not all practitioners report a change in career, but many report a deepened satisfaction in the career that they are in. ("I am much better in the courtroom," a lawyer recently confided to me.) The Pages help many of us to do our work better and to greater personal satisfaction. Stated simply, Morning Pages put us in touch with our need for change. Some of us need more radical change than others. Morning Pages adjust us to the degree that we need adjusting. When we write to our Creator precisely how we are and how we feel, the response

Action is character.

F. Scott Fitzgerald

back is specifically customized to our needs. Writing Morning Pages, we are forging a one-to-one, personal relationship to the Great Creator. There is great particularity in the ways that we are guided.

Start with three pages of longhand morning writing that says exactly where you are. Do this every morning. "Good morning. I am tired. I didn't sleep enough. I dreamed about drowning. I was Japanese . . ." Every morning, no matter how you feel, tell your Pages how you feel. Let your Pages become a morning habit. Something that you do first thing, a sort of Morning Report, a signing in. Very soon you will feel a shift, a sense of relief that you are telling someone, even if that someone is "the Universe," the whole truth.

I've always had a very comfortable relationship with No. 2 pencils.

WILLIAM STYRON

Morning Pages are the bedrock tool of a creative recovery. I have done Pages now for more than twenty years. In those years, I have probably not missed more than twenty days. Every day I tell the page how I am doing. Every day, the page tells me back that I am making the tiniest soupçon of progress. "At least I am writing Pages . . ." Year in, year out, the Pages nudge me forward ever so slightly. They may suggest I do a musical or try my hand at a novel again. They may suggest I paint my bedroom or make a commitment to a daily walk. They may tell me I need rest and more water.

In creativity, as in running, you have to start where you are. Let us say you are twenty pounds overweight and haven't written in fifteen years. Well, then, your first flyer at contacting help might read, "I am twenty pounds overweight. I haven't written in fifteen years."

Think of what you're doing as putting out your coordinates. Imagine yourself on a life raft bobbing in a vast sea. You want the big boat to save you, but it must know precisely where you are in order to effect a rescue. And so, you do not want to be vague. What you write in your Morning Pages gives the Universe precise information about exactly where you can be found. You want the Universe to help you, and, in order to help you, it needs an accurate account of where you are. So be specific. "I stopped writing fifteen years ago when my novel didn't sell and I thought, 'Oh, what's the use . . .' I still think, 'Oh, what's the use,' if I am honest."

Be trivial, be petty, whine, grump, groan, and complain. Morning Pages siphon off a haze of negativity through which we normally face our day. The negativity goes onto the page instead of just wafting around us as we make our way through our daily lives. "These pages are boring," you might complain. Write them anyway.

Sometimes we try too hard to have something to say. We feel desperate but we don't want to act desperate. We want to pose a little—even on the page. Posing gets us nowhere. We do better to just come clean. It can take getting used to, this nakedness on the page. We want to say, "I haven't written in a while," leaving it vague. We want to say, "I'm a little overweight." But it does us far more good to be accurate. That gives the Universe somewhere concrete to meet us.

It can be hard at first being naked on the page. We want to pretend we are in better shape than we really feel ourselves to be. We want to pretend we have momentous things to say when the truth may be that we yearn to say something but we don't know what. The truth is that we may feel trivial, like an also-ran. We can put this on the page. We can say, "I really have nothing much to say and so I am going to practice saying nothing much."

Little by little what we have to say and who we have to say it to will become clear to us. The truth, the whole truth, is a gradual process. We want to feel we are clearly defined but often we are not. Often we are vague and muddy around the edges. Often we have been making do with half-truths for a very long time. And so, when we first start writing, our writing is vague. We say, "I don't think I may like X" when what we mean is, "I absolutely hate X."

It is a good idea to have compassion for ourselves when we are starting out. It can take us a while to get our wheels to lurch free from the mud. It can be difficult to write: "I long to write and I am not writing." Just saying it makes the stakes higher.

There is no enlightenment outside of daily life.

THICH NHAT HANH

When every blessed thing you have is made of silver, or of gold, you long for simple pewter.

W. S. GILBERT

Who am I if I long to write and I am not writing? Am I a pretender? An also-ran? A coward?

When we first start writing our way out of the muck, we will be tempted to such flash judgments. These judgments are what have kept us so mired for so long. We call ourselves "cowards" instead of extending sympathy to ourselves. "Of course you're scared. Writing really matters to you." That is the compassionate overview that Morning Pages tend to bring.

As we make the commitment to undertaking three pages a day of longhand, we begin to sense that something is committing back. We might call that something the "Universe." We might call it "the Great Creator" or "God." It doesn't matter what we call it. We can feel it. We begin to contact a sense of wisdom not commonly our own. We start to take a longer and less apocalyptic view of our life. We begin to get an overview and the first gentle crumbs of progress are made. This can be very exciting and very humbling.

"You may not be writing what you long to write yet, but at least you are writing your Pages," we may tell ourselves. "You may still be twenty pounds overweight but yesterday you had yogurt instead of French toast and that's a step in the right direction."

Morning Pages are a gentle mentor. They help us make small course corrections rather than dramatic pronouncements. Because they are done one day at a time, they encourage us to live one day at a time. It is a rare day in which a tiny forward step cannot be taken. It is the job of Morning Pages to notice and encourage such small steps.

Our thoughts move across our mind; our hand moves across the page. It is very simple and very centering. We are simply writing down what meditators call our "cloud thoughts." We write down whatever it occurs to us to write, strictly stream of consciousness. Instead of sitting there "doing nothing" for twenty minutes, we are sitting there "doing something" for twenty minutes. This can appeal to our work ethic. Morning Pages are frequently called "positively addicting."

I'd rather have written Cheers *than anything I've written.*

KURT VONNEGUT

As I write I create myself
again and again.

JOY HARJO

Morning Pages are a simple, doable, and very positive practice. They invite change and they parse out change in small, di-
gestible increments. Over any considerable period of time, "the
Pages" function like a loyal, tough-love friend. If there is an issue we are avoiding they will broach it to us—and over and over
until we do something about it. "Julia, I was perfectly happy
drunk," I have been told. "Then I started doing Morning
Pages . . ."

Whether we are drunk in the outback or something less dramatic, Morning Pages will nudge us to make a change, until we
do make a change and as we make that change the Pages will
walk us through it. Above all else, Morning Pages are loyal. Unlike Manhattan psychiatrists, they do not take two weeks off
every August. Instead, they are always there for us, steady and
dependable. It's worth a try.

I cannot prove to you that Morning Pages will create a sense
of magic in your life, but I can ask you to experiment. Try the
pages for a few weeks. Try them for twelve weeks if you can.
(That's the period of time required to "groove" a new habit.)
Once you become accustomed to them, you may find them in-
dispensable. I have many students who have now been doing
Morning Pages for a decade or longer. Do I need to say that they
do them because they work?

The true object of all human
life is play.

G. K. CHESTERTON

Divining Rod

Set aside an early-morning hour—although you may
not need all of it. (Most people report that Morning
Pages take them a half an hour to forty-five minutes.)
Take your hand to the page and write three pages of
stream of consciousness writing. Remember that nothing
is too small or trivial to be included. You may find yourself grumpy or "boring." That's fine.

Morning Pages are not intended to be dramatic. They seldom sound good. That's all right. They are not intended to be "real writing." Expect them to be fragmented and to skitter topic to topic. Relax. Explore your own mind with curiosity, not judgment. There is no wrong way to do Morning Pages. Simply write down whatever comes to mind and do that for three pages. As a rule, I do suggest you use standard eight-and-one-half-by-eleven pages. If you use little pages, you will tend to edit your thoughts to fit the small format. Remember, your pages are for your eyes only. They are not to be shared with any audience other than your own consciousness. Do Morning Pages every day and be alert for the shifts that they will lead you to.

The first mistake of art is to assume that it is serious.

LESTER BANKS

Artist Dates

Today it is too warm for snow. The sky is a soft, silvery gray and a fine, light sleet is falling. New Yorkers venture out armed with umbrellas or turning their faces to the fresh, gentle mist. The weather is damp but not unpleasant. Suddenly we are on the cusp of spring. Central Park is the first place to show it. If you look closely, daffodils and hyacinths are pushing their buds upward through yesterday's snow.

This morning I walked two dogs in Central Park. I had my own dog, a naughty cocker spaniel named Tiger Lily, and my collaborator's dog, a sweet West Highland terrier named Charlotte. The dogs plunged through mud puddles and strained at their leashes in pursuit of squirrels. By walk's end, their coats were soaked and they came back inside "wet and wild," flinging themselves onto the Oriental carpets, rolling and twisting to dry their coats.

Have a variety of interests. . . . These interests relax the mind and lessen the tension on the nervous system. People with many interests live, not only longest, but happiest.

GEORGE MATTHEW ALLEN

The dogs enjoy a walk in any weather. They need their daily dose of adventure in order to be happy. All I need to say is, "Leashes!" for them to leap in the air, cavorting. "Hold still!" I have to beg in order to fasten the snaps to their collars. No matter how many times we walk the same route, it is never routine to them. There is always some fresh sight, some new smell for them to revel in. Ever obstreperous, Tiger Lily barks at children and lunges at passing Great Danes. Ever amiable, Charlotte greets children and dogs alike with a wriggle of glad expectancy. Surely we can all be friends . . .

There is no such thing as a missed day of dog walking. Even in the thickest snow or the fiercest cold we venture out. Each day's weather lends its flavor to the walk. It is the combination of routine and adventure that makes the walks so edifying. An adventure that can be counted on, that is a wonderful thing.

In seeking to nurture our creativity, we, too, need adventures that can be counted on. I call them "Artist Dates." As the name suggests, we are out to romance or woo our artist. We do so by taking a weekly solo expedition to do something that is just plain fun. As with any date, the planning is a part of the adventure. The anticipation is a large part of what makes it special. All week long we can look forward to our romantic rendezvous.

I live in Manhattan, a Mecca for artist dates. My apartment is on the Upper West Side, walking distance from The American Museum of Natural History. Up the great stairs and into the dim, cavernous halls I often take myself. I skip the special exhibits and go straight for the museum's staples. I love the dioramas, staged tableaux of wild animals captured in what appear to be their natural habitats. There are dozens of different types of gazelles. There are looming Alaskan brown bears, so huge they dwarf a grizzly. There are mountain goats and bighorn sheep. There are bison and water buffalo. Hippopotami wallow right before my eyes. Great apes cavort amid the tree tops.

I suppose the squeamish might see too much death in all the mounted scenarios. To me, it is all about the diversity of life. It is easy, encountering so many diverse creatures, to feel one has encountered the Great Creator. It is easy, seeing the care taken to twist a horn just so, to sketch in a finely tapering stripe, to believe we, too, are cared for. Clearly the Creator has its eye not only on the sparrow, but also on us.

The intuition that we are connected to a power greater than ourselves is one of the first fruits of Artist Dates. There is a sense of wonder that enters our lives the moment we slow down enough to give it access. We do not need to be admiring the natural world to feel our own spiritual nature coming awake.

Across the park from The American Museum of Natural History, perched high on Fifth Avenue, is the grand and glorious Metropolitan Museum of Art. An Artist Date there might begin with a visit to Asian Art. What could be more inspiring than the benign gaze of Buddha carved in stone centuries earlier and gazing at us still with perfect equanimity? A quiet steals over the senses. The timeless stone statues are unsigned, yet the artists live on in their work. As with the great cathedrals, the anonymity of the creators is part of what makes the hymn of praise so ecstatic. On an Artist Date, we sense the ecstasy of creation. We appreciate both the artist and the art.

But an artist date need not involve high art. Manhattan contains a fabric district and few dates are as satisfying as a visit to one of the huge commercial fabric stores. Is it velvet you are after? Here is crimson, burnt umber, regal purple. Perhaps you are looking for a heathery tweed? There it is, bolt on bolt of it, in all its misty glory. Now here is a fine pinstripe, there a natty herringbone. There seems to be no end to the diversity and the possibility of creation. "This has a fine hand," the aging salesman remarks, appreciatively stroking a smooth cashmere. Coats can be made and kilts. Sleek business suits. Drop-dead gorgeous chiffon dinner gowns. A suit for a college graduation. A Christening robe. Something for every occasion. From wedding gown to bathrobe, the imagination can conjure almost anything and it is in this act of conjuring that a sense of play is born.

A multitude of small delights constitute happiness.

CHARLES BAUDELAIRE

Each day comes bearing its own gifts. Untie the ribbons.

RUTH ANN SCHABACKER

Artist Dates fill us with exuberance. We see that we are not caught by the narrow confines of life as we have known it. No, the possibilities are endless. Just look at that taffeta . . .

Artist Dates bring us optimism. They awaken in us a sense of potential: our own and our world's. They help us to know that we are not alone. Rather, we sense that we are partnered by a large—and playful—*Something*. It is possible, we see, to make more of our life than we have made of it to date. Life is an adventure, not an ordeal, we start to intuit.

Artist Dates bring us a sense of enchantment. There is magic afoot and we encounter it more easily. On an Artist Date, we set our inner dial to "receive" and what we receive is often guidance and a heightened sense of well-being. We feel that we are in harmony, that there is a harmonic higher than our own that partners us at all turns. Agnosticism starts to fade as we encounter a spiritual experience. I do not ask you to believe any of this. I ask you to experiment and record for yourself the result.

An Artist Date is an adventure, a lark, a flier into the unknown. It asks you to have fun and to preplan that fun. For this reason, Artist Dates are notoriously hard to execute. Just try planning an adventure for yourself and watch your killjoy side fly into action. You are suddenly too busy to do anything so frivolous as have fun. Identify this resistance as a fear of intimacy—intimacy with your self.

It helps to think of the Artist Date as being analogous to the quality time a divorced parent spends with a child. Just as that parent will want to drag along the new significant other, so, too, we will want to bring a friend along. We will go to almost any length to keep from spending time alone with ourselves. Like the divorced parent, we are afraid of what we may hear if we actually give our inner creative youngster some time and attention and a chance to speak to us. It can be frightening to become intimate with ourselves, especially if we haven't been for some time. Expect to hear the unexpected.

"I want to go to a photo exhibit," may come bubbling up when you have decided on a "worthy" lecture on computers. "I

I want to be able to live without a crowded calendar. I want to be able to read a book without feeling guilty, or go to a concert when I like.

GOLDA MEIR

The aim of life is to live, and to live means to be aware, joyously, drunkenly, serenely, divinely aware.

HENRY MILLER

hate it here," may be the response when you take your inner artist to a very serious new drama. You can be pretty sure you will be caught off guard by something and that that something will give you food for thought.

Many times it is on an Artist Date that a recovering artist first experiences the recognizable presence of God—Good Orderly Direction. For some reason, Artist Dates tend to kick up our level of synchronicity, those experiences in which the hand of God or the finger of the Universe feels palpably present. Sometimes, opening the door the tiniest crack to our inner artist leads to large and significant breakthroughs.

Artist Dates tend to build on themselves. You have an interest in France and so you go to see a movie in French with subtitles. The next week, you attend a class on French cuisine. Three months later, you have signed up for French lessons at the local YMCA and you are contemplating taking a bicycle vacation through France. All you did was start to scratch a little itch . . .

Artist Dates connect us to a larger and more fascinating world than our normal beaten path. They remind us that we have many choices and that we make those choices daily. It is hard, when practicing Artist Dates, to feel convincingly trapped in a life we don't like. We become aware that we have the power to change many things: an apartment, a neighborhood, even a city. Doing Artist Dates, we begin to feel ourselves being led. We begin to have the novel feeling that we can even trust that leading. Ours is a fabulous world, far wealthier and more varied than we have allowed. It is on Artist Dates that we first begin to experience the world's abundance. It is often on an Artist Date that a recovering artist first learns to hear and to trust hunches. Hunches are often the way that the Universe leads us, and we need to be willing to follow such leadings a step at a time. "Follow your bliss," Joseph Campbell advised his students. For me, an Artist Date to a Rand McNally map and globe store led to a decade's worth of writing on Magellan, the great explorer.

Often, when we are working full tilt, we are tempted to skip Artist Dates because things "are going so well." The truth is that

Art is so wonderfully irrational, exuberantly pointless, but necessary all the same. Pointless and yet necessary, that's hard for a Puritan to understand.

GÜNTER GRASS

One must be a living man and a posthumous artist.

JEAN COCTEAU

when we are working full out, we should be doubling our Artist Dates because we are drawing heavily upon the inner well of images from which we make our art. Artist Dates replenish the inner well. They give us stocks to draw on. They make us wealthy.

Think of it like building a CB radio. When you are doing Morning Pages, you have the dial set to "send" and you are broadcasting, "This is what I like. This is what I don't like. This is what I want more of . . ." When the dial is moved over to Artist Date, you have suddenly switched to receive. You begin to be able to hear the Guidance coming back at you. Your radio kit is now fully functional. Because Morning Pages look like work and Artist Dates look like play, it is often much more difficult to do an Artist Date than it is to undertake the Pages. This is America. We understand "work." What we are baffled by is "play"— as in, "the play of ideas," a very literal phrase. It is difficult for us to do something that seems frivolous. We do not see how Artist Dates "work." We need to experiment with them despite our skepticism. Even the tiniest of Artist Dates will yield results.

Artist Dates are like yeast. It only takes a smidgen to create a large chain reaction.

One ought, every day at least, to hear a little song, read a good poem, see a fine picture, and if it were possible, to speak a few reasonable words.

JOHANN WOLFGANG
VON GOETHE

Being an artist means ceasing to take seriously that very serious person we are when we are not an artist.

JOSÉ ORTEGA Y GASSET

Divining Rod

Once a week, take yourself on a festive, solo expedition. Take the term "Artist Date" literally. It is half "artist" and half "date." Plan your date ahead of time and expect some resistance in trying to accomplish it. Expect, too, that your intimates may want to go with you. They are not allowed. It is your date with you, yourself, alone. You are out to "woo" your own creative consciousness. That is the "date" part of Artist Date. Think mystery rather than mastery. A date should expand your horizons by exploring territory a little bit outside of your usual realm.

An Artist Date is an adventure. It does not have to be "cultural." You may find yourself making a sortie to a new restaurant or stopping in at a hardware store or an art supply shop. Your Artist Date doesn't need to be big and threatening and expensive. It merely needs to entice you. A free flea market might be a better date for you than an evening at the theater. What you are after is the play of ideas—with the emphasis on the word "play."

I'm not a teacher: only a fellow traveler of whom you've asked the way. I pointed ahead—ahead of myself as well as you.

GEORGE BERNARD SHAW

Walks

It is a bright and sunny day. Spring is again in the air. Coats are left unbuttoned, heads uncovered. It is a good day for stretching the legs and New Yorkers, always great walkers, take to the streets in droves. This past winter was the coldest on record in fifty years. By way of contrast, this midforties day feels positively balmy. People are daft with the sunshine and fresh breezes. They run an extra errand on their lunch hour. It is good to be out and about.

For those of us working to increase our creativity, it is always good to be out and about, especially on our feet. Walking, the simplest of tools, is among the most profound. It makes us larger than we are. When we walk, we wake up our consciousness. We enliven our senses. We arrive at a sense of well-being. We experience "conscious contact" with a power greater than ourselves. That still, small voice is automatically amplified a footfall at a time. *"Solvitur ambulando,"* St. Augustine is said to have remarked. "It is solved by walking."

No matter what the "it" is, walking helps to unravel it. We may walk out stale from a day caught up with office politics. At first we walk rehearsing the day in our mind: "And then he said . . . and then I should have said . . ." But before long, our

No man can know where he is going unless he knows exactly where he has been and exactly how he arrived at his present place.

MAYA ANGELOU

Happiness walks on busy feet.

KITTE TURMELL

consciousness drops the bone we are worrying. Our negativity simply cannot stay in place as our body moves. Despite ourselves, despite our many heartfelt worries, there comes a creeping feeling of optimism. We notice the daffodils at the green grocer's and the large black buckets of pussy willows. We think about buying a pot of tulips. We settle, instead, on fragrant hyacinths. Yes, spring is afoot—a telling phrase. No coincidence, there is a "spring" to our stride.

Sometimes we walk out with a tangled personal situation that needs sorting. We have noticed something that needs attending to and then all during our busy day we have ignored it, shoving it beneath the rug of our consciousness. "But what about . . . ?" our problem nudges us despite our refusal to engage it. "What about . . . ?" it badgers.

When we walk out, the sorting process begins. We do not "solve" our dilemma. Instead, it keeps us company as we walk. It vies for our attention and then it fades away as the details of our walk begin to engross us. We notice the tortoiseshell cat perched on the windowsill. We notice the sign for a new needlepoint shop. We see that an optimistic someone has already planted a window box, then we laugh, realizing when right up upon it that the blooms are fake.

"But what about . . . ?" swims to our consciousness again. The pesky problem is still unsolved. We turn our attention to look at it but it sinks back down. Instead, we notice the mother and child just ahead of us. The mother pushes a stroller with little brother. The child pushes a matching stroller holding "dolly." Both of them step delicately over a mud puddle left over from yesterday's wet weather.

"I could try—" the thought comes suddenly to mind. It is, if not the perfect solution, at least a good possibility. Walking has turned the key.

Spiritual seekers have always walked. There are pilgrimages to Canterbury, to Mecca, to Jerusalem. There are pilgrimages around Kailas, the sacred Tibetan mountain. Aborigines go on Walkabout. Native Americans set out on Vision Quests. There is something in walking that tunes us to a higher key. Each footfall moves us up a step. We do not come home the same as we set out.

In order to be effective, a walk doesn't need to be long. A scant twenty minutes is usually enough to shift our consciousness to a broader and more expansive place. An hour's walk is a luxury. Taken once a week, a goodly walk puts the events of the week into perspective. It shows us an overview. It gives us valuable detachment. And, yes, it gives us words.

Walking is not just for writers but it is especially wonderful for them. Walking starts the writing engine humming. Dante is said to have been a walker. The British Lake Poets were great walkers. (It is no accident that poetry is divided into "feet.") The esteemed writing teacher Brenda Ueland swore by walks, for both herself and her students. She exclaimed, "I will tell you what I have learned for myself. For me, a long five- or six-mile walk helps and one must go alone and every day."

When we walk by ourselves, we find ourselves companioned. We set out alone but soon sense that the Divine is close at hand. It comes as intuition, as insight, as sudden conclusion. The shape of our life comes clear to us as we walk. We take note of the many causes for optimism. Without shame or scolding, walking puts a gentle end to self-involvement. Almost without noticing it, we become engaged with a world larger than ourselves and our concerns. A blue jay hops to a stone wall. A squirrel scampers along a tree branch. Our consciousness follows, entertained. We walk out with our pressing problems, but walking soon invites us to take a longer view. With little effort on our part, we find we attain a wiser perspective. As casual as a walk may seem, profound wisdom can be its by-product.

Statesman Søren Kierkegaard phrased it this way, "Above all, do not lose your desire to walk: every day I walk myself into a state of well-being and away from every illness; I have walked myself into my best thoughts, and I know of no thought so burdensome that one cannot walk away from it. . . ."

Walking makes us more whole. It mends the body/mind split by promoting the release of endorphins, tiny neural messengers

Belief consists in accepting the affirmations of the soul; unbelief, in denying them.

RALPH WALDO EMERSON

The only real voyage of discovery consists not in seeking new landscapes, but in having new eyes.

MARCEL PROUST

Solitude is as needful to the imagination as society is wholesome for the character.

JAMES RUSSELL LOWELL

of optimism. After a brisk walk, we feel a sense of well-being. Walking integrates our experience and grounds our perspective. It is an exercise in heightened and intensified spiritual listening. We may walk out with our own will set on certain agendas, but as we walk our will is tempered. As movement teacher Gabrielle Roth sees it, "If you just set people in motion, they'll heal themselves." A footfall at a time, our soul is tutored in divine timing. Walking back in, we may still want what we want, but we also come to see how our dreams and desires fit into a larger whole.

Walking makes us rightsized. We sense that we are far larger than we may sometimes feel and yet that there is a *Something* far larger than we ourselves are. We sense that *Something* holds us in benevolent regard. We sense that benevolence as we walk.

"It's just something I have to walk through," we often say, talking about hard times. What we don't realize is that all of life is something we have to walk through. As we take the phrase literally, we can begin to get help with our many difficult problems and dilemmas. Because it is such a simple tool and so readily available to all of us, we do not tend to think of "walking" as a sophisticated problem-solving stratagem.

And yet it is.

Seeds of discouragement will not grow in the thankful heart.

ANONYMOUS

We carry wisdom in our bodies. We carry memories and we carry, too, the medicine for what ails us. We can walk our way to sanity. We can walk our way to clarity. Baffled and confused, we can walk our way to knowing the "next right step."

In difficult times, many of us intuitively start walking. We may walk our way through a divorce, a breakup, or a job change. We may walk our way out of one identity and into another, newer and better-suited to us. Answers come to us while we walk—sometimes the answers come to us before the questions. We just get an itch to start walking and when we do, we then begin to get a sense of why.

Karen is in the middle of a nasty breakup. For the better part of a decade she was joined at the hip to Jim—this despite her friends' comments that the relationship did not seem healthy to them. "I lost myself in Jim," Karen describes it. "I gave up so many things to be with him. There were so many things I expected him to be for me. I do not remember who I am without him, and yet I must be somebody."

Striving to remember who she is, Karen has taken to walking. A fragment at a time, she finds pieces of herself come swimming back to her as she walks. "Today I started thinking about my acting career. I just let that go glimmering about four years ago."

Things that go glimmering away can also come glimmering back to us.

"I didn't get into the Actor's Studio, and I was so ashamed and embarrassed that I quit. Now I realize that many people audition over and over to get in there."

With every footfall, Karen comes more surely into possession of the parts of her that have been missing. By the time she has walked a mile, she is speculating what other audition pieces she could try.

The dark night of the soul is often illuminated by a good brisk walk. Ideas come to us as we walk and so does inspiration. Even if we can't go five or six miles, even if we can't go alone and we can't go every day, walking "works." We walk out with a problem and we come home, if not with a solution, at least with a different angle on what it is that has troubled us.

Right now, I am walking to romance a book idea. I want to write a book, and I want to write a book I would like to read. This means that I must ask myself, "What is it that truly interests me at this time?" In order to ask myself the question, I must get out of my head and into my body.

My body knows things that my head doesn't know yet. We speak of having a "body of knowledge" and this is a literal term. Our body embodies knowledge. We "know things in our bones." We "feel things in our marrow." And the best way to access this corporeal wisdom is to walk.

It is impossible to walk rapidly and be unhappy.

MOTHER TERESA

As soon as you trust yourself, you will know how to live.

JOHANN WOLFGANG VON GOETHE

I sing the body electric.

WALT WHITMAN

If we have listening ears, God speaks to us in our own language, whatever that language is.

MAHATMA GANDHI

Divining Rod

Once a week, take yourself out for a goodly walk. Twenty minutes is enough but an hour serves you even better. Stretch your legs and stretch your mind. Enjoy the sights and relish a new crop of insights. If it fits within your schedule, you may want to walk more than once a week. Many students report that they enjoy a couple of short twenty-minute walks and a weekly longish one. Expect that your walks will calm turbulent emotions and give you the time and space to "process" life as it occurs to you. Many students report that as they walk they feel a conscious contact with something spiritual that feels both larger and benevolent. You may well experience yourself as being "guided."

Creativity Contract

I, _____, commit myself to the regular use of the three basic tools. For the duration of this course, I will write Morning Pages daily and will take an Artist's Date and a Weekly Walk once a week. Additionally, I commit myself to excellent self-care, adequate sleep, good food, and gentle companionship.

_____(signature)

_____(date)

Uncovering a Sense of Optimism

This week inaugurates your creative journey. Hopes high, you set out. Some of you may feel giddy anticipation. Others of you may harbor lingering skepticism. No matter what your cache of secret feelings, now is the time for optimism. The tools you will use have worked for others and they will work for you, as well. You will become more free. You will become both larger and more strong. You cannot work on your creativity without discovering a sense of play. Your imagination will take flight. You will discover creative endurance. Great goodness lies ahead of you as you tap an internal spring. Focus on the positive and begin.

Being a Beginner

It's Monday, the ides of March. The week opens with spring weather, a high in the fifties. People wear their winter coats flung open like capes. There are runners out in their shirtsleeves. Just inside the entrance to the park, there is a scattering of purple crocuses, the first spring flowers. Intoxicated by the gentle wind, the dogs sniff the earth with increased urgency. They are excited by the change in seasons. The sun unlocks smells long frozen by winter.

It is a time for beginnings. At noon today I have my piano lesson. In piano, I am an absolute beginner. I take two lessons a

Even the lowliest, provided he is whole, can be happy, and in his own way, perfect.

JOHANN WOLFGANG
VON GOETHE

week and I slowly, very slowly, edge my way forward. My teacher, Chaim Freiberg, is a tall and handsome man, kind with a graceful humor. He comes to our lessons laden with strong coffee and homemade treats. He shares a sip of coffee, a bite of some Israeli delicacy he has made for his lunch. "Are we ready?" he will ask, always starting the lesson on a personal note.

"Let us try it together," he will say as he scoots his chair next to my piano bench and makes a rich-sounding duet from my simple melody. The duets are encouraging.

"You are doing very well," he tells me, although to my eye, I am probably his oldest and slowest student. "Let's try it again, and that's an 'A,'" he will gently correct me.

I have been taking piano for two years now. I have a small repertoire that I can play by heart and every week I edge a bit further into new territory. Most of the piano literature is simplified classics. I will pick out a theme by Brahms or Debussy, a beautiful melody line lifted from a larger work.

"Now let's try it again," Mr. Freiberg will urge me. When I stumble, he is all patience. "This note should be just a little longer," he will say.

"You play it once so I can hear it," I will ask. My ear is still better than my eye. When he plays the theme it sounds wonderful.

Mr. Freiberg is a composer as well as a teacher. When he wants me to master a new progression, he will write a piece of music incorporating the lesson that I need. His handwritten music is sketched out on blank paper. The notes are large and clumsy. I sometimes think this makes them easier for me to find. "Lullaby for Julia" is a haunting melody with its roots, like Mr. Freiberg's himself, in Israeli culture. I play the piece and cannot believe it hasn't been played for generations. But no. It is new, freshly minted, just for me. Who could resist such a teacher?

I was fifty-four years old when I finally began taking piano lessons. All through my forties I had bought the excuse that I was too old to start something new. Then one day it occurred to me that I would age whether I knew piano or not and that I might respect myself more as the world's oldest novice than as someone who stayed blocked and yearning. I began to search for a teacher, someone who could accommodate an older student who was trying to learn just for the sake of learning not with an agenda of becoming an accomplished pianist. When I found Mr. Freiberg's ad, it mentioned that he loved Broadway as well as the classics. I did, too, and so I thought we might be a match. So far, we have proven to be just that.

"You're doing very well," Mr. Freiberg tells me. "I think you may go far." I want to believe him. Like any youngster, I hero-worship my teacher.

We are never too old to be young at heart. Being young at heart means simply being willing to be a beginner. I have a special satchel that I carry my music papers in. I keep the satchel in a particular corner near the piano. Nothing else is allowed to take its place there. I am like a kindergartener with her first school bag.

It took courage to allow myself to pursue something that I loved. I had to allow myself the luxury of learning. I had to focus on process and not on finished product. I could not think about the distance I had to travel before I could call myself a pianist. I had to remember that I was learning to play the piano and that the word "play" was operative here.

To begin at all, I had to resign from competition. I had to stop comparing myself to my idols. My brother Christopher is a virtuoso keyboard player. I am friends with a magnificent classical pianist named Robert McDonald. When those men touch a piano it unlocks its mysteries for them. When I touch a key, it is all terra incognita.

The word "piano" means soft, and softly is how the instrument has entered my life. I can now play pieces that baffled me a year ago. Once in a while, during a lesson, I will catch myself thinking, "Oh, my God! I am actually playing this piece!" Mr. Freiberg is very low key. Sometimes on the days when I try the hardest and when my fingers are spaghetti, he will pull out some new trick, gently turning my attention to a new piece of music that he has written, something that he thinks I just might be able to master.

To win one's joy through struggle is better than to yield to melancholy.

ANDRÉ GIDE

"We will call this one 'Variations,'" he might say and then patiently sketch in the sheet music for five variations on a simple melodic theme. "What do you think of this?" he might ask. His music always has a soothing structure. It is built to be learned from and so one progression interlocks with the next so that the piece as a whole has a pleasing, organic quality.

"I like it," I always say and I always do like it. I have a book that holds some twenty-five of his original compositions. We always begin the lesson by playing through his homemade music before we go on to more formal books.

"Today was a very good lesson," Mr. Freiberg will sometimes tell me. I have noticed how often my "good" lessons come on the days when I had the most resistance, when I felt myself to be the most rusty. As a writer, I have learned that good writing and good moods do not necessarily go together. On some of my worst days, the best work emerges. It is evidently the same with music, and this is a lesson that I tell myself to remember.

I try to show up for my lessons without an expectation of great improvement. I try to love the process that I am in: learning to play the piano. It is the learning more than the piano that matters, I tell myself. I think of my friend Julianna McCarthy. At age seventy-seven, she has recently undertaken a Master's in poetry. "How is it going?" I ask her. She deadpans back, "It's going." When something is "going," we feel the flow. We are swept up by the current of life. What, I ask myself, could be better? Nothing comes to mind.

Happiness sneaks in through a door you didn't know you left open.

JOHN BARRYMORE

Divining Rod

Most of us have something we know we wish to do but find ourselves procrastinating about. For me, it was piano. For you, as for me, it might be a round of lessons— beginning modern dance, life drawing, acting, Italian. It might also be a deferred personal project like a play, novel, or nonfiction book. We tell ourselves we are "too old" to undertake our fancy and, in telling ourselves this, we rob ourselves of the opportunity to be a beginner. Being a beginner is very rewarding. It brings both excitement and self-respect.

Take pen in hand. Write about your deferred dream. Choose something enticing about which you have been procrastinating. On the page, allow yourself to imagine yourself actually doing what you long to do. How does it feel? What changes do you need to make to accommodate this new growth?

After you have written for enough time to fully explore your imaginary start, move from the visionary to the practical. Do the footwork necessary to begin. If piano lessons are your goal, start looking for a teacher. Muster the courage to make phone calls. Allow yourself to explore in your own behalf. For today, all you need is the grace to begin beginning. Think—and start—very small.

Encouragement

Winter is back. Small biting flakes pour from the sky. The forecast is for snow mixed with sleet and that is exactly what we are getting. It is a good day to stay inside, but that is not what's on the agenda. Today is lunch with Bruce Pomahac, a special occasion. For the sake of seeing Bruce, I will brave the weather and head downtown. With luck I will find a cab and the cab will drive sanely. Luck is with us. We find a cab. Dodging through traffic, wipers working furiously, we wind our way down to the corner of Twenty-ninth Street and Eighth Avenue. This is the site of Birrichino's, the Italian restaurant where we rendezvous.

To fill the hour and leave no crevice . . . that is happiness.

RALPH WALDO EMERSON

The only true happiness comes from squandering ourselves for a purpose.

WILLIAM COWPER

For the better part of three years now, my musical collaborator Emma Lively and I have met with Bruce once a week for lunch. It is much more than just a shared meal. It is a time of shared dreams and aspirations. All artists need coconspirators to cheer them on in their endeavors. Bruce is such a coconspirator for us. A sparkling man with a crisp wit and ready laugh, a composer himself, he is a source of experience, strength, and hope for us. He is the music director for the Rodgers and Hammerstein Organization, which means all productions of their work must be cleared through him. It is a large and demanding job. It is also work that he loves. For us, Bruce is the keeper of the flame, not only of Rodgers and Hammerstein's work but of our own. He is a treasure trove of Broadway stories. From his vantage point, he has seen it all.

As we struggle to persevere writing our own musicals, he is always ready with a quick word of encouragement, encouragement grounded in his long years of experience. Such encouragement is priceless for any artist. Today in particular we need a dose of Bruce's astringent optimism. Three weeks ago, we put up a staged reading of *The Medium at Large,* a musical we have been working on for four years. The reading was a "backers' audition," intended to entice investors into bankrolling our work. The cast was stellar, all Broadway veterans. Despite short rehearsal time, the two performances were just short of spectacular. We hoped for someone to step forward with a checkbook.

"That was one of the two best readings I have attended in all my years in the business," Bruce assured us in the aftermath. The show had played both days to jammed houses. Backers came and went, pausing to congratulate us on their way out. Our hopes were high. For months all of our attention had been focused on "pulling it off," and now we had. We were pleased with the work we had done, more than pleased with the work our director, cast, and musical director had done. There was nothing to fault. There were no "what if's," no "if only's." We had done ourselves proud. Shouldn't that create interest?

"Now what do we do?" we wondered in the wake of the showcase.

"Now you wait for the phone to ring," we were told. After months of action on the show's behalf, this sudden halt was terrifying. There was no more going to the piano to tinker with a song. There was no more going to the computer to tinker with a scene. There was no more tinkering, period. The die was cast.

Backers would like the show or they would not. It would or would not be up their alley. One producer e-mailed us that while she had liked our show, it was not as serious as the shows she was interested in backing. Our show was a romantic ghost comedy: "Sex can be very nice/ with a good poltergeist . . ." Her current shows concerned women in Bosnia and the threat of nuclear war. No, we were not a match, but she had enjoyed the show. We tried to take her e-mail in good humor, but our humor was wearing a little thin. Could we have done so much work for nothing?

A backer's audition costs about $15,000, what with renting a theater, paying a director and a musical director, paying actors a stipend, printing promotional materials and programs. If someone steps forward to go ahead with the show, it is clearly money well spent. If no one steps forward, it is money spent, period. And the money spent was hard-earned.

In the face of ominous-seeming quiet, Emma and I tried to count our blessings instead of the costs. We told ourselves: we learned our show is strong; we learned the music really plays; we learned the pacing is good; we learned the book of the show is funny . . .

We practiced our optimism like a mantra but in the days following our backers' audition, Emma and I fought with depression. When the showcase was over it was so *over*. Our phone wasn't ringing. Our e-mail was silent. So many people had seemed to enjoy the show so much, surely there must be *some* interest, we told ourselves. But silence reigned.

Needing reassurance, we phoned Bruce who gently reminded us that *Oklahoma!* fell on deaf ears when Rodgers and Hammerstein auditioned it on what is often called "the penthouse circuit." Hat in hand, they played the show through fifty times without getting a dime's backing. And they were Rodgers

The best things are nearest: breath in your nostrils, light in your eyes, flowers at your feet, duties at your hand, the path of God just before you. Then do not grasp at the stars, but do life's plain, common work as it comes, certain that daily duties and daily bread are the sweetest things of life.

ROBERT LOUIS STEVENSON

and Hammerstein! (At the time, Rodgers was the veteran of a long and successful collaboration with Lorenz Hart. Hammerstein was the veteran of a fruitful relationship with Jerome Kern.) As a combination, Rodgers and Hammerstein, they were a new entity, but surely *someone* should have been able to hear their potential. But no one did. Why should our luck be any better? Perhaps we had just joined the club.

"You're in the same boat now with everybody else," Bruce assured us.

It did help to hear that the odds were not stacked against us in particular. It did help to hear we were part of a time-honored tradition, that getting backing for a show was always difficult. There was something refreshing about looking the difficulties squarely in the face. Knowing the worst, we felt better. There is an old wives' tale that states that from conception to completion the average length of time for a musical to gestate is seven years. By that standard, Emma and I were right on schedule, just past the halfway mark and looking to stay the distance. But how did people do that? How did they keep their optimism and their courage intact? We needed help.

"You're lucky you've got other projects," Bruce told us. His hint was spoken as a true artist. He was reminding us that the joy had to lie in the process and not in the product. Doing the work was the best cure for the difficulty of doing the work.

And so, we decided to do what we knew how to do and went back to work on another show, *Magellan*. The minute we were back at the piano in creative waters, our anxiety eased. Focused on our work, we forgot our recent disappointment. All that mattered was getting *Magellan* right, and we had our work cut out for us there.

And then a director called—a Tony Award–winning director.

He wondered if he could submit the script of *The Medium* to The Goodspeed Opera House, a seedbed for new musicals. Could he? *Could he?* We said he could. We knew the director's work and were excited by it. It was wonderful that he liked the

Genius does what it must, talent does what it can.

EDWARD BULWER-LYTTON

show that he had seen. "He liked it! He liked it!" Emma and I exclaimed to ourselves over and over again. So we weren't so crazy after all. The show had played as well as we thought it had. Here was the proof. We readied a packet of materials for the director to submit.

No sooner had the director called than we got a tiny nibble from a producer. Then another tiny nibble. One producer wanted a synopsis of the script. Another producer wanted a reading copy and a demo CD to show to her partner. No one was saying, "Count me in," but there was at least a glimmering of interest.

"Just hang in there," Bruce told us now over lunch. "You are at the point where so many people get discouraged. It's good that you've got more than one project to work on. The waiting is hard. It's a tough business, a tough business." Bruce paused to break off a crust of Italian bread. His sympathy was hard-edged. His very presence constantly reminded us that we had to be in the business for the long haul.

If we go down into ourselves, we find that we possess exactly what we desire.

SIMONE WEIL

Outside the restaurant window, the storm continued to rage. The snow and sleet were now egged on by a nasty wind. Bruce, Emma, and I all ordered steaming bowls of split pea soup. I got a side order of homemade sausages.

"What do we do now?" I asked Bruce, although I thought I knew the answer.

"You keep the faith," he answered. "You keep the faith." With that he ladled up a sip of soup. I tried my own. It was hot and good. Suddenly the storm seemed less threatening. The day seemed less bleak. Thanks to Bruce, our optimism rallied. Perhaps we could keep the faith. Perhaps our backers' audition had not been in vain.

Divining Rod

Take pen in hand and make a list of people you can go to for encouragement. These people are your "believing mirrors." They may not be artists themselves and they need not be. What they must be is optimistic, believers in the essential goodness of life. You are a part of what they believe in. They reflect back to you your competency and potential. They are on your side and bring to your discussions a sense of optimism and hope. You owe it to yourself to be in regular contact with these individuals. Some of the names on your list may be people with whom you have fallen out of contact. Pick up the telephone. Drop them a call or a line. Tag base with your believing mirrors. You may wish to tell them that you have undertaken work with this book and that they can expect to be hearing from you more regularly.

Focusing

Last night, I taught down in SoHo. The students handed me index cards, recording just what they had done for their Artist Date this week. "I went to see the Chuck Close exhibit at the Met." "I went to a trim store in the fabric district." "I went to my very first yoga class." The Manhattan revealed through their index cards is rich and varied. "I went to a samurai movie." "I went to a children's magic show without a child to accompany me." "I went to the Twenty-eighth Street flower market." "I went to see *The Producers*." Teaching a class in Manhattan gives me the flavor of Manhattan, a glimpse of the many lives it is possible to lead here.

But I am living one life in particular, and that life must be fully inhabited for me to thrive as an artist. Sometimes, it is difficult for me to commit to my Manhattan life. I miss New Mexico with its purple folded mountains, its vast savannahs of silvery-green sage. I miss the scent of pinion on the wind. I miss the canyons populated by fir trees.

In Manhattan, the canyons are made from concrete. They are beautiful, but I must train myself to see their beauty. Last night on the way down to class, the cab passed through Greenwich Village. It was snowing and from the taxi window, I spotted a crowded flower stand at a corner Korean grocer's. Through the silvery snow, the flowers flared bright with unexpected intensity.

"Look how beautiful," my companion breathed. And beautiful it was—if I took the time to see it. I had to force myself to focus. I had to take myself by the nape of the neck and give myself a mental shake. "There! Look at that!"

As an artist, I must take the time to see. My artist's eye must be schooled in the particular. It is not healthy for me as an artist to be tuned to the inner movie, always watching the "what if, if only I had's" as they unspool on the inner screen. ("What if I'd kept my ranch in New Mexico?" "If only I still had my horses.")

"What if" and "if only" are poison for any artist. They throw us into the past. They dull our lens on the passing world. And it is in the passing world that inspiration lies in wait for us. For an artist to be vital, for the work to hold up, there must be primacy given to the here and now. I know this but lately must work to practice it. If I live in the "then" instead of in the "now," the art dries up. My writing loses its snap and vigor. It becomes vague and generic. I do not see the bucket of jonquils, flaring like struck gold through the wet city night.

Lately, the inner movie has been compelling me. I have felt an undertow pulling me out of my daily life and into a twilight world of fears and regrets. I have had trouble holding on to my optimism. I have felt myself slipping away from the life I have now and into a half world of the life I might have had, if only . . . If only I had chosen differently . . . If only I had chosen better . . .

I worry that this is the knife edge of depression beginning. It frightens me as I feel my mind starting to skip toward the cliff

The thing about performance, even if it's only an illusion, is that it is a celebration of the fact that we do contain within ourselves infinite possibilities.

DANIEL DAY-LEWIS

edge. My family has a history of depression. My father was hospitalized many times for manic depression. My mother was hospitalized for depression, period. They were fragile, gifted people and I sometimes feel that my legacy from them is both their fragility and their gifts. I must work to husband my own optimism. I must cling to the small and positive: walking the dogs, putting words to the page, taking time at the keys. I must not entertain the large and overwhelming. For me that is romancing trouble.

A veteran myself of three breakdowns, I have had to learn to live each day very carefully. I must write. I must walk. I must pray. I must content myself with small amounts of progress. Above all, I must not binge on drama and despair. That was what I did during my black, drinking twenties. Now I am a sober alcoholic. My sobriety and my sanity require daily maintenance. For me, self-pity is the rim of the glass. I cannot afford to think, "Poor me, poor me." It leads to "Pour me a drink."

No bird soars too high if he soars with his own wings.

WILLIAM BLAKE

Divining Rod

We can choose to focus on the positive or on the negative. We can choose to see the beautiful or the ugly. We speak of "training our eyes" on something and that is a literal phrase. Our eyes can be trained to focus on those areas of life that reward us with grace and beauty.

Take pen in hand. Number from one to five. Make a list of five beautiful things you have recently spotted. For example, the little white dog coming into your building. The Harlequin Great Dane going out. The stargazer lilies at the Korean grocer's. The golden yellow gingko tree midway down your block. The crescent moon rising over the skyline. Each day yields beauties enough for a short list. You may wish to make writing this list a nightly practice.

Grounding

It is a starry night. Even in Manhattan where the lights from skyscrapers compete with the sky, the stars tonight are clearly visible, drawing the earth to scale. In Manhattan, my apartment is one set of lights amid millions. In the galaxy, Manhattan is just a sprinkling of lights on something known as planet Earth. It is all a matter of perspective. Seated at my writing desk, looking out at the glittering lights, I strive for a sense of optimism, a feeling that as small as I am, what I am doing still matters in the scheme of things.

Boredom is not an end-product. It is comparatively rather an early stage in life and art.

F. SCOTT FITZGERALD

Optimism is partially the happy accident of psychodynamics and partially a trained response. Some people seem to be born optimists. The rest of us need to work at it a little. One way I work at my optimism is by talking with my friend Larry Lonergan. Larry is a spiritualist medium. He lives with one foot in this world and one foot in the next. It is from Spirit and a carefully maintained spiritual practice that Larry garners his optimistic bent. When I need to feel better, I dial Larry's number for a dose of optimism. His is a farseeing perspective. He always holds the long view.

"You are on the verge," Larry told me just this afternoon. "There are many things pending. You just need to keep the faith while things unfold." Unfortunately, Spirit is vague about timing. "They say it will be 'soon' but they do not tell me what 'soon' means," Larry said ruefully. He sounded a little guilty that the other side wasn't more forthcoming. Still, "soon" means something. It is the encouragement I need today.

What "soon" means to me is to keep on trying. Don't quit right before the miracle. Show up at the page. Show up at the keys. Bite the bullet and focus. I have *Magellan,* the opera I am working on that needs more attention. I need to listen to it and flesh it out with more music where it is needed. If I go to the keys, music will come to meet me there. I simply must be willing to go to the keys.

I cannot give up just because the going is tough right now.

Babies are necessary to grown-ups. A new baby is like the beginning of all things—wonder, hope, a dream of possibilities . . . Babies are almost the only remaining link with nature, with the natural world of living things from which we spring.

EDA J. LeSHAN

"Soon" there will be more interest. I must be ready to receive that interest by having kept the faith myself. This means I must buck the tide of discouragement. I must see my fifty-eight years as years of valuable experience, not merely "age." This perspective can be tricky to maintain.

Ours is a youth-oriented culture. We are trained by television and the media to focus on those who are young. Our pop stars are youngsters. Their fortunes are immense and their futures bright. We do not read much or hear much about life in the arts for older people. We do not have many role models for doing what we must do—and that is persevere.

I am friends with a pianist who is midstride on what promises to be a long and brilliant career. Now in his fifties, he finds the traveling side of touring more grueling than it once was. He still tours and tours widely, but he husbands his energies more carefully than he did in his twenties, thirties, and forties. When jet lag strikes, he tells himself, "This is just chemical. You don't really hate your life." As a mature artist, long accustomed to the public eye, he has learned to talk to himself in private. Feeling overwhelmed or beset, he lectures himself, "Don't be a hothead. Don't overreact. Is this really worth your getting upset about it?" What he is telling himself, in many forms, is "Consider the big picture. Take the longer view." When I speak with him, he tells me to do the same thing.

If we have some spiritual underpinnings, it is easier to take the longer view. Meditation gives us the sense of something larger and other than ourselves. My pianist friend both runs and swims, two forms of active meditation. He also puts in long hours at the keyboard, hours when he is connected to higher realms. Myself, I walk for Guidance. Additionally, Morning Pages give me a connection to the divine and a connection, too, to what might be called "divine intention," a sort of overarching benevolence that I count on when the going gets rough.

One thing that I didn't anticipate when I was younger is how often the going gets rough. As an older artist, I tend to work on larger projects, projects that require years rather than months or weeks to germinate and come to fruition. There is no instant feedback loop. Nothing that says to me often and loudly, "You are doing fine." In order to have that sense of reassurance, I need to work at a spiritual practice—my Morning Pages, my Artist Dates, and my walks—and I must listen also to my friends. I call Bruce or I call my friend the pianist. I can piggyback on their faith when my own faith wears thin. And my faith does wear thin.

With the best of intentions and the most diligent of practices, it still wears thin. Fatigue can make it hard to have faith. Too much busyness can make it hard to have faith. Too much or too little solitude can impact faith. For that matter, so can a bout of hunger or overwork, anything carried to an extreme. Faith thrives on routine. Look at any monastery and you will see that. Faith keeps on keeping on.

Right now, my sister Libby is my walking exemplar of faith. She is an animal portrait artist and she has been suffering for nearly a year from an injured painting arm. The injury occurred when she was shied into by a startled horse. The horse was frightened by the sight of a large standard poodle wearing a snow-white ruff because he himself had been injured. My sister doesn't blame the horse for being spooked or the poodle for looking spooky, but she estimates that a thousand pounds of pressure was suddenly thrown onto her arm. Blinded by fear, the horse charged directly into her, catching her arm at a skew angle.

"I thought my arm was broken," she recalls. "It hurt so badly." She had it x-rayed immediately. An injury to her painting arm, after all, was an injury to her livelihood. The elbow seemed to be the center of trouble. She was put on ibuprofen and sent to physical therapy. A year of treatment followed and none of it truly helped. Whenever she painted for more than a few minutes, her arm would start to throb. She tried working with a sling. She tried bracing her arm. There were days when she could barely hold a brush.

Because her income depended on her ability to paint, there were many days when she fought panic. "I tell myself it's one day at a time," she would phone and tell me then. I could hear

Great art is the outward expression of an inner life in the artist, and this inner life will result in his personal vision of the world. No amount of skillful invention can replace the essential element of imagination.

EDWARD HOPPER

the anxiety eddying in her voice. "So I'll paint just a little today and then I'll let the arm rest."

Finally, on the advice of an older friend, she went to a chiropractor who told her it was not her elbow that was injured at all but her shoulder where the pain originated. The shoulder was dislocated. It had "separated" from its proper position. The chiropractor manipulated the shoulder back into alignment, which helped considerably—but not enough. A rotator cuff may be torn. Libby is now waiting for the results of a belated MRI. "I am good for about a half hour now," she says.

Accustomed to long days at the easel, a half hour seems barely enough time to get started, and yet she has managed to keep painting at the altered pace. She works on her commissions daily, a tiny piece at a time, but work she does and the commissions, somehow, get finished, although her daily fear is that they won't.

It is art that makes life, makes interest, makes importance . . . And I know of no substitute whatever for the force and beauty of its process.

HENRY JAMES

Suddenly saddled with abundant free time and nothing but nerves to fill it with, she has also turned to the page and begun writing a book. "I had to do something with my creative energy or it was going to turn in on me," she says. "I don't know what will come of the book but at least I have done something productive."

The doing of something productive regardless of the outcome is an act of faith. The doing of a small something when a large something is too much for us is perhaps especially an act of faith. Faith means going forward by whatever means we can.

"Just do the next right thing," twelve-step programs advise their members. Their advice is good advice for the artist. For the alcoholic, sobriety is achieved one day at a time. For the artist, so is a creative career. My sister edges forward on a portrait today. That is all she can do and all that she needs to do. The slogan "Easy does it" applies as much to her as it does to someone battling the bottle a day at a time.

A new moon is rising. It is a thin sliver of hopefulness. They say the new moon blesses beginnings. I believe that. From her studio window in Racine, Wisconsin, my sister spies the moon. It washes her hay field with silver. That same moon rises over Manhattan. I see it above the roofs of brownstones. I call my sister.

"Just keep on keeping on," I tell both my sister and myself as I face the blank page and she faces the blank easel. As the sickle moon peers in her studio window, my sister readies a canvas for the start of a new portrait. She keeps the faith.

Divining Rod

The smallest and gentlest acts keep us grounded. As we husband our lives with care and attention, we are rewarded with feelings of peace and accomplishment. What actions keep you grounded? Morning Pages may be one such action—as is making your bed. Making a nightly list of daily beauties may help to ground you—as does regularly opening all of your mail. It may help you to pick up scattered clothes or to do your mending. You may get grounded, as I do, by a phone call to your sister or another believing mirror. Doing all the dishes and leaving yourself nightly with a clean sink may be yet another source of grounding and self-esteem. Some people love to vacuum. Take pen in hand and list five homely actions that are grounding for you. Execute one of them.

Art is the sex of the imagination.

GEORGE JEAN NATHAN

Possibilities

Right now, although snow still blankets the ground of Central Park, golden crocuses have joined the purple ones in popping into bloom. Sheltered by a stone wall, the parti-colored flowers push upward through the snow. "Welcome to the Park," they seem to say. "Welcome to spring."

Twenty feet further on, a forsythia bush flares brightly, bursting into bud. Despite the chill air, green-gold rosettes garland its branches. Very soon there will be yellow blossoms, the golden bushes lighting the park like bonfires, signaling "spring." Even now, four plump-breasted robins hop through the snow, picking for tidbits beneath the frozen crust. Robins, too, mean spring, despite the appearance of winter.

Today I am bundled into an oversized coat. With my layer upon layer, I am a little too warm—and I look like someone out of *Doctor Zhivago*. I have the two dogs with me, straining at their leashes, and they, too, are bundled into coats. While I admire the early flowers, Tiger Lily plunges in pursuit of a robin. I laugh and tell myself she is a perfect artist's dog, always chasing something that is just out of reach—a possibility.

This morning, I spent my own time chasing an opera. I hear the music to *Magellan* in my head and I see the production of it in my mind's eye. Yet I must labor to bring what I see and what I hear into concrete notes on a page. I have been sketching in *Magellan* for nearly six years now, adding this sprig of melody, this scrap of lyric. Magellan's journey was large and grand. I am striving to make something to match it but I must work a little at a time, always laboring to bring into form something just beyond my reach. I am like Tiger Lily, leaping after that elusive bird. One day, I will catch it. At the least, I will certainly try.

As artists, we must learn to try. We must learn to act affirmatively. We must learn to act as though spring is at hand—because it is. We are the spring that we are waiting for. Wherever creativity is afoot, so is a blossoming. All creative acts are acts of initiative. Whether we are playing a concerto, perfecting a plié, scribing a novel or sketching a sketch, we start with nothing— "the verdant void"—and impregnate it with our own creative spark. Art is born, but not without labor on our part.

In order to make art, we must be willing to labor. We must be willing to reach inside and draw forth what we find there. On an inner plane, we are all connected to a larger whole. This is what is meant by inspiration, this connection to something greater than ourselves. But it begins with where we are and what we are. It begins with possibility.

Honesty is the starting off point of possibility. Honesty begins with specificity. I am typing at a small Chinese lacquer desk, looking north out a large window to a view of Manhattan. I am on the eleventh floor and my view overlooks the tops of many town houses. If I edge to the left of my desk, I can look out across Central Park. I can see across the reservoir rimmed by cherry trees that will soon be a pale pink froth as the season turns. For tonight, though, the park looms dark. Yesterday's snow has melted. Now I am left with ink-black branches. Soon they will be leafy green, but not yet. For tonight, the trees resemble line drawings of trees.

An artist is someone who turns his coat inside out and falls in love with the color of the lining.

Jeanne Tardiveau

Looking due north out my writing window, I stare across the tops of town houses and into the flanks of two large skyscrapers. The skyscrapers feature large, square windows. I can watch the blue-gray flickering light of television streaming from many of them. On my desk, I keep a pair of birding binoculars. I could train them on my neighbors if I were so inclined. I do not do it. Spying on a neighbor raises the possibility that a neighbor could be spying on me. That is a thought I prefer to avoid—but it is possible. Entertaining the possible is the province of art. It is the possible that sets the creative engine humming.

"It is possible," the artist thinks, "that I can write a play."

"It is possible I can make a sculpture."

"It is possible I can make a film."

Out of the notion, "I can" comes the next thought: "I think I will." The impulse is playful. It doesn't consider the odds. It is an impulse born of pure faith. The artist has a vision and that vision includes the successful completion of the art he has in mind. An artist is like a lover who cannot pause to entertain the possibility of being spurned. He must press his suit. His whole impulse is to love.

Like the crocus that pushes into spring willy-nilly, the artist also pushes forward into growth. The crocus lies beneath the snow waiting for the slightest touch of warmth to spring forth. Like the crocus, the artist does not pause to ask if his work is timely or welcome. Critical reception will perhaps be chilly like an unseasonal snow but, like the crocus, the artist survives.

There are only two ways to live your life. One is as though nothing is a miracle. The other is as though everything is a miracle.

ALBERT EINSTEIN

Divining Rod

Very often we are our own wet blanket. We do not allow ourselves to see and to seize our opportunities. The following exercise is designed to catch you off guard and allow you to see your "coulds" rather than your "shoulds."

Take pen in hand and number from one to ten. Use the phrase, "I could try_____" and fill in the blank with whatever comes to mind. For example, "I could try writing poems again" or "I could try practicing Italian every night for half an hour." Write very rapidly and do not concern yourself with the practicality of your responses.

CHECK-IN

1. **How many days this week did you do your Morning Pages?** If you skipped a day, why did you skip it? How was the experience of writing them for you? Are you experiencing more clarity? A wider range of emotions? A greater sense of detachment, purpose, and calm? Did anything surprise you? Is there a "repeating" issue asking to be dealt with?

2. **Did you do your Artist Date this week?** Did you note an improved sense of well-being? What did you do and how did it feel? Remember, Artist Dates can be difficult and you may need to coax yourself into taking them.

3. **Did you get out on your Weekly Walk?** How did that feel? What emotions or insights surfaced for you? Were you able to walk more than once? What did your walk do for your optimism and sense of perspective?

4. **Were there any other issues this week that felt significant to you in your self-discovery?** Describe them.

Uncovering a Sense of Reality

As you explore your inner world, your outer world will come more sharply into focus. As you face your imagined barriers, you will encounter real ones, as well. This week's work will help you to become more grounded and farseeing. As you seek your own internal support, as well as the support of friends, your creativity will become more steady. As you undertake small actions on your own behalf—watering the garden, as it were—larger actions will seem more possible. A sense of your own power will return to you.

Claustrophobia

A fierce wind rattles the windows. The sky is a glowering gray. The clouds move across the heavens in fast forward. It is bitter cold again, a day to stay inside. It is a day that invites claustrophobia.

So much of an artist's career hinges on the sense that we are going somewhere, that we are not just trapped by the four walls of wherever we are. For creative sanity, I must believe that if I just do the next right thing, a path will unfold for me. I must believe there is a divine plan for me and my work.

As an artist, I must believe in higher forces, sources of inspiration, movements of destiny. I must believe in something larger and wiser than myself. Some artists believe in God. Others

Action may not always bring happiness, but there is no happiness without action.

WILLIAM JAMES

believe in Art. No matter what we call it, a belief in it is necessary for our sheer artistic survival.

If I believe my writing is leading me somewhere—somewhere beyond what I can see—then I can endure the cabin fever of a day like today. If there is enough of a sense of adventure in the work itself then I do not need to plunge into the outdoors seeking the feeling of an adventure. And so, I must turn to the page. I must find my adventure within my own creative consciousness. I must keep the drama to the page.

Today I received a phone call from a young writer. It was the third call I've had from her in so many days. Each day, she has called in with some new misadventure. Her friends are misbehaving. Life itself seems to be misbehaving. Things have not been going her way, and she blames the stress in her life for her not settling down to work. I know how she feels, but I am also growing suspicious. Artists love drama and when we do not create it on the page or on the stage, we often create it in our lives. It is my suspicion that the young writer's life will stay stressful and dramatic until she decides to go back to work. Once she is working, the drama will settle down.

"But you don't understand," I can hear her wailing at me.

I understand all too clearly. How many valuable writing hours have I myself wasted on drama? Focused on things that were out of my control, I failed to use the power that I did have, the power to create. It is the voice of my own experience that says to me that when too many people start behaving too badly, I probably am just not working hard enough. Over the years, I have ruefully noticed that when I am on track in my writing, everyone seems to behave much better.

We hear so often that the artist's temperament is restless, irritable, and discontented. All of that is very true—when we are not working. Let us get in a good day at the page or the easel and we are suddenly sunny and user-friendly. It is the blocked artist who is such a study in malcontent. Artists have an itch that nothing can scratch except work.

"But I can't work. I am too upset," the young writer tells me.

Trouble is only opportunity in workclothes.

Henry J. Kaiser

I know how she feels but I also know that if she would just start working, her life would settle down and with it her emotions. "You don't understand how they are treating me," the young writer insists. "They're really acting terrible."

What I understand is that she is not working and that she is prickly. Most of the time her friends behave very well. Most of the time she is able to allow them to behave as they need to. It is only when she is not working that her friends develop mysterious ticks and flaws. It is only when she is not working that her normally very nice boyfriend suddenly becomes the monster. It is when her mind is not on her work that it is so closely focused on the workings of everyone else's personality. Her own personality is what is on tilt, but she can't see that.

"You think everything comes down to work," she accuses me.

"I think a lot does."

"You'd be upset, too," the young writer tells me.

I listen to her and I believe her. Drama is contagious. Already I am wanting her friends to shape up and fly right. I am wanting her life to become easier. Listening to her woes, I am becoming upset. I want to "fix" things for her. It takes me a moment to realize that nothing probably needs fixing. Everything will fall into perspective if she simply gets to the page. In the meanwhile, I can simply get to the page. Clad in a pair of red plaid pajamas, I settle in at my writing desk. The day is claustrophobic but the adventure of writing is not.

It is not irritating to be where one is. It is only irritating to think one would like to be somewhere else.

JOHN CAGE

Divining Rod

Often we are restless, irritable, and discontent because we are not cherishing the life we have. Any life— and I mean any—has some things in it that are well worth noticing and appreciating.

Take pen in hand. Number from one to ten. List ten

things that you can cherish in the life you've actually got. An example might be, "I cherish my good views from this apartment," or "I cherish my proximity to good walking trails," or "I cherish the amount of sunlight I get in my bedroom." What you cherish may surprise you. (You might not cherish what you think you "should.") Allow yourself to be as whimsical as the Spirit moves you to be.

Inhabiting the Present

Art is not to be taught in academies. It is what one looks at, not what one listens to, that makes the artist. The real schools should be the streets.

OSCAR WILDE

The day is cold and crisp. The flowers in Central Park shiver in the chill. We are back to winter again although now we are nearing April and such throwbacks are increasingly rare. A wicked wind nips at the windows. I am suffering a throwback of my own right now. I have received a writing packet from my sister Libby. The packet is an excerpt from the book she is writing. It details her first trip to Europe two decades ago. She includes many letters that she sent to me then and I realize now, reading, that she was writing to me when my daughter, Domenica, was still just a seven-year-old. The past tears at my heart.

Scanning the letters, I see my daughter when she reached just to my hip pocket. I remember our catch phrase for when we needed to cross a street or go somewhere else that was dangerous: "On your mother's hip," I would tell her. In the letters, my sister is in Italy. She sees many beautiful brown-eyed children and their chocolate eyes remind her of Domenica. As she writes to me, I am living still in the Hollywood Hills. I own a silken black horse named Jazz. I am young and wild. The me that Libby writes to still exists, caught now in the body of a fifty-eight-year-old woman. Oh, the past was sweet.

I am on dangerous ground. My mind wants to gild my memories. It wants to present the past in soft focus, as muzzy and sentimental as a greeting card. It doesn't want to remember the long days spent drinking, the dangerous twilight rides, jumping my horse while drunk. My mind wants to remember chilled white wine and elegant dinner parties, not the scotch, neat, burning its way into my system every morning. No, I cannot afford to romance my past. It does not serve me. To stay emotionally sober, I must focus the lens of my perceptions clearly on the now. This is what serves me both as a person and as an artist.

In order to function well as an artist, I must love the present. I must function in the present, savoring the sweet that is to be found there. I must put the Hollywood Hills far behind me. I live on a different coast in a different time. I must be able to look out my writing-room window and cherish the current view: red brick town houses, roof gardens, the backs of apartment buildings with their fire escapes clinging to their flanks. Pigeons flock along the roof lines but far above them I must note the high-soaring sea gulls—Manhattan is a seaport, after all. And what's this? A shuffling at my feet. I must smile at the dogs coming in to disturb my work, reminding me that we have yet to go to the park today. "What about us?" the dogs insist. "Forget the past."

The present is complicated enough. Putting aside my sister's book, I must be able to field the phone call from my daughter, now twenty-nine. She hopes she is not interrupting my writing. With excitement, she tells me that she has been offered a part-time job training horses and that she thinks she may take it, needing something positive to do besides wait for the next audition. My daughter, an actress-writer-director, now lives near the Hollywood Hills. She rides a mustang through the high canyons. She traces the very trails I used to ride with Jazz.

Man is always more than he can know of himself; consequently his accomplishments, time and again, will come as a surprise to him.

GOLO MANN

Divining Rod

We need to fall in love with ourselves. One of the best ways to do this is to view yourself as a character, one you are fascinated by. If you observe yourself closely enough, you are very interesting. Think of the Brontës' novels about "ordinary" people. With this tool, you will become your own biographer.

Take pen in hand. Set aside about a half hour's writing time. You are going to write about yourself in the third person. Do not write, "I am fifty-six years old and I live in New York." Instead, write, "She/he is fifty-six years old and lives in New York." Sketch in your life and your surroundings exactly as they are just now. Talk about what you love and what you hate. Talk about what you want more of and what you want less of. Place yourself smack in the middle of life and describe that life in succulent detail. "She lives in a spacious apartment high above the city. Once an eagle came to roost on her eleventh-story balcony . . ."

Every man feels instinctively that all the beautiful sentiments in the world weigh less than a single lovely action.

JAMES RUSSELL LOWELL

Staying in Training

There are as many kinds of beauty as there are habitual ways of seeking happiness.

CHARLES BAUDELAIRE

In ten days, I am leaving for Paris. I will be there for one week and in order to prepare myself, I am studying French, which I haven't spoken in nearly forty years. Every day, for an hour, Emma and I park ourselves on matching leather couches and scowl intently as we repeat the cues from an audiolingual learning program. "*Bonjour, Madame. Bonjour, Monsieur.*" We learn how to ask directions to our hotel, how to accept a dinner date, how to order wine and beer. I keep waiting for the part of the program where the speaker orders a Perrier or a coffee. Instead, I am tutored in how to dicker about prices. *"Onze euros? C'est trop cher."* Emma and I have yet to do our French today. With luck, we will get to it in late afternoon, settled in on our couches as the sun sets outside the window. With luck, the lesson will seem sweet to me. Making art has taught me that the tiniest smidgen of progress is something to be savored.

As an artist, I must cherish each tiny bit of track as I am able to lay it down. Two pages further on the book? Very good. Two phone calls made on behalf of the musical? Also good. I must scan the horizon for the next right thing and do that thing, however tiny it may seem. A career must be husbanded. Care must be taken. Every day must bring some small bit of progress. How would an artist with any self-worth act? Act that way. Tonight I am traveling to the East Village to hear two singers do a cabaret. The singers, a male and female duo, are friends of mine and I want to support them. They are both Broadway stars and the evening's work will not advance them a notch, but it has allowed them to fill their days with something productive, something done for sheer love. He is about to do a show at Lincoln Center. She is about to head off to Europe as the lead in a new musical. The evening's program, romantic duets, will showcase sides of themselves that are not currently at play. I will make the trek to hear them sing so they will know I am voting in favor of their dreams.

It is all too easy as an artist to allow the shape of our career to be dictated to us by others. We can so easily wait to be chosen. Such passivity invites despair. To remain healthy and vital, artists must stay proactive in their own behalf. Writers must write for the love of writing and not merely, or only, to fulfill a book contract. Actors must consciously choose ways to keep acting when they are not winning auditions. Singers must find ways to sing in between Broadway parts.

Artists are very much like athletes. As an artist, I must be alert to keeping myself in effective training. Like a creative triathlete, I must take care to be well-rounded. I must take stock of my talents and take the time and care to try to use them fully. This is what my musical friends are doing. This is what I myself must do.

Beauty is an ecstasy; it is as simple as hunger.

W. SOMERSET MAUGHAM

If poetry is like an orgasm, an academic can be likened to someone who studies the passion stains on the bedsheets.

IRVING LAYTON

Just at the moment, I am writing nonfiction. It is a very particular kind of writing and to do it I must be alert in very precise ways. I must constantly tune into my environment in a very grounded and factual way. Nonfiction writing requires the "grit" of facts. Specificity in all forms is very helpful but it also produces a kind of emotional myopia. As a balance, I am also listening to opera, which is headier and more romantic and expansive. Opera allows my dreamer to step front and center. On a day when I allow myself to move between the two forms, I feel more balanced. Too much nonfiction and I feel I have my nose to the grindstone. Too much opera and I fear that I will simply drift away from life as I know it. Mixing the two, taking small steps forward in each, I find harmony, even optimism.

It's late afternoon. A nippy wind tugs at the windows. There is a window in the living room that can be kept shut only when tied with a ribbon. Even at that, the cold air leaks in and the ribbon flutters in the draft. It is sunset. Time to begin the day's French. Emma and I settle in to concentrate. *"Bonsoir, Madame."* The window creaks open. The phone shrills. It is my sister Libby with very good news about her injured arm. Her MRI has given her a fresh diagnosis. "I am doing the happy dance," she says. "What is wrong with me is just bursitis, not a torn rotator cuff. It can and will be fixed."

"Très bien, Libby," I tell her. She will soon be back to more hours at the easel.

"Très bien," she replies, laughing.

Art is an experience, not the formulation of a problem.

LINDSAY ANDERSON

Art for art's sake . . . It is the best evidence we can have of our dignity.

E. M. FORSTER

Divining Rod

It is all too easy as an artist to bewail the "odds stacked against us." It is harder—but necessary—to improve those odds by taking small actions in our own behalf. This is the power of perseverance, what I call "laying track." No matter how trapped we may feel by large cultural crosscurrents, there is always some small something that we can do in favor of our artist.

Take pen in hand. Number from one to five and list five small actions you could take on your own behalf. Any small action will suffice. For example, in preparation for my French trip, I can "Work with French tapes one hour daily." I can "Buy a small French-English dictionary." I can "Buy a guidebook to Paris." Such small actions can add up to a large sense of optimism. From your list, take one forward-moving action.

Were I called on to define very briefly the term art, I should call it "the reproduction of what the senses perceive in nature through the veil of the soul."

EDGAR ALLAN POE

Perfectionism

We have been graced with another spring day. The sky is a luminous blue. The breeze is fresh. The forsythia in the park edge closer to full bloom. The dogs are ecstatic. So many smells. So much adventure. It does not take much to make them happy.

I am a more difficult case. I would be happy, if only . . . Regret still plucks at my sleeve. I must work to muster optimism. What is the "next right thing"? I ask myself. Ah, yes.

Art is a private thing. The artist makes it for himself.

TRISTAN TZARA

Today is a teaching day for me, which means that I begin the day by reviewing the lesson that I will be teaching tonight. This week's work centers on perfectionism and the crippling impact it can have on our creativity. As always, reviewing the work, I see that I have not really grown beyond the lesson at hand. Creativity is a spiral path; we pass through the same issues over and over again at slightly differing altitudes. I have written twenty books, some more easily than others. My own perfectionism is not banished, just disguised. Now I call it "having standards."

I recently threw away two hundred pages of work, judging it simply "not good enough." Perhaps with more patience, the work could have been improved. Perhaps with more self-forgiveness, the work could have been seen as promising. But perfectionism is not patient, not self-forgiving. It is self-castigating. It is loveless. It allows the critic in us to have ascendancy and the final say. My critic has been ruling the roost lately.

At the moment, I grapple with my critic on a daily basis. It makes it difficult to write. Because he is such a permanent fixture in my creative pantheon, I have named my critic. He is called "Nigel." In my mind's eye, he is a gay man with impossibly high aesthetic standards. My work is never good enough for Nigel. He is always ready with a red pencil. According to Nigel, who has never been known to say anything nice, it is the critic's job to be critical.

"A critic is critical," Nigel assures me. He wants to get his hands on all of my work—and the sooner the better, in his opinion, if not mine. Perhaps all creators have their Nigels. Perhaps everyone's Nigel feels they don't quite measure up.

Like my Nigel, everyone's critic has doubts, second thoughts, third thoughts. The critic analyzes everything to the point of extinction. Everything must always be groomed and manicured. Everything must measure up to some mysterious and elusive standard.

The critic lacks generosity. It's in a hurry to reach final draft, polished form. It does not want to wait and see where a thought is going. Forget first drafts. Forget the charming roundabout. It prefers dull declarative sentences. The critic loves logic and it fears inspiration.

I sometimes think of the critic as a character left over from caveman times, times concerned with sheer survival. The critic hunches at the edge of the clearing and watches for dangerous intruders. If we send in an original thought, that thought is often shooed away. To the critic, an original thought may appear disturbing, even dangerous. It wants to see what it has seen before. It has seen a cow but it has never seen a zebra. Don't try to tell it that a zebra might be interesting. Those stripes don't look like such a good idea. Get those zebras out of here! Give us some nice, docile cows for our creative clearing. That's more to the critic's liking.

To the critic, ease feels foreign—and suspicious. Work should be work, shouldn't it? Surely nothing can simply flow? Damn the colloquial! Every thought, each sentence, must be carefully weighed. Nothing can begin without knowing the ending. There is no room for exploration, for ambiguity. The critic is a nervous man. The critic likes known routes.

The critic believes in product, not process. Do not try to simply rough something in. Forget sketching. That's not good enough. The critic does not like us to have the joy of creation. It is interested in fixing things, not in creating things. It insists there must always be something to fix.

I have recently been rereading Dorothea Brande's excellent book, *Becoming a Writer.* She carefully distinguishes between two functions of the writer, the creative impulse and the critical one. She believes these two functions must be taught to work independently. It is her belief that the critic can be trained to stand aside, that we can learn to write freely and then to invite our critic in for the second draft process when its discernment may prove valuable.

In order to train the two separate functions, she recommends a practice of early morning writing. (She does not call this practice "Morning Pages" and I knew nothing of her theories when I myself devised Morning Pages as a creative practice.) Like mine, her morning writing cannot be done "wrong." The critic's vote does not count. From this the critic learns that it must sometimes stand aside, that it will not be allowed to strangle the embryonic art as it struggles to emerge.

I do believe that Morning Pages can train the critic to stand aside. I believe that our critic can be trained and tamed—just not permanently. I myself have enjoyed long periods where Nigel was largely silent and I was free to do my first-draft work. Such periods are blissful. Such periods have always been interrupted, however, because the critic is patient. It is cunning, baf-

The artistic temperament is a disease that affects amateurs.

G. K. Chesterton

fling, and powerful. It is never permanently paralyzed. It will wait until we are tired, until we let down our guard. It will wait until it senses some weakness and then it will one more time insist that it should have the upper hand. "I am not so sure this is any good," the critic will weigh in. It seems only reasonable to consider the doubt that it raises. And that first doubt leads to another and another.

My friend Julianna McCarthy, a consummate actress, asserts that for artists it is lethal to pick up the first doubt. The critic will tempt us to drink of this poison. The critic likes us crippled and dependent. It likes to hoard its power and lord it over us. Rarely does the critic offer us constructive criticism. The critic is a black-and-white thinker. Our work isn't flawed or improvable. It is terrible. Condemnation is the critic's stock in trade.

An artist is a man of action.

JOSEPH CONRAD

I am thinking now of the last time I taught perfectionism—or rather, how to avoid it. I was greeted at the start of the class by a nervous young woman. She wanted just a moment for a word with me. She looked tormented.

"I think I may have done something really wrong," she told me. "I am a jazz pianist. For my Artist Date this week, I decided to take myself to a jam session. I got there and when I heard the first man play, I thought, 'This is impossible. He's so good. I will never be as good as he is.' I just sat slumped in my chair, defeated. I suppose I could have tried to get up and play something but I really felt like, 'Oh, what's the use?' I just slunk home. What was the matter with me, do you think?"

"I think you suffered a bout of perfectionism," I told her. "You took your critic with you on that date."

"Yes, I suppose I did."

"I think you listened to your critic and raised the jumps too high too fast."

"I think maybe I did." Just having the diagnosis gave the young woman relief.

Perfectionism doesn't believe in practice shots. It doesn't believe in improvement. Perfectionism has never heard that anything worth doing is worth doing badly—and that if we allow ourselves to do something badly we might in time become quite good at it. Perfectionism measures our beginner's work against the finished work of masters. Perfectionism thrives on comparison and competition. It doesn't know how to say, "Good try," or "Job well done." The critic does not believe in creative glee—or any glee at all, for that matter. No, perfectionism is a serious matter.

As artists, we must learn to be alert whenever things become too serious. When we stop being able to laugh we often stop being able to create. Our perfectionist takes center stage, the critic cracks the whip and sends our artist cowering. The larger our perfectionist looms, the smaller our talent seems to become. It is our perfectionist that needs to be miniaturized. A little laughter goes a long way toward drawing things to scale.

The first prerogative of an artist in any medium is to make a fool of himself.

PAULINE KAEL

When I become too serious, my pets come to my rescue. At my most morose, Charlotte will nudge at me insisting that now is the perfect time for a game of toss the ratty. My dogs do not believe in perfectionism. Out and about on a spring day, they do not criticize themselves. They do not say, "Look at those extra pounds the winter put on you." Tugging at their leashes, they chase squirrels they will never catch, and they do so with enthusiasm. My dogs know a thing or two about the art of being happy. I watch them and learn.

Divining Rod

All of us carry an Inner Censor. The censor is in charge of keeping us small. Negative and critical, it is always at our creative throat. As we become more accomplished, our critic becomes ever more sly and skillful in its attack. Let us say you are a writer. At first, the critic will attack you for being unpublished. After you do publish, your critic will tell you you are a one-book author. After many books, the critic will say you are repeating yourself and are a has-been.

As you become increasingly distinguished, your critic's attack will become more subtle and subversive. Artists do not seem to outgrow their critics, but we can learn to evade them. For many of us, it helps to name and describe our Censor. This transforms it from the voice of authority into a cartoon character. I have my Nigel but students have had censors as diverse as Bruce the shark from *Jaws* and "Sister Mary Priss, a thin-lipped ruler-toting dictator who always finds fault with what I do."

Take pen in hand. Identify, name, and describe your Censor. What does it look like? What does it sound like? Is its voice cruel or bullying? What does it say? Where did this voice come from? Sometimes it is as recognizable as a parent or a negative grammar-school teacher. Sometimes our critic seems to come from out of nowhere but it is still convincing in its attack.

Whether you can "really" draw or not, sketch your critic in action. Search through magazines until you find an image that sums up your critic. Clip it and mount it. By reducing your critic to a cartoon character, you lessen its power.

Everyone needs to work. Even a lion cannot sleep, expecting a deer to enter his mouth.

HITOPADESHA

Taking Action

This morning there was a light haze over Manhattan. The air was damp and balmy but it was not clear. The day was torn between rain and shine. It could have gone either way. For me, the weather perfectly mirrored my inner dilemma. Wanting to move ahead but uncertain as to just how, I myself have not been clear. When I am not clear, I am frustrated. Recently, I have been frustrated a lot.

Aggravated, I have tried to treat myself with tenderness. I have tried to remind myself that I have been here before, in creative limbo, and that sooner or later something shifts. Eventually, always, there is a break in the weather and a way to move ahead. It is all a matter of having patience, I told myself—but today I was not patient. I was socked in, on the verge of turbulence, just like the day itself.

At ten a.m., I took a cab south. I was meeting with my collaborator Emma and director Randall Myler. We were set to rendezvous at The Big Cup to brainstorm ways in which we could go further with our musical *The Medium at Large.*

The Big Cup was a Chelsea coffee bar. It featured gay men, loud music, and strong coffee as well as scones, muffins, cookies, brownies, and croissants. While rock music pounded over the sound system, morning diners pore over the day's paper or check their e-mails. Emma and I settled in with coffee with almond syrup and a chai latte.

"How are you doing?" Emma asked me.

"How are *you* doing?" I asked her back.

We were frustrated and we felt we had run out of ways to go forward. We were hoping that Randy would have some ideas. So much of the trick with a creative career is maintaining optimism and forward motion. So much consists of doing the next right thing, however tiny. Often we get discouraged because we are unable, left to our own devices, to see a next right step. Discouragement acts as blinders. This is where friends come in handy. This is where brainstorming matters.

Friends often have ideas that we may not have entertained. Sometimes it helps to talk to someone who is not in our field and doesn't know the rules that we, sometimes unconsciously, are playing by. "Have you tried . . . ?" someone will ask and it will be something so simple that it—simply—hadn't occurred to us. There are many different ways to skin the cat and some of those ways are going to be outside of our peripheral vision. A good friend can be like borrowing a radar dish—suddenly we are scooping up all sorts of signals where before there were none.

Inspiration follows aspiration.

RABINDRANATH TAGORE

Dressed in an oversized plaid shirt and blue jeans, Randy arrived. He is a director and directors are nothing if not direct. Propped forward on his chair to be heard above the din, he was full of suggestions. "Have you tried . . . ?" he asked and, "Did you think of . . . ?" Very often, the answer was, "No." Emma and I talked with him for an hour, taking copious notes.

From Randy's perspective, we were far from stuck high and dry. There were all sorts of tiny ways to go forward. If we were willing—and we were—there were any number of things that we could do. And there was something to be said, too, for patience. Randy himself once incubated a musical for nineteen years. Our four on *The Medium* was nothing to him. We barely had our feet wet, but if we wanted to get them wet further . . . We left The Big Cup buzzed on caffeine and buoyed up by Randy's enthusiasm.

I would not say that the weather had cleared by the time we took our cab back north, but I myself felt clearer. I could see some usable track ahead. There was a playwriting contest Emma and I could enter. There was another director we could call. There was a theater out on Long Island that might be perfect for a small production. There was a producer that we could tag base with . . .

One more time, Emma and I were back to small, doable actions. We were able to see the shape of the day. We would get on the phone and make the calls that seemed intimidating but necessary. We would ready a packet for submission . . .

Late in the afternoon, we walked in the park. The morning's haze had given way to a clear, steady light. The park was filled with joggers and strollers. Dog owners lolled along the reservoir path. We noted that white crocuses had joined the purple and the gold. We saw that several forsythia bushes were actually blooming. On a sheltered hillside, jonquils were budding. Soon they would be open. We had entered the playwriting contest. We had called the producer. We were waiting for a call back from the director. We had checked out the theater on the Internet. By the time we got to the park, we were ready to celebrate a day well done.

"It's amazing," Emma said to me, "what a difference it makes

It will never rain roses. When we want to have more roses, we must plant more roses.

GEORGE ELIOT

to be able to take an action. It is the difference between optimism and despair."

A squirrel skittered along a stone wall. Tiger Lily, my cocker spaniel, took off after it. Emma and I laughed with delight. We were having the same fun, chasing our brilliant careers.

Divining Rod

This tool asks you to engage the help of a friend. You may wish to choose someone from your previous list of encouraging friends. What you are after is a really good brainstorming session. You want your friend's input on the next steps that you might take regarding your art. For your self, this will be an exercise in open-mindedness. It is astonishingly easy to dismiss our friends' input as too naïve to be really workable. Don't be so sure. Friends are often cannier than we think, and they may suggest directions that are far more promising than the tried-and-true routes we are so discouraged by. Do not dismiss this tool until you have tried it. Now is the time to practice assertiveness on your artist's behalf.

You will need to call a friend and set a formal date. Explain to your friend that you are meeting on behalf of your artist. A dinner date or a coffee date is ideal. You will need time enough to settle in and really explore. In preparation for your date, you might wish to jot down a list of the actions that you have taken and those you think it is possible to take. These you can share with your friend to start the ball rolling.

You may also wish to set out your goals related to your project. As our friends may be quick to point out, sometimes our goals are too farsighted. (We may ultimately want to see our show on Broadway while our more tan-

The shortest answer is doing.

ENGLISH PROVERB

gible, reachable goal might better be to secure a good workshop production.) Use your friend to help you generate a doable list of next steps. Remember it is fair game to ask your friend for spiritual help as well an intellectual input. It is quite legitimate to say, "Can you put my project in your prayers?" Even our most secular-minded friends may display the surprising willingness to be a spiritual support for our dreams. "I'm not so long on prayers, but I could send you good vibes," one friend of mine phrased it.

No great discovery was ever made without a bold guess.

ISAAC NEWTON

CHECK-IN

1. **How many days this week did you do your Morning Pages?** If you skipped a day, why did you skip it? How was the experience of writing them for you? Are you experiencing more clarity? A wider range of emotions? A greater sense of detachment, purpose, and calm? Did anything surprise you? Is there a "repeating" issue asking to be dealt with?

2. **Did you do your Artist Date this week?** Did you note an improved sense of well-being? What did you do and how did it feel? Remember, Artist Dates can be difficult and you may need to coax yourself into taking them.

3. **Did you get out on your Weekly Walk?** How did that feel? What emotions or insights surfaced for you? Were you able to walk more than once? What did your walk do for your optimism and sense of perspective?

4. **Were there any other issues this week that felt significant to you in your self-discovery?** Describe them.

Uncovering a Sense of Support

Critical to any creative journey is a sense of creative support. You must practice discernment, weeding out that which does not serve and watering the shoots you want to foster. This week's tasks invite you to consciously interact with those who are positive on your behalf. Reaching out to others for their belief, you will also reach within and steady your personal confidence. If you had the faith, what might you try? This week's explorations will lead you into knowing your own mind.

Friends to the Work

Early this morning my phone rang. It was a fellow writer checking in. We have made a plan to piggyback on each other's energy for a while. She is having a hard time writing a book proposal. I am having a hard time writing, period. Her last proposal didn't sell and she is discouraged. Stymied, she goes to the page and comes up dry. She is struggling with a stubborn block. I struggle with blocks myself, and so I am a willing conspirator to help dismantle hers.

I love the idea for her new proposal and am convinced it will sell quickly and well. She needs only to finish up her first draft and then do some quick fixes to the top of the proposal, adding in more anecdotes to make it more reader-friendly. Crippled by fear and discouragement, she has found it impossible to do this work, work normally well within her range. A survivor of sim-

Good friends, good books and a sleepy conscience: this is the ideal life.

MARK TWAIN

The worst solitude is to be destitute of sincere friendship.

FRANCIS BACON

ilar blocks, I am a compassionate witness to her creative struggle. Her check-in call helps send me to the page. We are both in this together—"this" being a life in the arts.

There is a lot of mythology around the artist as a loner. As my friend novelist Tim Farrington ruefully phrases it, "The lonely genius stereotype, the semiautistic gifted person slaving passionately away in noble isolation." Well put, Tim, and complete hooey. The artist's life need not be isolated and lonely—we are just tutored to believe that it is. And such tutoring can be a self-fulfilling prophecy. An artist who needs help and support may be loath to ask for them. After all, aren't "real" artists beyond such needs? In a word, no.

We're fed a great deal of romance surrounding the lonely lot of the artist. We picture the garret from *La Bohème,* see the lone, starving artist, struggling with depression, struggling with sheer eccentricity. *We are trained to see artists in this way.* Over a recent weekend, teaching in San Francisco, I asked for a show of hands from all the people who believed an artist's life would be lonely. In a room filled with two hundred people, nearly two hundred hands went up. Believing this, we can try to live it out—a prospect that makes for a great deal of pain. Who wants to try writing a novel if the act is going to cost us all our friends? And so novels go untried and artists go on blocked.

The truth is that creativity occurs in clusters. Consider Paris in the twenties and the cluster that built up around Gertrude Stein's hospitality. Consider the Bloomsbury Group convening for Thursday night cocktails and inadvertently launching a movement. It can be argued that successful art is built on successful friendships. It can certainly be said that friends are what enable an artist to go the distance. Let me give you a case in point.

I recently attended the book signing of a red-hot New York writer. She had three novels out to rave reviews from the normally dyspeptic *New York Times.* She had a play opening in Moscow and another in New York. Her career was sizzling. After her well-attended signing, I was invited to dinner with her friends. We filled a long sixteen-person trestle table in a trendy

East Side bistro—included were the members of not one but two writers' groups that the red-hot writer attended—and had attended for all the years she was shaping her sizzle-worthy work.

"I owe it all to you," she called down the table at one point. Her friends hooted derisively in response, but on questioning did admit to having read certain pivotal drafts and offering notes. They had been for her "believing mirrors," mirroring back her competency and her talent. They had cheered her on, step by step, draft by draft. They had offered suggestions, reservations, encouragement, advice.

Am I suggesting that we should make art by committee? Hardly. Remember that the writer still had to write her drafts solo, but she did so with the support of her friends. Draft by draft they cheered her onward, signaling "Yes!" as the work came into focus. They believed in it. They believed in her. She, in turn, could believe in their belief when her own belief felt shaky. They formed a cheering section to hurrah her over the finish line. With their support, she made it.

I recently had my own experience with the power of friends to keep a project on track. I wrote a novel, a slender romantic novel, a love story about two misfits who lived in Manhattan. When I finished my first draft, I sent it to an editor and two friends. The editor was someone with whom I had worked repeatedly on nonfiction. The friends were people who had been reading my work in rough to polished form for nearly twenty years.

"Good start, keep moving," my friends signaled back. "This book is a really good time." They loved the little book even in seed form. The editor, by way of contrast, had grave problems with the central premise—and a lot of problems with the rest of it, too. Her notes cut me to the core—where my friends stood waiting to cheer me on.

"She's off. She just doesn't get it. Maybe she's never had a dysfunctional relationship," they opined. "Just keep at it. The book is delightful."

"Are you sure?"

Work and love—these are the basics. Without them there is neurosis.

THEODOR REIK

"Oh, Julia, don't give up on it because of one person's opinion."

And so, egged on by my friends, I set aside the editor's notes and went back to work. A second, third, fourth, fifth draft flushed out the first. The book began to make the rounds of professional readers, as well as my friends. Other editors loved it. On impulse, I sent the finished book back to editor number one.

"Now I get it!" she exclaimed. "It's terrific. I guess the lesson here is never to send me an early draft!"

I didn't say to her, "How can you be so blithe about your change of heart? I could have committed suicide over your first notes!"

For me, the lesson was the value of friendship—and the unique value of friends to my work. I knew that without my friends' help I would have abandoned the novel. I would have taken the editor's notes too closely to heart and given up on my book, telling myself, perhaps, that I had delusions of grandeur thinking I could pull off a romantic comedy. Arguably, I wouldn't even have seen this as self-destructive, just "realistic." (Today, thanks to my perseverance, the novel is pubished by St. Martin's Press.)

Friendship is one of the most tangible things in a world which offers fewer and fewer supports.

KENNETH BRANAGH

Ruefully, I thought back to an earlier novel I had scuttled, not yet trusting the power of friends. I had again sent the book to two friends and one editor. The editor wrote back, "Divide the number of roses and sunsets by two and publish!" I thought the note was sarcastic and, despite my friends' pleas that they liked the book and that roses and sunsets *could* be cut, I put the novel in a bottom drawer where it lived out its days.

You might be thinking from all of this that I am a hypersensitive writer. I think that I am. But I think that most artists are hypersensitive—or, in the word of famed writing teacher Natalie Goldberg, *delicate*. It's not that we can't take criticism, but that we often cannot take it in a balanced way. This is where friends come in.

Friends help us to weigh the positive against the negative. They help us to know when we have been savaged and when we just *feel* like we have been savaged. They help us to sort out when criticism has a point and when it is pointless. They help us to tell the difference between being bludgeoned and *feeling* bludgeoned. These are distinctions it is difficult to come to on your own.

I call it those people in whom we trust completely and with good reason "before, during, and after" friends. They are our true benefactors, our believing mirrors, mirroring back to our-selves our strengths and possibilities. It takes a while for a person to earn a place on this bench. They must prove themselves, over time, to be not only softhearted but also hardheaded. They must be tough-minded without being nasty. They must be user-friendly without being mushy. To be a believing mirror, they must, like a good mirror, have a clean, clear surface that allows them to mirror back without distortion what they are asked to reflect upon. There is nothing of more benefit to a career than a set of good believing mirrors. I know this from hard-won ex-perience.

Not all work will be inspired. Not all work will point in the right direction. Friends who know our work, our body of work, will be quick to notice when a new direction is struck. They make good sounding boards to discuss the validity of the direction we are trying, whether we are moving fruitfully for-ward into new terrain or have simply gone off on a tangent. Over time, friends will form opinions as to our vein of gold, that area of the creative field we may work most successfully. "Try another mystery," they may urge or, "I love it when you write romantic comedy."

Writing is not the only art form that benefits from friendly vision. "I see you've been really working on your backgrounds," a portrait painter might be told. "I like what you did in the sec-ond movement," a choreographer might hear. Ideally, a friendly viewer takes to mind both where the work has already been and where it might be trying to go. There is a sense both of history and of possibility. Sometimes a friend to our work will actively seek to open doors on our behalf.

Friends may not know better than we the direction work

Too many people miss the silver lining because they're expecting the gold.

Maurice Setter

I figure if I have my health, can pay the rent and I have my friends, I call it "content."

LAUREN BACALL

needs to take, but they may know at least as well. When I was working on my poetry album, *This Earth,* with composer Tim Wheater, he urged me to focus on political poems, not romantic ones. The resulting album won *Publishers Weekly'*s "best original score." I doubt a more confessional album would have succeeded so well.

Friends may be able to tell us when we are working badly and when our critic is simply working overtime. A straightforward, "It sounds fine to me," may be the indicator we are on the right track and not, as our fears told us, meandering blindly. Unfortunately our own Inner Critic is not a trustworthy guide as to the caliber of our work. Sometimes—rarely—our critic will let the second-rate work slip past. More often, our critic will mercilessly attack work that does not deserve such attack. This is where the validating support of friends comes into play.

"This work is rubbish," our critic may announce.

"I'm not so sure about that. It seems sound to me," a friend may opine.

Listening to our friendly viewers over a hyperactive inner critic is a learned skill. All too often, it is fear that prevents an artist from stepping onto center stage. The shy creator may be comfortable creating but uncomfortable with the resultant spotlight. Here, too, is where the championship of our friends is pivotal. As artists, we need to have those who can root for us as we gather ourselves to take some terrifying leap of artistic faith. We may call such a friend to say, "I am afraid to send off my article but I am going to go mail it now." We may phone back to say, "I just mailed it." In 12-step lingo, this is known as a "sandwich call." Something difficult sandwiched in between our supports.

Belief is contagious and sometimes when we cannot believe in ourselves we can at least believe in the belief of others. "Maybe I'm not so bad," we might think. "Maybe I should take another stab at it." And then we do.

Divining Rod

You have made a list of encouraging friends. You are now asked to put that list into further action. By phone, e-mail, or letter, contact your believing mirrors. Catch them up on where you are on your projects. Be specific about the areas where you feel you need help. You have brainstormed in depth with one of them and now you are scanning your web of friends for further help and guidance.

Do not be surprised by the loving input you may receive. Our friends can be quite wise regarding the proper care and maintenance of our artist. Very often, when we are driven in our art, we fail to take loving actions toward ourselves. We neglect to celebrate the many small victories as they pass. Let us say you have just finished a draft of a project and you are now focused on the work—and future drafts—that remain to be done. A friend may very well suggest that you celebrate the work you have already accomplished. Schedule a dinner to do precisely that.

Allow your friends to be friendly. As you are more open with them about your hopes, dreams, and disappointments, they are able to be more supportive to you in your process. For you, the challenge is adequate self-disclosure. Try trusting your friends rather than playing the Lone Ranger. This flies in the face of our cultural mythology that tells us artists are loners. We need not be loners. (Successful artists seldom are.) Remember that success occurs in clusters and is born of generosity. Allow your friends the chance to be generous.

Always be a little kinder than necessary.

SIR JAMES M. BARRIE

Discouragement

There is nothing on this earth more to be prized than true friendship.

ST. THOMAS AQUINAS

As artists, we do not often marinate ourselves in self-satisfaction. We do not often think, "This is the greatest"—although it might be. It takes constant vigilance not to slip into negativity, or simple apathy. It takes courage to believe over any given period of time that we are getting better and not sliding into decline. To keep on keeping on takes energy and commitment, two variables we may need to borrow. Novelist Tim Farrington describes a day's work as "pushing the boulder uphill." For many an artist, on many a day, he is quite right.

Often, it is tenacity, not talent, that rules the day. Aided by our friends' support, we are able to be tenacious, to try one more round of submissions, to knock on one more gallery door. William Kennedy's novel *Ironweed* underwent fifty submissions before hitting pay dirt—and this book went on to receive the National Book Award!

For most artists, discouragement is the private hell we do not talk about. In my case, for example, I am discouraged on two fronts right now. The first front is *Avalon,* the musical I've worked on for seven years. It is currently sitting in limbo. In my manager's words, it is generating "respectful interest" but no real takers. The second disheartening front is my novel, which keeps getting "almost" bought. It is difficult, living through "almosts." How many more times can I bear to hear that "the editorial side loved the book but it didn't make it past sales and marketing"? It does no good to muster defenses like, "Editors are loving it." Until we have a "yes," we have a "no." And "no's" are difficult to live with. I try to practice that art. Every day I read the poems of Ernest Holmes. I pray not to be cynical. I pray not to close my heart.

Tomorrow, *Avalon* may find a producer. Tomorrow, my novel may find a publisher. For today, the assignment is to stay faithful, to keep on acting as if, to put words to the page despite their difficulty, to maintain optimism despite pessimism, to keep on keeping on. For this, I need help. I have learned to ask for it.

"Any good word yet?" Larry Lonergan asks when I talk with him. In the face of my discouragement, he stubbornly insists that good news is coming. He believes that the novel will sell and that *Avalon* will find a home. On the days when my belief wobbles, I piggyback my belief onto his. Faced with his faith, I find my own. I do not sabotage myself. I keep on stubbornly working. So much of keeping on is just keeping on.

It's late afternoon. I have just talked with my friend the struggling writer. She reported in that she had managed to complete a page of work and that the proposal again seemed to be edging forward. "Thank you so much," she told me. "It was possible to write knowing I was going to talk with you later."

"I got some work done today, too," I told her. "And I may have pages that I can salvage from the two hundred pages I pitched out. That would be a miracle." Together we laughed. The real miracle was the relief of one artist sharing with another. We were in the writers' boat together.

He who sees a need and waits to be asked for help is as unkind as if he had refused it.

DANTE ALIGHIERI

Divining Rod

This tool requires a little legwork and a little footwork. You may wish to take yourself to your local bookstore or else let your fingers do the walking and go to Barnes and Noble or amazon.com. You are looking for a biography or an autobiography that details the artist's life. You are on the look out for experience, strength, and hope. You want to hear from the horse's mouth exactly how disappointments have been survived. It helps to know that the greats have had hard times too and that your own hard times merely make you part of the club.

There is no wilderness like a life without friends; friendship multiplies blessings and minimizes misfortunes; it is a unique remedy against adversity, and it soothes the soul.

BALTASAR GRACIAN

In writing musicals, I look to books about Rodgers and Hammerstein. Their success is laudable but very hard won. Rodgers once faced such discouragement that he almost quit the music business to become a lingerie salesman. Hammerstein survived more than a decade's bitter disappointment between his early success with Jerome Kern and his later success with Rodgers. Sometimes, when I am most bitterly disappointed, I will take myself to the page and ask, "What would Oscar Hammerstein tell me?" Then I listen for whatever guidance seems to come through. Very often I receive wisdom that does not seem to be my own or the product of my own imaginings. I am always told to persevere.

Take pen in hand. Number from one to five and select five mentors from among the deceased. Focusing on one of them, ask for any help and input that they might have for you at the current time. Sit quietly and listen to hear what guidance comes to you. Write out what you "hear." Very often you will find that there is a wisdom available to you that does not seem to be your own.

Joining Humanity

Spring has gone back into hiding. Today the day is cold, drab, and gray. The park is emptier than it has been. The streets seem emptier, too, as if people are staying indoors and applying themselves to the task at hand. For me, the task at hand is an ordinary day of work. I have gotten a phone call from my friend the writer and she has said she will be working a short day, but work she will. Already it feels comfortable, our routine of checking in with each other. It makes the workday more doable, makes it something shared between friends.

It is the ego's dicey proposition that as artists we should always be "special" and different. The ego likes to be set apart. It likes to look down its nose at the rest of humanity. Such isolation is actually damaging. It is like the reverse of the Midas touch turning everything golden into a problem. Let us say we have fear—as all humans do—the ego would have us having "artistic fear" which sounds like a specialized something that perhaps only an expert, and an expensive expert at that, could help us cope with.

If we have plain old ordinary fear then we are within reach of a solution. Fear has been with humankind for millennia and we do know what to do about it—pray about it, talk about it, feel the fear, and do it anyway. "Artistic" fear, on the other hand, sounds somehow nastier and more virulent, like it just might not yield to ordinary solutions—and yet it does, the moment we become humble enough to try ordinary solutions.

I know what things are good: friendship and work and conversation.

RUPERT BROOKE

It is only by courting humility that we stand a chance as artists. When we choose to join the human condition rather than set ourselves apart from it, we begin at once to experience relief. If we stop calling our writer's block "writer's block" and begin using words like "resistance" and "procrastination" we are suddenly no longer in rarefied territory.

One of the greatest disservices we can do to ourselves as artists is to make our work too special and too different from everybody else's work. To the degree to which we can normalize our day, we have a chance to be both productive and happy. Let us say, as is often the case, we are resistant to getting down to work. We have a choice. We can buy into our resistance— Writer's block! Painter's block!—or we can simply say, "I don't feel like working today, and I'll bet an awful lot of other people are in the same boat."

The minute we identify with the rest of humankind, we are on the right track. The minute we set ourselves apart, we are in trouble. When we start thinking that as artists we are very different from other people, we start to feel marginalized and hopeless. When we realize that we are probably in pretty much

If a man write a better book, preach a better sermon, or make a better mouse-trap than his neighbor, tho' he build his house in the woods, the world will make a beaten path to his door.

RALPH WALDO EMERSON

the same boat as everyone else, we begin to edge toward solution. Our shared humanity is the solution. Our "specialness" is the problem.

"It's hard, starting a novel" can be normalized into "It's hard starting any new project." "How will I ever meet this portrait deadline?" becomes "How will I ever meet this work deadline?" The fact of being a novelist or a portrait artist matters less than the all-too-human thought "I am not sure I can pull it off this time." All workers face this fear. It's normal.

"I am having trouble starting, please stick me in the prayer pot," we may ask our friends, reducing our resistance from a gigantic block into something more manageable.

"My critic is going bananas, please pray for me to get a little break," we may ask, reducing our critic from a godly authority figure into a mere annoyance.

Any time our work process becomes something we can share with our "normal" friends, we are on the road to health. Everyone may not experience writer's block, but everyone has experience with resistance. When we stop insisting on being special, an "artist," we can begin to solicit commonsense solutions, which our friends may have plenty to offer. All we need to do is ask for help.

The human being does not exist who has not procrastinated. Many human beings have devised stratagems to deal with their procrastination. Suddenly, we can avail ourselves of their help. We don't need to talk to another writer to be understood. "I know I should, but I just can't make myself" is something anyone can understand. Suddenly starting on the novel is just a chore, no more glorified than cleaning out the broom closet. You'll feel better once you've made a stab at it. Which you can, with a little help from your friends.

"Work for a half an hour and call me back to say you've started," a friend may suggest who spends her days editing tiresome legal briefs and knows a thing or two about procrastination.

"Schedule yourself a treat or a bribe," another friend weighs in. "Work first. Bribe second. I always allow myself a half hour of reading the tabloids after scrubbing the bathrooms."

"Take a sheet of paper and list all of your angers and resentments about the project," a third friend interjects. "That really helped me when my boss gave me an impossible assignment." Suddenly we are on the road to recovery. Our creative dilemma has become a human dilemma.

All human beings are creative. The more we can accept and welcome that fact, the more normal our own creativity can become. If it is "normal," then it can be shared with everyone. If it can be shared with everyone, then there is lots of help available to us when we get discouraged. Our friends will understand.

The ego doesn't like the proposition that artwork is like any other work. The ego likes mysterious and self-serving hokum like, "Artwork requires inspiration." Hooey. As any honest artist will tell you, inspiration is far more often a by-product of work than its cause.

We don't feel inspired, far from it, but we begin anyway and something in the act of beginning seems to jump-start a flow of ideas. In cozy retrospect, we can call such ideas "inspiration," but as they occur they are far more workaday. One thing seems to lead to another and another, and before we know it an "inspired" day's work has transpired. The only genuinely inspired part of that day was the very beginning when we decided to accept the Nike slogan, "Just do it."

Outside my writing-room window, the gray day edges toward charcoal. Night is settling in. Tonight there is no showy sunset, no final flourish to the day. It is simply another day finished, another day's work done and that, too, is good. A quick check-in call to my friend the writer reveals that she, too, has again had a productive day. Tonight she goes to her writers' group, pages in hand. It feels good to be turning out proposal pages again, to be one more time moving forward. "I am just so glad to be working," she says, laughing. It feels good to be a

Friendship is a strong and habitual inclination in two persons to promote the good and happiness in one another.

EUSTACE BUDGELL

worker among workers, a friend amid friends. We will write again tomorrow.

Without wearing any mask we are conscious of, we have a special face for each friend.

OLIVER WENDELL HOLMES

Divining Rod

You are asked to turn one more time to your list of encouraging friends. You are about to use this list again but a little differently. You are now to choose one name from among your supporters and to call that friend not to talk about your creative troubles but to listen to the details of his or her everyday life. This is an exercise in turnaround and it will serve you well. Henry Miller advised young artists to develop an interest in people and that interest is what you are working at now. Tell your friend, "I was just missing you, and I realized I wanted to know much more about how your life was actually going."

Listening to our friends as well as speaking to them of our own lives is very grounding. The more we know of what they are up to, the more we can feel that despite the essential isolation of the creative path, we are living a life in community. We can think, "I may be writing right now, but Ed is at his law firm and Sonia is still seeing clients. Libby is feeding her horses right about now, and Larry is heading out on his daily constitutional." Knowing our friends' schedules gives us a sense of companionship as we face the page or the easel. The bottom line is that we make art about the human condition and our lives must be rich with experience in order for our art to remain vital.

Sobriety

For about a month now, I have been working with a young writer on the film adaptation of one of my novels. Every day we rendezvous by phone and put in an hour's work on the script. Little by little, we chip away at the problems and work our way toward a solution. We are on draft three now, and with each draft the movie comes more into focus. There is nothing very mysterious about making the movie better. All it takes is our focused time and attention. Nothing could be simpler. Nothing could be more rewarding. And yet, each day, when it is time for the work phone call, it is tempting to just get on the phone and socialize. We laugh about our resistance, but it is hard, settling in to work. The ego doesn't like punching in and doing work on a schedule. The ego likes more mystery and hokum.

The idea that the biggest secret of making art might just be making some art is a conclusion the ego works very hard to avoid. The ego wants us to be "in the mood" to make art at the very least. And yet, as any working artist will honestly tell you, waiting for the mood is a huge time waster. We are married to our art and just as the first caress can lead to interest between a long married couple, the first lick of work can lead to an appetite for work. In other words, mood more often follows action than instigates it.

How the ego wants it to be different!

The ego doesn't like the proposition that there is one divine mind working through all things and available to each of us. No, according to the ego, we each have a limited store of creativity. We each tap—or don't tap—our creative potential and there's no use praying for more creativity because we're not going to get it. And who can believe that God is interested in our art anyhow? The ego discounts and discards the actual spiritual experience of countless artists.

Artists know that when we are working at our best some-

I regard the theater as a serious business, one that makes or should make man more human, which is to say, less alone.

ARTHUR MILLER

thing larger than ourselves is working through us. We are a conduit, a channel for a greater creativity than our own limited resources. In fact, we are tapped into an infinite flow of creative ideas, ideas that come through us but are not really our own. How the ego hates this proposition. You mean we can ask for more creativity? Yes. You mean we can count on a greater flow of creativity? Yes. You mean all of us actually are creative and can be still more creative? Yes.

The ego doesn't like this. It is far too democratic and egalitarian for the ego to stomach. The ego loves competition, not camaraderie. What the ego has in mind is a small tribe of "real" artists who are "special" and "different." If we listen to the ego, we become dangerously marginalized. Our art becomes more difficult for us to make because we are too busy trying to make ourselves into artists. We become focused on "How am I doing?" rather than "What am I doing?" Our attention strays from process to product—and we, as much as our work, become the product we are producing. "Do I look like a real artist?" we wonder.

The ego loves to keep us wondering. The ego likes uncertainty because wherever there is uncertainty there is grounds for obsession, particularly self-obsession, the ego's favorite plaything. The ego wants us to think about being an artist rather than simply be one. The ego doesn't want art to boil down to the very basic question of process.

If we accept the premise that all human beings are creative, then it becomes "normal" behavior to be creative. If it is normal to be creative, then we can expect our friends to support and encourage it—and not just our officially "creative" friends, either.

As we demythologize creativity, we exorcise a great many demons. We have no need for the demon of feeling special and different, isolated and alone. If creativity is normal, then it can be committed right in the heart of our family and friends—which is where creativity needs to be committed. I wrote my first novel in an upstairs bedroom at my parents' house. My parents were hospitalized, I was doing stand-in duty as parent-in-residence, and in the hours when my sisters and brothers didn't need me, I wrote a novel.

"I'm going to go upstairs and write for a while," became as normal a sentence as, "I'm going to go downstairs and tackle some of the laundry." My novel was simply one more job I had set for myself. I cooked meals, did laundry, helped kids with their homework, and I wrote. Just as I couldn't let the laundry pile up, or the dishes pile up, I couldn't let the writing pile up, either. A certain regular amount of writing was required.

Making writing part of normal life instead of something special and apart from it served me very well. I didn't have the language for it then, but my writing life was "sober." By "sober" I mean nondramatic. When I actually did get physically clean and sober, in 1978, one of the first areas my new friends helped me to address was the issue of emotional sobriety in my work life. Work needed to be daily and doable, I was told. "One day at a time" and "Easy does it" were slogans I could actually apply to my writing. Desperate to find sanity and a sober life, I did as I was told.

I learned to write daily, one day at a time, one page at a time. I learned to set a sober quota on work—for me, three pages daily—and to consider my workday "done" when my quota was fulfilled. As directed, I posted a sign in my work area, "Okay, God, you take care of the quality; I'll take care of the quantity." The sign was intended to keep me from bingeing on negative emotions. There was no point, I was taught, in indulging in emotional benders related to work. Work was something to be normalized. My ego was best kept out of it.

If I were writing a screenplay, my quota was three script pages a day. If it were a novel, three novel pages a day. Eventually nonfiction books yielded to the same three-page-a-day formula. Three pages were long enough to feel I had done *something* and short enough to allow room to do something more or else—visit with friends, for example, or take in a movie.

Because it was not allowed to take over my whole life, work

Problems are messages.

SHAKTI GAWAIN

allowed me to have a life. My only job was three pages a day. If I did them first thing in the morning, then I had the whole rest of the day to fill with preoccupations other than myself.

I learned, in the early years of sober writing, to make the sandwich calls that said, "I'm going to write for a while now," and then, "I've finished writing for the day." It wasn't always to another writer that I called in my work commitment. Sometimes it was to an actor or a singer or a "nonartistic" friend. Friends of all stripes could be friends to my work. Work was nothing glorified. It was one more chore. I went to work at my typewriter the same way my friend Jackie went to work at her dress shop. I showed up. I ignored my resistance. I did my *pages.* When my pages were through for the day, so was my identity as a self-conscious writer. For the remainder of the day, I was a girlfriend, a mother, a sister—many different roles beside "artist."

Freed from the weight of my entire identity, writing became something I did more lightly. Writing itself became easier, less tortured, less self-important. I became a woman who wrote, not a woman writer. As my identity as a writer became a garment worn more loosely, I discovered I had many other identities that I could inhabit with greater ease. My friendship base broadened. I could be friends with a lawyer and a kindergarten teacher. I could be friends with a painter and a housewife. You didn't have to be an artist to be my friend. I didn't have to *act like* an artist to be your friend. What we had in common was our shared identity as *human beings.* This was special enough for me.

It remains special enough for me. Now that I am an older artist, I find I must consciously fight the temptation to *pose* as an artist. With a substantial résumé to point to, I must work harder to take myself lightly. The rules of creation remain exactly the same and I do well when I adhere to them. Three pages a day. Keep it simple and keep it doable. When it's done, it's done.

Working at my work a day at a time, I have written twenty books now plus a great deal of music and a number of plays and screenplays. It has all been accomplished by the "easy does it"

When a woman tells the truth, she is creating the possibility for more truth around her.

ADRIENNE RICH

method. I try to be a conduit and a channel. I try not to be self-conscious, not to be worried about how "I" am doing. For three pages daily, I "listen" and write down what I "hear." In a sense, I cannot take credit for what I accomplish. My productivity has really been born of cooperation. This cooperation is what I can model for artists younger than myself. I "show up" for work. They can do the same.

"We got through it!" exclaimed the young writer when I worked with her today. Indeed, we had finished another draft. Our movie is starting to have flesh on the page. The characters are behaving like characters. The scenes are unfurling like scenes. This is exciting—exciting enough that I am tempted to binge on the work. Fortunately, I know better. I am going to Paris for eight days and while I am gone, the young writer will have time to write certain scenes we now know are missing. When I get back, we will go through the draft process again, working again a little at a time. We will do *un peu,* as they say in Paris—or they do if I remember any of my high school French.

Love the moment, and the energy of that moment will spread beyond all boundaries.

CORITA KENT

Divining Rod

Most of us accomplish too little because we are expecting to accomplish too much. Daunted by the size of the task we wish to accomplish, we freeze up. We are defeated before we begin. And so, we do not begin. For example, we want to write a novel but see it as an enormous expenditure of time that we just don't have. "I'd love to," we say, "but—" It is only when a creative career is broken down into daily increments that it becomes doable.

A novel, after all, is written one page at a time. If we set a daily quota of three pages, that means we will have ninety pages in a month, 180 pages in two months,

She became for me an island of light, fun, wisdom, where I could run with my discoveries and torments and hopes at any time of day and find welcome.

MAY SARTON

270 pages in three months and in a scant four months we will have 360 pages—the length of a modest novel.

Books are not the only art form that lends itself to a gentle quota. Piano can be learned in a scant twenty to thirty minutes a day. That same half hour can be spent at the easel. Or at the barre. Although we love them and even crave them, we do not really need vast savannahs of time to work at our art. What we need is the willingness to work at our art in the time that we have actually got.

Take pen in hand. Explore the following questions. What art form could you begin practicing if you actually tried "easy does it" as a work practice? What art form do you tell yourself you have no time for? Is it really true? When in your day can you find twenty minutes to spare for working on your art? How do you kill time—TV? The phone?—and can you stop doing that? What is your artistic goal and what is a daily, workable amount that you can reasonably expect from yourself? Can that amount be lessened? What amount of work can you accomplish daily without drama? That is your sober quota.

The Best Kind of Friends

Who would have thought Paris would be about people and not about things? What could be more striking than the Eiffel Tower ablaze each night with dazzling lights, the glittering Seine rippling through the city? What could be more enticing than the roadside stands selling freshly made crepes, the corner cafés with their café crème and chocolat chaud? All true, but for me, Paris was a city of friendships.

Although April in Paris is a time of budding trees and brilliant gardens, the sights to be seen in Paris are often not out and about in the streets but in the carefully lit rooms of galleries, most especially in the Musée d'Orsay which houses a brilliant collection of Impressionist paintings. There we have a record of friendships celebrated and talents generously nurtured by well-chosen friends. Gauguin and Van Gogh, Picasso and Matisse—these artists brought out the best in each other and were wise enough to know it. Their work cross-pollinated each other's. Their friendship made it possible for each of them to go the distance. What did the Impressionists most love to paint? Lunch with each other.

Part of husbanding our talent lies in finding those who are generous enough to reflect us back as talented. Creativity flourishes in an atmosphere of acceptance. As we learn to number friends to our work among our friends, that work can strengthen and bloom. It could be argued that friendship is often the determining factor between a career that flourishes and one that languishes. We are responsible for choosing our friends.

Ah, duty is an icy shadow.
AUGUSTA EVANS

During my twenties, I was married to young filmmaker Martin Scorsese. He numbered among his friends George Lucas, Steven Spielberg, Brian De Palma, and Francis Coppola. Not one of those men was yet famous. All were upwardly mobile and generous in their support of one another's emerging talents. They screened early cuts of their films for comments and input. I remember a sequence of *New York, New York* being reversed and revamped at George Lucas's suggestion. As each member of this creative cluster percolated upward, they continued to pool their resources. It was routine for one director to suggest to another a talented young actor he had found. Scorsese suggested De Niro to Coppola for *The Godfather: Part II.* Every one benefited from one another's generosity. And no one was famous to begin with—although all would become so with one another's help.

One of the reasons our society has become such a mess is that we're isolated from each other.
MAGGIE KUHN

It helps to remember that the famous do not begin as the famous, they merely begin as the gifted and interesting. All of us have friends we can call both gifted and interesting. We require even more of certain friends—that they be gifted and interesting and *generous*—generous enough to reflect us back as also gifted and interesting. This is what makes a mere friend into a "believing mirror."

For many of us, believing mirrors can take a little getting used to. Often, we have grown up surrounded by fun-house mirrors that reflected our dreams to us as egotistical, grandiose, even preposterous. It takes generosity not to diminish the dream of another. True believing mirrors are always generous.

How do we know if we have encountered a true believing mirror? There is a feeling of excitement and possibility. There may be a positive comment that we can cherish and replay. ("Why girls, this song could win you an Oscar," remarked one believing mirror on first hearing a melody of mine and Emma's. We were thrilled.) There will be no hint of cynicism, no suggestion that your dream is *crazy*. There will be the ring of sincerity and blessed optimism.

Believing mirrors are believers, first of all, in the basic good of life. Setting aside chic skepticism, they are upbeat and encouraging. They believe in the college try. What's more, they believe in trying again. They are realists. They expect good things, but they know good things take work. They assume you will do the work because your dreams are good and worthy. They will help you if they can.

What they cannot know is exactly how much help they already are giving us simply by existing. One positive friend may be all that it takes for us to keep on keeping on. Let me give you a case in point.

In 1946, Tennessee Williams was ill and believed he might be dying. With death-bed courage, he wrote a letter to Carson McCullers, whom he greatly admired. "I wanted to meet her before I died," he later wrote, and so he invited her to Nantucket, where he was summering. "This tall girl came down the gangplank, wearing a baseball cap and slacks." Their friendship was forged.

The summer unfurled with long conversations, long swims in the ocean, long writing sessions at opposite ends of a kitchen

Remember, Ginger Rogers did everything Fred Astaire did, but she did it backwards and in high heels.

FAITH WHITTLESEY

Life was meant to be lived, and curiosity must be kept alive. One must never, for whatever reason, turn his back on life.

ELEANOR ROOSEVELT

table where he worked on *Summer and Smoke* and she worked on the theatrical adaptation of *The Member of the Wedding*. For both writers, the friendship was catalytic and timely, offering each rich encouragement from a respected source. Williams did not die. Instead, he staged a renaissance. McCullers offered him friendship and "spuds Carson," which were baked potatoes with olives, onions, and cheese in them. He thrived on both.

For Williams and McCullers, their pairing was the timely meeting of a believing mirror. Their relationship refreshed and rejuvenated them. McCullers later referred to the summer as one of "sun and friendship." Both the sun and the friendship were sorely needed.

Williams and McCullers had each won early critical acclaim followed by years of sharper criticism that both took too much to heart. In sharing with each other, they were able to alleviate the wounds left by the critical establishment and return to an appreciation of the work itself, the sheer joy and self-respect to be found in doing it. Over and over, in his correspondence with others, Williams would draw the focus back to what McCullers had "produced." An appreciation of the heroism of artistic production against all odds—that is the gift of a true believing mirror. I have enjoyed that gift for some years now.

I have been friends for twenty years with Sonia Choquette. Often, when I am despondent over my work, when Larry has not been able to convince me of my merits, it is Sonia whom I will call. She believes in me and believes in the ultimate success of my body of work. "Look at all you've done over the past year," she will urge me. "You've written a novel, you've written a prayer book, you've worked on an opera. Why, you're doing better than you think."

It is a function of believing mirrors to focus us always on the positive, on the bottom line of our "doing better than you think." Sonia will remind me that I *am* writing when my critic is telling me I am not writing well. Sonia will raise the possibility that perhaps what I am writing threatens the critic, and that

From the first time I met the little girl, until her death recently, a period of a little over seventy years, we were friends.

MRS. MARY E. ACKLEY

is why it is so vituperative right now. It is not that a believing mirror ignores negativity, it is more that a believing mirror considers the negative but still votes on the side of the positive.

A rejected novel "just needs to find the right people." A delayed musical is "just waiting for the climate in the market to be right." Both of these views are forward-looking, refusing to be discouraged. More than almost anything else, a believing mirror is stubborn. It is loyal and it is farseeing. A believing mirror conveys dignity. It says, "Look at all you've done."

A believing mirror focuses on our process as an artist. It finds dignity in the fact of making art, not in the fact of having made it as an artist—although a believing mirror always allows that it believes we will do that, too. A believing mirror does not believe in a capricious and withholding universe. It believes in rewards for work well done. "You've done too much good work for it to come to nothing," a believing mirror will say.

Creativity is an act of faith and believing mirrors give us faith in our faith. *Catch-22* was submitted twenty-two times before it was accepted as a novel for publication. It took powerful faith to continue the submission process. "Powerful faith" is a gift of believing mirrors. For a writer, a literary agent may be a believing mirror. For an artist, a dealer. But there are many nonprofessional relationships that nurture our self-belief. Friends, spouses, siblings, parents—any of these may be a source of believing eyes.

There is something healthy at the heart of every artist, something that welcomes the "ah hah" of inspiration in whatever form it comes. Take the odd-couple pairing of Irving Berlin and Cole Porter, united by their mutual appreciation of each other's genius and by no other circumstance. Berlin came from the ghetto and extreme poverty. Porter came from privilege. Berlin was a conventionally married man. Porter was a celebrated homosexual living in a marriage of convenience. Even their melodic approaches could not have been more different, and yet the men admired each other and struck up a lively and enduring correspondence. To the outside world, their alliance was un-

One needs something to believe in, something for which one can have wholehearted enthusiasm.

HANNAH SENESH

I'm not going to limit myself just because people won't accept the fact that I can do something else.

DOLLY PARTON

likely. As believing mirrors, they saw and mirrored back to each other the talent both worked to cultivate.

There is a purity to the connection between believing mirrors, an ability to see past the differences to the divine spark within. It is this ability to see past appearances that marks many of the more famous artistic alliances. At a pivotal point in their fledgling careers, Fitzgerald and Hemingway forged a friendship of believing mirrors. Talk about an attraction of opposites! Fitzgerald was delicate and self-destructive. Hemingway was full of bravado and machismo. What they had in common was admiration for each other's work. Fitzgerald brought Hemingway to Scribner's and helped him get paying career legs under him. Hemingway urged Fitzgerald to trust his imagination and write freely. "For Christ's sake, write and don't worry about what the boys say, whether it will be a masterpiece or what."

There can be a bottom-line tough-mindedness to believing mirrors, a tendency to focus on the use of talent and to ignore the rest. In my relationship with novelist Tim Farrington, many daily details are exchanged but the bottom-line question is always, "Are you writing?" As Farrington has phrased it to me, "Writing rights all." And so, I can talk to him about my fears, my misgivings, and my doubts, and he will always bring it back to the question of my talents and whether I am using them.

Assumed in a believing-mirror relationship is the fact that it is God's will for us to use our talents. This in itself is radical. We have often been raised with a false sense of modesty. We have been taught it is better, somehow more spiritual, to be small not large. We have been tutored to hamper our own creative flight with doubts as to whether such flight is seemly. A believing mirror wants us to soar. To them, our bigger self is our true self, the self to aspire to.

Pivotal to self-expression is the idea that there is a benevolent, interested Universe that wants us to expand. Without such belief, we may buy into our self-doubt and by doing so sharply limit what we are able to attain. We may think, "Wouldn't it be lovely" and then automatically dampen our enthusiasm with

A seeker went to ask a sage for guidance on the Sufi way. The sage counseled, "If you have never trodden the path of love, go away and fall in love. Then come back and see us."

JAMI

"That could never happen"—but perhaps it could. It is the function of a believing mirror to keep us focused on the "Perhaps it could."

For a believing mirror, nothing is too good to be true. Spiritually grounded even if not conventionally religious, a believing mirror focuses on the divine spark of genius within us all. Because that divine spark is godly in origin, anything is possible. When we are connected to the Divine within us, nothing is beyond our reach.

Elmer Green, known to the world as the father of biofeedback, speaks of the existence of what he calls "lifetrons." Tiny energy units galvanized by intention, lifetrons set up a flow of benign coincidence. It is my contention that when we set up an alliance of believing mirrors, we catalyze lifetrons into service on our behalf. Christ spoke of this when he said, "Whenever two or more are gathered together in my name, there I am in the midst."

There is a sacred quality to an alliance of believing mirrors. We are dedicated to seeing each other as pure spiritual potential. Our human personalities, our foibles and flaws, are somehow overlooked. We are focused on the big picture of what is right with ourselves rather than on the smaller and more limiting picture of what is wrong. A believing mirror sees our shortcomings as mere stumbling blocks not the behemoths they sometimes appear to ourselves.

Today I spoke to a believing mirror about the fear and doubt I experienced on a current creative project. When I wound down, my friend said, "So. This is just the period on this project" when you will have to be patient." Note the optimism in this diagnosis. "The period" (it will end) "on this project" (one of many you've done) "when you will have to be patient" (as you assuredly have the emotional maturity to be). I got off the phone and turned back to the project with renewed calm and determination. Surely I was patient enough to do just a little more.

The renewed determination to "do just a little more" characterizes a believing-mirror exchange. Because they are certain we are going to succeed eventually, believing mirrors are in no panicked haste. They remind us to simply take the next right step, faithfully believing that everything is unfolding exactly as it should. If you tell a believing mirror of a sudden and dramatic breakthrough, they may act as if there is nothing either sudden or dramatic about it. To them, it is simply the continued unfurling of something right and proper.

The idea of your dream as "something right and proper" is yet another earmark of a believing mirror's faith. They want you to succeed, so every circumstance that reinforces your success is seen as natural and good. Believing mirrors do not worry you will get too big for your britches. They may worry about whether or not your britches are big enough for you. Theirs is a refreshing perspective.

In Paris, the city of friendship, it is still possible to go to a café called Deux Magots and enjoy a hot chocolate where Hemingway and Fitzgerald met each other over drinks. It is possible to go to a bookstore called Shakespeare and Company and celebrate the friendship that James Joyce enjoyed with its proprietor. It is possible, buying Parisian postcards, to celebrate your own circle of believing mirrors, each of whom deserves a note. Writing those notes, it is possible to feel both gratitude and hope.

Divining Rod

Picasso credited Matisse with catalyzing some his own most inspired work. Friends who are friends to our work are often such catalysts. Believing mirrors point us

A friend is one before whom I may think out loud.

RALPH WALDO EMERSON

in new, promising, and fruitful directions. For this they deserve our appreciation and thanks.

Take pen in hand. Go to the page and recall there, in specific detail, the ways in which your believing mirrors have helped you to persevere. (As a jog to memory, it may help to go project by project.) It is easy for me to say that my friends Sonia and Larry are responsible for my having the courage to continue working on my musical *The Medium at Large.* It is to my literary agent Susan Raihofer that I owe a vote of thanks for her ongoing belief in my novel *Mozart's Ghost. The Artist's Way* I owe to the belief and support of Mark Bryan. Tim Wheater is the person whom I thank for my play *Love in the DMZ.*

Survey your own list of believing mirrors and recall the precise ways in which their optimism and strength have become your own. It is time for a timely thank-you. A phone call, a postcard, a brief letter—any of these are ways to contact and nurture our believing mirrors. Take time now to make a connection of gratitude. Your believing mirrors may turn your thanks aside, saying, "Oh, c'mon, it's nothing," but we know that it is not.

Believing Mirrors in Action

Paris is six hours ahead of New York and so, coming back to New York, I found myself in the grips of jet lag. It was bad enough as I walked the dogs in the park, each leaden step an insult to the balmy spring day. It was far worse when I sat myself down to write. Seated at the computer, jet lag bore a remarkable resemblance to writer's block. Fortunately, my phone rang.

"How is your writing going?" my friend Rhonda wanted to know. I told her that my writing felt painfully cramped and stilted. "It has for days," I added dramatically.

"Oh, I remember when it felt that way on your last project," she chortled. "Then before you knew it that project was sailing along and then it was finished. I'm sure it will be the same on this project."

I did not ask Rhonda where she got her insane optimism. I knew the answer to that. Rhonda is a friend to my work and has been for many years now. A determined optimist, she expects the best both of me and of the Universe. *Of course* I will be able to write through what she might call this "resistant patch." A believing mirror does not expect creation to be without difficulty but it does expect for that difficulty to be mastered. No, no self-pity around Rhonda.

So next, I complained by e-mail to Tim Farrington that I was in the "slog, slog, slog" section of working on a new book. He shot back briskly, "Slog, slog, slog stage of a new book is great you know." I wanted to slug him. Then he added, "Ignore that Inner Critic; they never let up." I wanted to say, "Some days it's easier to ignore the Inner Critic than other days," but I knew he already knew that.

Still feeling sorry for myself, I called my friend Natalie Goldberg, the famous writing teacher.

"I had a bad writing day," I whined to her.

"Well, you know that goes with the territory," she shot back. "You have to be in it for the whole enchilada, the bad writing days and the good."

Something in what Natalie said surrendered me. Yes, of course. How could I forget that bad writing days just came with the territory? I was in it for the long haul, and the long haul was what my friends expected of me. That was why Rhonda could be almost gleeful reminding me of bad writing spells from the past. That was why Tim Farrington could assure me I was actually in a great stage. That was why Natalie could listen to my whining and cheerily remind me that it came with the territory, that I had signed on for the whole enchilada.

I was shopping for drama and not finding any among my friends. Larry and Sonia were both stubbornly optimistic. I was wanting a bad writing day to mean "throw in the towel." They were reminding me it just meant my hat was in the ring. Annoying as I found it when no one would cosign my drama, my believing mirrors were functioning perfectly, refusing to let me derail myself too far. A bad writing day, even a whole string of bad writing days, was nothing to get myself wound up about. If Tim Farrington could tell me the Inner Critic never lets up, that was the voice of his experience speaking and he wasn't talking about quitting the writing game. Clearly, instead of licking my wounds, I just needed to toughen up a little. One more time, I needed to get emotionally sober.

Owing perhaps to jet lag, a genuine biochemical event, I was on a "dry drunk," an emotional bender that closely resembled the real thing. Unless I wanted to court a breakdown—or a drink—I needed to snap out of it. A good glimpse of myself in a believing mirror showed me how distorted my thinking was. Tempted to more drama by beating myself up, I reminded myself that all of us undergo bouts of distorted thinking. No one, and certainly not me, is immune. We need our believing mirrors for timely rescue. We *all* need our believing mirrors.

If artists are not essentially self-destructive by nature, we do tend to binges of relentless self-criticism and it is during such periods that we must rely on the more temperate judgment of our believing mirrors. In my own case, I have found that my Inner Critic's most scathing comments are often reserved for what will later appear to be my strongest work. When I was writing my recent book *Walking in This World,* my critic worked overtime to assure me how terribly I was writing, what a rotten job I was doing trying to marshal my ideas onto the page. Bedeviled and beset, working uphill all the way, I finally gave a stack of the essays over to be read by a believing mirror.

"I think this writing is good, actually very strong," the diagnosis came back, puzzled. "Tell me again exactly what you think is wrong with this."

Of course, there was no way to say *exactly* what I felt was wrong with the work. My critic wasn't armed with a rational attack. It had stuck with vague, impossible to fix pejoratives, words like "weak."

"I just thought it was weak or something."

"No, I don't think so. I actually think the essays are strong."

When I showed the same stack of essays to a second believing mirror and once again met with praise not pans, I began to get a little bit excited. Maybe my critic was so active not because the work was bad but because the work was good. My believing mirrors thought it was and they had a track record of accuracy.

Believing mirrors are not flatterers. They know too well that we are counting on them for objectivity. Some of my believing mirrors are very tough critics. I know that to pass muster with them, I must really be able to pass muster. Believing mirrors do not always come back 100 percent in our court. A believing mirror may say, "Mmmm. There was something a little wobbly in the second half." They may say, "Your voice seemed muffled somehow. Did you say what you really meant?" Or, "I felt you were evading an issue here." Such reservations, spoken with our best interests at heart, mean, "Back to the drawing board, something's not right here."

This afternoon, my phone rang. It was Ed Towle, one of my oldest friends and one of my most trusted readers. He was calling from his car in L.A. He was trapped in traffic and found himself wondering how my writing was going.

"I'm trapped in traffic, too," I laughed. "I have so many ideas right now, and I'm not getting them on the page in any order."

"It's a first draft for Christ sake. You're not supposed to have any order. You're not supposed to know how it fits together because it doesn't yet. That's for later."

Ed is himself one of the finest writers I know. It is encour-

The greatest good you can do for another is not just to share your riches, but to reveal to him his own.

BENJAMIN DISRAELI

aging to me that he doesn't believe in an overplotted linear first draft. Talking to him, I begin to relax. I start to think, "Oh, yes, my books always start out as a mess. It always takes multiple drafts to put them in shape."

The word "always" is comforting. I have written before, it reminds me, and I will write again. Writing is a messy process and that's equal parts "mess" and "process." When I relax into my known writing history, I begin to loosen up. This book is no worse or harder than any other book. It's just worse and harder because it's the current book.

I have been friends with Ed Towle for twenty-five years. We started reading each other's writing just after we graduated from Georgetown. Ed was one of the earliest readers of *The Artist's Way* and his comments helped shape that and future books. "Perhaps," I think, "I should trust him now. He tells me to keep on keeping on."

"Trust" is one of the key elements in finding a believing mirror. We need to trust the sensibility of the friend we are dealing with. We cannot feel they're talking through their hat. We cannot feel they are just humoring us. Such humoring is not what we need. We need friends who are tough-minded enough to tell us what they see.

It is nine p.m. on Holy Saturday night. That makes it three a.m. in Paris, already Easter, and my constitution is by now somewhere mid-Atlantic. My body clock might be reading midnight. Rather than trying to write more tonight, I am going to make an early night of it. My little cocker spaniel, as if sensing this, has already made a nest for herself at the foot of my bed. I have a fine collection of tabloids, reading guaranteed to put me to sleep. Last night, happily, I dreamed I was writing a novel.

Love, and do as you will.

St. Augustine of Hippo

Divining Rod

Our friends are not always available to us. Sometimes we will be struck by doubt or despair and find that we must act in our own behalf to muster the courage to continue. We may be in a foreign country or simply in a different time zone. Our friends may be temporarily caught up in their own busy affairs. It is at times like this that we most need a note of encouragement—even if we have to write it ourselves.

Take pen in hand. Write yourself a letter of encouragement, singling out the many things that you have done well. Give yourself the respect of a job well done—even if your work has not yet met with worldly acceptance. Be specific in your praise. Give yourself the review that you wish that would receive. For example, upon receiving a rejection letter, you might counter that news with "Dear Julia: Your novel *Mozart's Ghost* is a delightful—and very inventive—confection. Your characters are clear and warmly drawn. Your dialogue sparkles . . ." Post this letter where you can read and enjoy it.

CHECK-IN

1. **How many days this week did you do your Morning Pages?** If you skipped a day, why did you skip it? How was the experience of writing them for you? Are you experiencing more clarity? A wider range of emotions? A greater sense of detachment, purpose, and calm? Did anything surprise you? Is there a "repeating" issue asking to be dealt with?

2. **Did you do your Artist Date this week?** Did you note an improved sense of well-being? What did you do and how did

it feel? Remember, Artist Dates can be difficult and you may need to coax yourself into taking them.

3. **Did you get out on your Weekly Walk?** How did that feel? What emotions or insights surfaced for you? Were you able to walk more than once? What did your walk do for your optimism and sense of perspective?

4. **Were there any other issues this week that felt significant to you in your self-discovery?** Describe them.

Uncovering a Sense of Balance

Pivotal to any creative journey is the ability to resist the cliff's edge of drama. All of us are tempted to binge on negativity. It is the careful husbanding of optimism that allows us to move productively forward. This week's spiritual toolkit is aimed at dismantling the hobgoblins of fear and distrust that poison your well. You will align yourself with a Higher Power that extends itself in benevolent ways on your behalf. Sketchbook in hand, you will practice being in the now, where there is always sufficient safety for you to experience balance.

The Rim of the Glass

I am back from Paris but my body has not yet joined me in New York. I am still on Paris time and that throws me off kilter. Awake in the night, I find myself replaying a laundry list of fears. I pray. I write. I go back to bed. I do not like it, the lying awake, the negativity. One more time, it reminds me too strongly of the drinking days, of the many early mornings when I woke up shaking, fighting off despair and self-loathing. "I am not drinking," I remind myself. "I haven't had a drink in many years, and I do not need to have one now. I am just scared." I wish I could place a phone call to one of my close friends, but it's late and they are sleeping. Awake and restless, I turn to the keys. The familiar tapping of the keys is comforting.

I have mentioned that I am close friends with Larry Lonergan. He sees humor and divine timing where I see catastrophe. When I am in trouble, I frequently go see Larry to see what it is *Spirit* has to say about my dilemma. And Spirit, as told to me by Larry, is often blunt.

"You're wearing yourself out," he said to me today. "There's nothing wrong with you except your attitude. Are you getting out at all? Spirit thinks you're keeping your nose too close to the grindstone. Are you?" (I was.)

Over the years, Larry has batted close to a thousand. He will say, "You're going to write a short book before the longer one and the idea will come to you shortly." I may wail, "But, Larry, I have no ideas" only to have an idea strike me, an idea for a short book, that I *will* write before tackling the longer book. Over the years, I've learned to trust Larry's input. He does not always say what I want him to say, but what he does say tends to hold up in my experience. Sometimes what he says seems uncanny to me.

"An idea is going to come sailing in on you from out of the blue," he once said. "It looks like a romantic comedy. Have you been thinking about writing a comedy lately?"

It would have done no good to say, "Larry, all that's on my mind is tragedy." Walking in Central Park, admiring a plump robin, an idea came—and an idea for romantic comedy at that.

Sometimes I almost feel I am cheating, being able to number both Larry and Sonia Choquette among my friends. I feel like I have two guardrails up that help me to keep my car on the road. When my own headlights fail me, theirs kick in. They light up enough of the road that I am able to keep driving ahead.

"I'm worried about money," I wail.

"Your money's fine. You're just scared by being off your writing routine," I hear back. (Sonia is fond of telling me I thrive on routine. Which I do.)

As I am grappling with writing this book on the importance of persevering faith and enduring friendships, I turn to my friends for the faith and support to do it. I write to my friend Tim Farrington that I am toiling through a tough first draft and that I hate slogging. Tim fires a writerly letter back.

When unhappy, one doubts everything; when happy, one doubts nothing.

JOSEPH ROUX

"I think you're supposed to hate slogging. I thought that's what slogging was all about. I'll pray for a day of optimism and joyful productivity for you soon . . . you'll find your groove. . . . I know it sounds Pollyanna-ish but you're in God's hands and the Spirit will move when it moves. Our job is to show up, and you're doing your job. The rest is God's, it actually really truly is. . . . Just be you at the keyboard, in the hands of God. Wait, listen, love the silence, and eventually the silence will sing for you, as it always has and always will."

"Eventually the silence will sing for you . . ." How lucky I am to have a friend who can believe this and articulate it for me. I am lucky in my friendships, but I am also careful in them. I avoid people who are too negative because I have my own well-known-to-me negativity to deal with. I know all too well how a negative day can become a negative week if I am not careful. I must be vigilant at maintaining optimism. I must be skilled at titrating my energy so that there is "enough" belief to see me through.

And so, I seek out people who are optimistic, self-starting, and farseeing. I seek out people who are experienced in the difficulty of trusting themselves and who have learned to do it against the odds. As professional seers, both Sonia and Larry had to learn to live with being "different" from their fellows. Both had to learn how to keep their own counsel when what they saw—how much they saw—differed from consensus reality.

As an artist, I, too, must be able to see into the future. I must be able to cast an idea forward and see it fleshed out and standing on its own, a real creation. A book, a film, or a play begins as a notion, a blueprint, and that blueprint must be held in mind for the book to gather weight. As the writer, a book must be "real" for me before it can be real for anyone else. If I hold a book as "real," then I can find others who can also see it. It takes a special sort of constructive imagination to be able to look at the bare bones of a creative project and see it in the mind's eye as fully clothed. This special skill is what I have looked for over the years as I have slowly and carefully collected my believing mirrors.

Make a virtue of necessity.

GEOFFREY CHAUCER

It is five a.m. I am still awake and lonely, still on Paris time. Frightened, I am writing to muster courage. Comfortless, I try to write of what comforts me. What comforts me are my friends. It is still too early to call them. They live in earlier time zones and are still abed. I lie in bed deliberately counting my blessings. I know I am meant to place my dependency on God, but God can seem distant. "God speaks to me through people," I was taught when I was newly sober. Seeking to be emotionally sober now, two and a half decades later, God still speaks to me through people. I need to hear Sonia's familiar voice although I know that what she will say to me is, "You're fine. Jet lag is just a biochemical event. It will pass."

"It will pass," that is a touchstone of emotional sobriety. "It will pass," I tell myself. That done, I mercifully drift to sleep.

Divining Rod

Bedtime is a time of hobgoblins and convincing, although groundless, fears. Many of us grew up with the comforting words of a childhood prayer that ran, "Now I lay me down to sleep. I pray the Lord my soul to keep. And if I die before I wake, I pray the Lord my soul to take." Older and more sophisticated now, we often consider ourselves to be beyond such prayers—but are we? The night can make children of us all.

Take pen in hand. You are to write yourself a simple bedtime prayer. What gentle well wishes do you tell your frightened soul? You might try something along the lines of, "Dear God, I am going to sleep now and I need your help. I ask you to turn my troublesome day to good account. Please give me peaceful slumber and the blessing of feeling your presence. Guard and guide me while I sleep.

Allow me to wake with a clear idea of your will for me. May I do your will always . . ."

Faith

I have accepted fear as a part of life—specifically the fear of change . . . I have gone ahead despite the pounding in the heart that says: turn back . . .

ERICA JONG

The flowering trees along Columbus Avenue are packed with blossoms, white and pink. They are like oversized wands of cotton candy poking into the air. Walking back from my piano lesson this afternoon, I passed a street vendor doing a brisk business in sunglasses. Clearly spring is here and, judging by the vendors' wares, New York's notorious summer is lurking, just waiting to pounce. I was told as much today. When I came up in the elevator, I shared it with a woman and her large wooly dog.

"I am afraid it's too hot for him already," the dog owner confided in me. "He is bred to retrieve birds in the extreme cold. He's not bred to withstand heat." She sounded worried. The weather outside was barely balmy, not at all hot. Still, her big dog did look winded. He sat on the elevator floor and gently huffed.

"Maybe he will get a chance to get used to it a little by little," I suggested. That was how I myself planned to adjust to New York's legendary summer heat.

"Maybe." The dog owner sounded doubtful, as though my optimism were wildly out of line with reality as she knew it. Like her dog, she had a soulful, doleful gaze. I couldn't wait to slip out on my floor. Vigilant about my own negativity, I wanted to cling to my optimism. I could choose to project impending doom or impending happiness. My vote went to happiness.

Optimism is an elected attitude, a form of emotional courage. It is a habit that can and must be learned if we are to survive as artists. So often, "things" look so bleak. The book doesn't sell. The play is not produced. The audition goes brilliantly but the part goes to someone else. In order to survive

*For everything you have missed,
you have gained something else.*

RALPH WALDO EMERSON

such disappointments, we must master optimism, not as a form of denial but as a deeply rooted faith that we are somehow partnered in ways that we cannot see. We must look for the silver lining, knowing that there *always* is one.

As artists, we must cultivate faith. We must learn to see beyond appearances. We must trust that there is something larger and more benevolent than the apparent odds stacked against us. For the sake of sheer survival, we artists must learn to have a deep and abiding belief in our own work and its worthiness, despite the world's apparent acceptance or rejection. As artists, we have a vocation. There is Something that "calls" to us to work. In answering that call and making art, we keep our side of the bargain. Our efforts will be rewarded, although not perhaps in the ways that we had planned.

As artists, we must be in it for the long haul, not just the showy seasons of success. As artists, we are subject to cycles of acceptance. There will be bleak seasons and fruitful seasons. There will be successes and there will be failures. We cannot control the reception of our work. We must find our dignity in the doing. We must learn to say that our work, even if unsung, does count for something.

There is dignity in the act of making art, no matter how that art is received. Much of the best work I have ever written has never been published or produced. Faith tells me that there must be some reason for that that I cannot yet see. I cling to my faith and turn aside bitterness. I work although my work has come to "nothing." I have whole novels that haven't yet sold. I have fine plays that have seen no productions. My artist's faith tells me to keep on writing, that there must be a way, and a reason, to keep on keeping on. Faith allows for a career to take detours. Faith allows for a career to even grind to an apparent outward halt. Faith takes, always, the longer view. It divorces our creative practice from its current reception.

As artists, we must be resilient. Delicate as we are, we must also be stalwart. We must take our cue from the natural world and vow to be like the perennial flowers, stubbornly reappearing season after season. There is some simple dignity that lies in the labor of doing the art for art's sake and not for the glory and acclaim that we hope will accrue. I am a writer and writers write. Every day that I write, I am keeping my side of the bargain.

There are many days when I do not "feel" like writing. These are the days when I tell myself I have nothing to say, the days when I want to say, "Oh, what's the use" and count my thwarted art as the reason I do not go on. "Why try? It will come to nothing anyway," I catch myself thinking.

On those days I write anyway. Such thinking is the rim of the glass of despair. Despair is the poisonous drink an artist cannot afford to even sip. In order to go forward on these days, I must be willing to be small, not large. I must be willing to write from a spirit of service, to write simply because writers write. It does no good to demand to always be brilliant. That demand is an instant prescription for writer's block. No, in order to write, I must be willing to write badly and to have the faith that if I go forward "writing badly," some purpose is still be being served.

We are creations and we are intended, in turn, to be creative ourselves. Like the fruit trees, we are intended to blossom. The trees put forth their froth whether there will be admiring eyes or not. So, too, we are intended to flower in our art even if our art does not meet with a welcoming reception. We must make art for the sheer sake of making art. That is being true to our nature. That is being true to our path.

A prudent man will think more important to him what fate has conceded him, than what it has denied.

BALTASAR GRACIAN

Divining Rod

Most of us focus not on what we have done and have accomplished but upon those things we have yet to do. Most of us can make a quick list of dreams that are yet to be fulfilled. And yet, we have done many things well and in order for us to have true self-worth we must value the worthy things that we have done.

Take pen in hand. Number from one to ten. List ten things which you have accomplished already that you are proud of. My list includes teaching my daughter to horseback ride, learning to play the piano, studying French, studying Italian, completing a children's album, and designing a beautiful apartment. Your own list will reflect your own values. You may wish to praise yourself for more than ten accomplishments. When I am teaching a class, I sometimes ask students to enumerate fifty.

Greed's worst point is its ingratitude.

SENECA

Keep It Simple

It is a shiny bright new-penny day. The sky is cloudless, clear blue from horizon to horizon. Spring is leaping tree to tree in Central Park. Joggers are out in happy throngs. Young parents, singly and in pairs, push baby carriages along the cinder paths. The weather is so intoxicating it announces firmly, "Winter is truly over." Two nights ago, driving home from SoHo in a taxi, I passed a church with a gloriously blooming magnolia tree gracing its gate. Even as I type this, the tree beneath my writing window is bursting into leaf.

This morning I got a call from the blocked writer. She was due to start again at the top of her proposal and make some fixes. She said she knew what she had to write but she was hoping to find some inspiration before she could start. She thought she would do some reading to see if other people had been brilliant before her, if something in what they wrote might not spark something in her.

"I thought I would read some really great writers to see if I can get inspired," she said. My stomach sank as I listened to her plan. "What I need to do is come up with something really interesting," she continued. "The beginning of this proposal has to be brilliant, really fascinating." With stakes like that, no wonder she was blocked!

Gently, I told her I thought she might get more blocked shopping for brilliance, that she might do better simply to be willing to write—badly if necessary—and then see what comes of that. Very often our "bad" writing contains the seeds of our "good" writing within it. We resign from being perfect and, when we do, perfection steals in unawares. The trick lies in losing our self-consciousness. There are stratagems that help with that, chief among them trying to be of service.

"Have you ever tried to write from a spirit of service?" I asked her.

"I have trouble with the whole idea of spirituality," she answered with a trace of petulant rebellion. After a beat, she added, "But at this point I am desperate enough to try anything."

I suggested she post the little sign I had been taught to use, "Okay, God, you take care of the quality, I will take care of the quantity." From the silence on the line, I could practically hear her thinking, "How corny." Politely, she got off the call.

In order to be unblocked, I am willing to be corny. I have learned through hard experience that my artist needs to be babied. It needs a sense of safety. (Successful nursery rhymes are nothing if not corny.) I might wish it were different, but the part of me that creates is young and vulnerable. To ensure my productivity, I must be protective of this inner innocent. This means I need to keep things very simple.

I cannot control the outer world, but I can control the inner world I create in. That world can be Utopian in its simplicity. As in kindergarten, the rules must be gentle and fair. Such innocence serves me well. It has and does keep me productive. Hence, the posting of corny signs. Hence, the setting of very modest quotas. I do not want my artist getting discouraged, not when I can prevent it.

As an artist, I do best when reaching for humility. I must be

Be a good animal, true to your instincts.

D. H. LAWRENCE

willing to be just a worker among workers, just an artist among artists. Competition has no place in this scenario. Competition creates stress. Stress creates constriction and constriction creates block. Think of your artist as an emotional youngster. For that youngster, it's scary to be the center of attention. The glare of the spotlight can create the paralysis of block.

To function freely as an artist, I must take the focus off of winning, off of being the brightest and the best. I must give up such ego-driven notions as being "fascinating" and "brilliant." (Those judgments are for critics to make in due time, not in my own beleaguered mind.) I need a safe, critic-free arena in which to do my work. Then, with the ground rules in place, I must gently go forward. Simpleminded as it sounds, I must simply write—a word at a time, a sentence at a time, a paragraph and a page at a time. My quota must be daily and doable. Just a little, done daily, adds up to quite a lot. What we produce can always be improved, but produce we must. "Easy does it" and the corny slogan about taking care of the quantity and not the quality allow us to produce.

For me, it is good to talk with the blocked writer because in her I hear my own temptation to block. There is always a good reason why she cannot write just yet. Listening, I hear my own temptation to indulge in drama and realize my own need to keep the drama on the page. Sharing my "tricks," reminds me to use the tricks I have found. My Morning Pages are one stratagem I use daily to keep me from indulging in drama. In my pages, I write about my fears and then I make a short list of what it is I might be able to do about those fears. For example, on any given day, I can panic about money OR I can write— which earns money. My daily list always includes "write." When I am writing, my money seems oddly able to take care of itself.

So many things are out of our control, but making art *is* in our control. There is always a small and doable creative something we can do if we are willing to move ahead without a guarantee. We may not be able to work at our art on the level that we wish we could, but we can always do something.

What we call fate does not come into us from the outside, but emerges from us.

RAINER MARIA RILKE

The ghosts you chase you never catch.

JOHN MALKOVICH

I cannot guarantee how an editor will respond to my work, but I can write daily. An actor cannot guarantee winning an audition, but he can always work on a new monologue that will put him one leg up on a future audition. A singer can work on scales. A songwriter may not be able to get a record deal but he can write another song. In other words, we can always make things for love. Extending ourselves in love toward our art nurtures feelings of dignity. When we commit ourselves to the process of art and not to the need to produce a saleable product, we begin to experience the joy of creation.

The bright day draws toward a close. The setting sun gilds the newly emerging leaves. The whole world seems lit by optimism. On the phone with my friend the blocked writer, I get the great good news that she decided not to start by reading but instead to try actually writing. She has posted my corny sign. To her great satisfaction, she managed two full pages and once again has a sense of where she needs to aim tomorrow. Telling me of her victory over her block, her voice is calm and centered. Just for today, the drama stayed on the page. There might be a God after all.

One drink is too many for me and a thousand not enough.

BRENDAN BEHAN

Divining Rod

All of us have need of a calm oasis that speaks to us of beauty and serenity. For some of us, this will be a spot in nature, perhaps a grove of pine trees or a meandering stream. For those of us who live in the city, the spot of beauty may be man-made—a church or synagogue that feels far removed from the city's hustle and bustle.

Set aside a half hour's time and take yourself to a spot that speaks to your spirit. You may wish to take a notebook or simply to sit quietly, allowing your thoughts and impressions to bubble up unimpeded. A towering tree may evoke a sense of dignity and wisdom. A stained-glass window can evoke a sense of awe. Allow yourself to feel the transcendent feelings that come upon you. Enjoy a sense of communion with a power greater than yourself. You may find yourself experiencing insights about how your life could be more fully your own. When you leave your place of beauty, you will take with you a renewed sense of optimism and potential.

Alcohol doesn't console, it doesn't fill up anyone's psychological gaps, all it replaces is the lack of God.

MARGUERITE DURAS

No Regrets

Last night I went to a sophisticated New York dinner party, the kind of party that is so sophisticated you want to slash your wrists after it. The dinner-table conversation was rife with hot gossip, the "inside scoop" on the publishing world and how crooked and rigged and rotten it was. I listened with a tightening feeling in my chest. I was trying to write this book and if I gave a moment's thought to how futile it all was, I would be on the brink of suicide.

Wishing for a lighthearted and soignée persona, I instead sat at the dinner table numb with escalating terror. Names piled on names, each one fancier and shinier than the last. Brittle laughter echoed all around me. I felt dumbstruck, like a hayseed. I cursed my naive Midwestern roots. How would I ever be able to keep up a conversation with these "real" New Yorkers? What was there to say to people who put their faith in *The New York Times* and in who you knew? My books, dubbed "self-help" and mentioning God, are of the type *The New York Times* chooses not to review, and yet my publishing experience has to date been positive. Was that just a crazy fluke? It certainly didn't make for chic storytelling.

The party wore on. More names were dropped. Forget being

Drunkenness is temporary suicide.

BERTRAND RUSSELL

just a "famous" writer. These writers were so famous they had famous editors. Imagine having Jacqueline Onassis on the other end of the editorial phone! By comparison, my whole career had been made around the edges, without the imprimatur of the powers that be. I didn't know anybody "important." What I knew, all I knew, was how to write—and that often felt in question to me.

For me to survive as a writer, there had better be a God, something larger and more powerful than *The New York Times.* Without such a God, I am lost. My career is hopeless, my dreams are futile, and I am helpless against the odds. With such a God, I just might have a chance. I need to carefully hoard my optimism. I need to side with Oscar Hammerstein who called cynicism the cause of grief and grief the enemy of his art. "Anything that kills my enthusiasm is the enemy," he declared. As an artist, I need to believe I have a chance. As artists we all need to believe we have a chance—because we do. I believe that the Great Creator loves other artists and is active on our behalf to find us a break. I believe this not only because I have to believe this, but also because it is my experience.

It is a risky, block-inducing business, thinking about the odds stacked against us, the people we should have known, the times we should have been more astute politically. When we compare ourselves to others, there will always be someone who is doing better than we are. There will always be someone who is more successful, who has played his or her cards "right" while we have bungled ours. When we compare ourselves to others, there will always be people who are one "up" to our one "down." When we meet them, we feel discouraged. When we feel discouraged, we shut down. Shut down, we "block" and our productivity dwindles. Yes, the business of comparison is a dangerous business. Sitting at that dinner, although I certainly knew better, I was busily drawing comparisons. In those comparisons, I came up woefully short.

As artists, we do much better trying to keep things simple. We do better to compare ourselves solely to ourselves. Self-inventory is useful, while self-flagellation is not. Without calling

Drunkenness is nothing but voluntary madness.

SENECA

The main motive for "nonattachment" is a desire to escape from the pain of living, and above all from love, which, sexual or nonsexual, is hard work.

GEORGE ORWELL

*I did not find you outside,
oh Lord, because I made the
mistake of seeking outside
You who were within.*

ST. AUGUSTINE OF HIPPO

*God does not die when we
cease to believe in a personal
deity, but we die on the day
when our lives cease to be
illuminated by the steady
radiance, renewed daily, of a
wonder, the source of which
is beyond all reason.*

DAG HAMMARSKJÖLD

our whole identity into question, there are inquiries that we can fruitfully ask. How am I developing as an artist? Am I doing the work necessary for me to mature? Did I work today? Yes? Well, that's good. Working today is what gives us currency and self-respect. It is what cannot be taken away from us. There is dignity in work. Not working is what makes an artist crazy. An artist who is not working can get into all sorts of trouble. Trouble even worse than a New York dinner party.

There are always reasons not to work. There are always other things vying for our attention. Then, too, there is the attractive and seductive notion that if we don't work now, later it will be easier, we will somehow be more "in the mood." We will enjoy blessed confidence and joie de vivre. In my experience, that magical "later" never comes. Work is called "work" for a reason. It may be good, it may be rewarding, but it is often hard. And besides, "mood" is a dangerous friend.

Sometimes when my writing is the hardest, it turns out to be the best. Sometimes, when my writing is the easiest, it has just that flaw, it's too easy. I didn't examine what I was saying closely enough. On rereading, it strikes me as glib or at least not careful enough. If writing must be one thing, it must be filled with care. We must tell the truth. How else to earn our reader's respect? On my hardest days, there is still some precarious good being eked out. I have tried and that trying counts for something. Compared to not trying, it counts for a lot.

Yesterday I got a phone call from an old and beloved colleague who is not working. Did I realize, the colleague wanted to know, how very much money we could have made if I had just decided a few things differently a decade or so ago? Why, so-and-so was raking in a fortune. We had just left money sitting on the table. If only I would have listened to him more carefully I would be much, much more solvent. . . . Who wouldn't like to be more solvent? Why couldn't I have been smarter? My colleague had just been thinking about it all, he said. He sounded sad and angry. In fact, he sounded just this side of bitter and discouraged.

I listened to his thoughts and found myself thinking about

the way I needed to believe that we are guided at all times, and that we do the best we can by the light we have to see by. If God is all powerful, and I believe that God is, then there is no such thing as an irreparable mistake. If I ask for guidance and my course needs correcting, I will get the guidance necessary to correct my course. There is no need for harsh recriminations. There is no need to count back over the past looking for wrong turns. The decisions of a decade ago must be seen as the best decisions we could have made at the time. In any case, a decade past is a decade past and there is no changing things. Today can perhaps be done better but the past cannot be undone. If my colleague had been working on something constructive and forward-looking, I think he would have known that. Not working, he was scratching at the past, raking it over and over again, like a dog rubbing raw its own hide.

In order for us to go forward, we must live in the now. We must take the day that we have been given and make of it what we can. We cannot change the past. We can only regret it, and such dwelling leaches optimism from the day at hand. It is one more way to be blocked and a sadly effective one—if only . . . If only things were different, but they're not!

Talking with my sad colleague, I feel myself one more time on the slippery slope. The past is seductive. I must struggle to keep it in its place. It is too easy for the mind to seize upon some golden moment and to believe the great lie that since then everything has been ashes. "What's the use?" and "Why try?" are what come of such distorted thinking. It takes vigilance to keep from gilding the past. Each day, I must find something to love in the day at hand.

Today the temperature has climbed to the mideighties and New Yorkers are muttering in the streets. Walking back from piano, I heard the couple behind me, "It's a shame we don't get a real spring. We're slipping right past spring and into summer." For a moment, I joined them in their despair. I had a New York summer coming up after all, and it might be really hard. Then, catching myself, I snapped out of it. The day was glorious, albeit

Greater happiness comes with simplicity than with complexity.

BUDDHA

a little warm. The dreaded summer was still not at hand. The trees were barely leafing yet and there were jonquils blooming at their feet. We were, in fact, having spring.

The reward of a thing well done is to have done it.

RALPH WALDO EMERSON

When one door closes, another opens, but we often look so long and so regretfully upon the closed door that we do not see the one which has opened for us.

ALEXANDER GRAHAM BELL

Divining Rod

When we focus on the beauty of the now, we are able to let go of regrets about the then. When the adventure of each day's passage is celebrated, it reinforces our sense that we are in the right time and place. In other words, rather than gilding the past, we must make an attempt to gild the present. Few things do this as effectively as sketching.

Buy yourself a blank notebook. My favorite size is about five-by-seven. I like the kind with black leather covers that can easily be located at an art's supply store. Notebook in hand, proceed through an ordinary day— but take the time to do a little sketching. You may have to wait at a doctor's office. Sketch the waiting room. You may take yourself out for a cappuccino. Draw the café. If you are meeting a friend for drinks, ask if you can try a quick line drawing. Many of us find that although we are not "real" artists, we have a charming talent for the amateur sketch. Allow yourself to carry your notebook with you as a companion. You are seeking to become enchanted with yourself as a character. As you illustrate your life, you also illuminate it. There is more of interest than you at first realized.

CHECK-IN

1. **How many days this week did you do your Morning Pages?** If you skipped a day, why did you skip it? How was the experience of writing them for you? Are you experiencing more clarity? A wider range of emotions? A greater sense of detachment, purpose, and calm? Did anything surprise you? Is there a "repeating" issue asking to be dealt with?

2. **Did you do your Artist Date this week?** Did you note an improved sense of well-being? What did you do and how did it feel? Remember, Artist Dates can be difficult and you may need to coax yourself into taking them.

3. **Did you get out on your Weekly Walk?** How did that feel? What emotions or insights surfaced for you? Were you able to walk more than once? What did your walk do for your optimism and sense of perspective?

4. **Were there any other issues this week that felt significant to you in your self-discovery?** Describe them.

Happiness hates the timid!

EUGENE O'NEILL

Uncovering a Sense of Autonomy

Essential to any creative unfolding is a sense of
self-direction. We are the "origin" in "original." The
tasks of this week will help you to specify exactly
who and where you are, locating the powerful currents
that trace through your life. Listing your loves will
allow you to move closer to them. Listing your fears
will allow you to move beyond them. God lives in
the details, the concrete, knowable facts of your life.
As you explore your psyche and its place in your
environment, your compass will become ever more
accurate in pointing you true north.

The Doctor's Advice

Today was an untidy day with a doctor's appointment smack in
the middle of my writing time. I took a cab down to the
appointment—sixty blocks south through busy streets—while
spring enticingly hovered in the air. I found the address and
dodged my way through some yellow tape where a sidewalk was
being repaired. I rode up in the elevator. I made it to the appointment with minutes to spare. The reading material offered
in the waiting room featured an article on Google. If I were to
search myself on the web, I might find a portrait of a wild-
haired, highly strung woman with the caption, "She would
rather be writing."

"You seem overwhelmed," I was greeted. The doctor sur-
veyed me gravely. I did feel overwhelmed. I wanted to be at

*Happiness is when what you
think, what you say, and what
you do are in harmony.*

Mahatma Gandhi

I find that it is not the circumstances in which we are placed, but the spirit in which we face them, that constitutes our comfort.

ELIZABETH T. KING

home, sticking to my simple grid, not out and about in the city. I needed to be at my desk, putting words to the page. Whenever I am not writing enough, I feel overwhelmed. And appointments like the one I was keeping take large nasty bites out of the time I have earmarked for writing.

"I am not writing enough," I complained tersely. "It makes me tense." The doctor eyed me and I eyed the doctor. I did not want to be there.

"Maybe you should rent a cabin in the country and go away for the summer and write," I was advised, somberly. "Country places aren't that expensive," he added, perhaps seeing dollar signs flash before my eyes.

What? Was the doctor crazy? I pictured myself in the country, somewhere in the middle of nowhere with nothing to do but stare at the page. Wasn't that the greased slide to writer's block? Wasn't I really better off staying right where I was and doing just what I was doing?

I didn't want to rent a cabin in the country. I wanted to write right where I was, smack in the middle of New York City. I wanted to write about the excitement of the flower district, the garment district, the antique district. I wanted to write about exactly where I was planted, in the rich soil of a bustling metropolis. I wanted to write, period. I had a lust to simply lay some track, to put some words to my experience, to try to achieve an optimistic balance by putting things onto the page. My daily quota of three pages felt skimpy. It was just enough to keep me grounded, but barely. The rest of my life seemed suddenly to be wildly out of whack and I knew from experience that if I could just write through it steadily enough, life would calm back down. "Keep the drama on the page," I lectured myself. But drama seemed to follow me everywhere, even to the doctor's.

For the past several days, my phone messages, lengthy and dramatic, have been from people who are not functioning in their art. "Call me," they say, but to call them is to invite their drama to spill over into my life.

I must be serene in the place where I am planted. At the moment, that is right in the middle of Manhattan. It is hard listening to their messages, listening to the endless variety of things that can be put before work. I say before "work" but what I mean is before emotional sobriety, the simple grid of a positive life lived one day at a time. Such a life must be free of frenzy, free of the frantic rushing here and there that cannibalizes tranquility. To be emotionally sober, I must set my own gentle pace. I try to do that but lately I have felt jostled and pressed. The "world" has been too much with me.

Yesterday I went to dinner with a fancy lady writer, and she advised me at some length of the many things in the city of which I really ought to be availing myself. "When would I find time to write?" I caught myself thinking. There are many things that give me pleasure, but there are few things that give me as much pleasure as the joy of making something. No, for me I must cling to my grid and keep things very, very simple. I tell myself this almost as a mantra. Despite myself, despite all that I "know," I feel myself spiraling into drama and despair. "Just keep it simple," I tell myself daily in my Morning Pages. Go to the keys. Go to the typewriter. Go for a walk. Edge forward a little. Guard yourself against despair. Try to sleep. If you do find yourself lying awake at night, count your blessings and not your fears. The first blessing is that you are sober, if not emotionally, at least physically. Do not sip at the glass of despair.

Acceptance makes any event put on a new face.

Henry S. Haskins

That which does not kill me makes me stronger.

Friedrich Nietzsche

Divining Rod

When you begin to slide into despair, it is because you have lost your sense of grounding. Therefore, the tool to apply is one of gentle well-being. Put simply, your need is to count your blessings. Gratitude is a homely but effective antidote to despair.

Man needs difficulties; they are necessary for health.

CARL JUNG

Take pen in hand. Number from one to twenty-five. Begin with the big things. In my case, I start with, "I am sober today." And then, "I have my health." And then, onward to, "I have a safe place to live," and "My rent is paid." From the large, move to the small, "I like my bed. It is very comfortable." "I love my flannel sheets. They are cozy." You may find as many people as objects on your list. "I am grateful for my friendship with Sonia." "I am grateful for my rapport with my daughter." Area by area, survey your life and look at the sheer number of positives that you have. Yes, today you may have had a rejection letter on your novel, but you did go forward on some new writing. You did write your Morning Pages. Grief and loss come to all of us but gratitude lists help us to keep things in proportion. The half-empty glass is actually half full. It is all a matter of perception.

The Abyss

Another night of insomnia has worked its wicked magic. If sleep mends the raveled sleeve of care, the lack of sleep creates cares. I tell myself that all is well, but my mind does not believe this. Exhausted, fairly staggering with fatigue, it lurches from worry to worry. I tell myself not to project. I tell myself to live one day at a time, but my mind doesn't listen to my advice. It evades the careful fences I have set up for it. Instead I am rehearsing my catastrophic future. In that future, I wander homeless through Manhattan's maze.

I know that these imaginings are both negative and dramatic. I know that they probably will not come to pass, but I also know that when I had my first and worst nervous breakdown, I did wander alone through the streets of London. The police scooped me up and took me to a locked ward. I barely knew my name.

What happened once could happen again, I fear. Yes, I fear. That is the task my mind has set for itself, the endless surveying of worst-possible scenarios. Despite myself, I am romancing trouble. Despite myself, I stray near the edge of the cliff.

Right now I am not long on resilience. I am not long on faith. I am standing on the edge of a great chasm. That chasm I call "the abyss." The Devil lives in that chasm, and if I stand too close to the edge of the cliff, he gets his hands around my ankles. For a week now he has had a very good grip, and I have been struggling not to be pulled down. I have been filled with fear and with anxiety.

The Devil always comes at me through despair. The Devil talks about the odds stacked against me and how foolish I have been. The Devil likes to say, "What's the use? Game over." The Devil comes at me as anxiety and the thing I cannot fix. The Devil comes at me, above all, as a drink. The Devil wants me to think that if I just have a drink, everything will be better, at least more bearable. There is nothing that taking a drink is going to make better. The Devil tells me I am about to lose "everything" and I think that perhaps I am. The Devil would certainly like to paralyze me with fear so that losing things becomes more likely.

As I have felt myself sliding toward the cliff, I have reached out to find help, hands to hold on to, a tree to grasp. I have, a little at a time, found what I was looking for. I talked with my friend Bernice, a wise Jungian therapist, who told me to inch my way back gently, to work my emotional recovery the same way I did when I was struggling to get sober the first time. That means being willing to try working just the slogans of sobriety— "One day at a time," "Live and let live," "Let go and let God," "Easy does it." Just now, writing this little essay, talking about the abyss, I am working "Easy does it." I am trying to write something small, something centered in the day that I am in. What has me so frightened, I wonder?

I think the abyss began yawning open for me when I read a

Human life begins on the far side of despair.

JEAN-PAUL SARTRE

new book about Bill Wilson, the cofounder of AA. In that book, Bill was revealed to be a depressive womanizer who begged for a drink on his deathbed. Reading these things, I felt shaken. Would I still be craving a drink as I lay dying? Would there be no respite? No grace? I called friends to talk about it, and they said, "So? He was human." They sloughed off my concerns. I felt that I was dealing with more than, "So he was human." I was dealing with a fear that the center would not hold.

"Do you think you had him on a pedestal?" I was asked. I didn't think so.

"Everyone who taught me sobriety is dead," one woman told me.

I didn't find it comforting to think about that. I have been scared enough thinking about the age of the people I love, most of them in their seventies. As my mind rehearses its negative scripts, I mentally attend funerals. So many of my closest friends are so old!

"Just for today, they are still with you," I tell myself. Just for today you can phone them and hear their voices. Just for today, you are all still in this together. You are not alone.

Change is not made without inconvenience, even from worse to better.

SAMUEL JOHNSON

Divining Rod

When large fears overrun us, we must turn to tiny yet revolutionary actions. We must, despite our fears, "Whistle a happy tune." When tragedy seems to loom from all corners, it is a good time for comedy. "This too shall pass" applies to our despair but sometimes we must practice a little creative distraction to allow time to pass. Therefore, I am suggesting to you what has been suggested to me: when the chips are down, rent a comedy. When the chips are very down, rent five of them.

Stage your own minifilm festival. In 12-step parlance, this is called "acting as if." A little laughter can go a long way toward lightening the heart.

Bringing Up Baby, It Happened One Night, The Philadelphia Story, The Princess Bride, Damn Yankees, Splash. These titles and many more serve as worthy distractions from our existential angst. (Now is not the time to rent *The Razor's Edge* or *Leaving Las Vegas.*) When you feel yourself to be in critical condition, you must treat yourself as gently as you would a sick friend.

Flagellating ourselves is not virtue. It is self-obsession. What we are in need of in our darkest times, is the magic of a little self-forgetting. It is not the moment to pore over the ills of the world. It is not time to get serious about becoming a better person. You are already a fine person, you have just lost the perspective that tells you so. Be gentle with yourself. Now is not a time for inventory and self-searching. Those activities are better left to when you are more balanced. And you will again be balanced. Allow laughter to lead the way.

What you really value is what you miss, not what you have.

JORGE LUIS BORGES

Going Back to Basics

I have just set up a typewriter in the corner of my bedroom. I have moved the computer to one side and I tell myself that someday I might get back to using it, but not now. For right now, I want to get back to basics, and basics for me are the comforting clicks of a typewriter trotting forward and the slow and steady accumulation of pages.

I am trying to take Bernice's sound advice and back myself away from the cliff. To end the emotional bender of terror, I must

Reflect upon your present blessings, of which every man has many; not on your past misfortunes, of which all men have some.

CHARLES DICKENS

set myself a gentle and familiar routine. In order to feel sane and steady, I must keep things sane and steady. I must set a mental discipline not to imagine the worst, not to let my mind go skittering toward the cliff. "One day at a time," I tell myself and for today I have a roof over my head and work to do. I am not homeless. I am not broke and desperate. I may be near a breakdown again but I am not having one yet. And the "yet" may never come. I cannot afford drama. I need clarity and gentleness and I need, as experience has taught me, to keep things very basic.

Creatively, I am a creature of habit. My daily habits form the grid that I must cling to right now. I need to do a few simple things and to keep doing them. I do my Morning Pages. I take my Artist Dates. I walk. Whenever I fall off my simple grid, it is quite a tumble. Whenever I pick up the first doubt and allow that doubt to spiral me deep into despair, I need my basics to get me emotionally sober again. And so, I needed to get a typewriter and I needed to roll a piece of paper into the machine. I needed to have the tactile reassurance of a book unfolding, and unfolding a page at a time in an old-fashioned and orderly way. One day at a time, one page at a time. This is what I can live with.

I feel hopelessly old-fashioned. I have been trying to write on a computer but that has not worked for me. It is too modern, too confusing. One press of a button and I can zoom anywhere in the manuscript. I found myself pushing buttons and then wandering, lost, in the maze of words that I found. Just as my mind skittered from fear to fear, the computer skittered from essay to essay. Surely someone knows how to use this machine correctly and it is an advantage to them, but not to me. The computer only mirrors and amplifies my own confusion.

It was comforting today when I found a store that still sells typewriters and Mark, the man who helped me, listened to my panic for a moment before asking gently, "Are you a writer?" I confessed that I was. "We have writers all over the city," he assured me. "There are a lot of people who can't work on a computer." He named a writer I greatly admired. She was a long-standing client. I do not know if she works on a Selectric, like I do, but I do know that she calls in and gets Mark, who hears her anxiety about having an old familiar machine and he gets her one.

My friend Natalie Goldberg writes longhand. My friend Ed Towle uses speckled books. I write my Morning Pages longhand but when it is time for me to think book, I want the horse and carriage of a typewriter. (It occurs to me that a part of a typewriter is called "the carriage." I think that name is no coincidence.) With the safety of my typewriter set up in the corner of my room, I feel my terror starting to ebb away.

This afternoon I talked once again with my friend Bernice. One more time, she listened to my fears and then she reiterated to me, "You are still on an emotional binge. The anxiety is like a drink. Your system is drunk with anxiety. You need to do tiny things to move yourself back from the chasm." I needed to wash my hair. I needed to clean my room. I needed to fold clothes, straighten sheets. I needed small, concrete actions in the life that I actually have, not in the terrible life that I imagine as coming toward me. So, what are the facts? Facts, unlike fears, are sober. These are the facts:

I am sitting at a window facing north. The tree below my window is coming into leaf. The leaves are tender and bright, unfolding daily like tiny flags. Since last I wrote a book, I have moved from my old quiet apartment on Riverside Drive to a new apartment more in the midst of things. It's being in the midst of things that is tricky for me. The world feels too much with me. I get overwhelmed and I want someplace safe and quiet in which to dream and work. New York does not feel safe and it does not feel quiet. It is many other things: vibrant, chock-full of life, bristling and bustling with excitement. But no, not quiet. I must seek quiet out here. I can do that one day at a time.

Just at the moment, I am balanced on a knife edge. I am trying to find my sea legs again and I am needing to be very gentle to find them. I tell myself that I will be all right, that it is just a matter of going forward a day at a time, doing the small and doable things that will lead me one more time to a feeling of stability.

Every form of addiction is bad, no matter whether the narcotic be alcohol or morphine or idealism.

CARL JUNG

Today I was in the Greek diner on the corner of my block. An old woman was there with her companion. She edged her way forward with a cane. "I am eighty-eight," she said, to no one in particular. Her face was fine and alive. In my building, down on the eighth floor, lives a ninety-two-year-old who always puts on fresh makeup and wears her scarves tied just so. The idea of growing older in New York scares me. The city seems so overwhelming, and how much more so to a senior citizen? What courage it takes to live here! But I do live here, and I will live here for the foreseeable future. That future looms large and frightening to me. "God does not give us more than we can handle," I am told but I wonder if God doesn't overestimate me just a little. Or perhaps, and this is likely, I underestimate God.

Any coward can fight a battle when he's sure of winning, but give me a man who has plucked to fight when he is sure of losing.

GEORGE ELIOT

Divining Rod

When we are at our bleakest, we often "know" better. On my blackest days, I can remember my sunny days. It is just that I doubt that I will ever get back to them. At times like this, continuity and consistency are the keys to winning through. Tiny positive actions yield large results. And so we must look to the small and the doable rather than to the large and seemingly unfixable.

Sticking to our grid of positive actions adds to our shaky self-esteem. There is power to be found in perseverance. As 12-steppers say, "Don't quit five minutes before the miracle." And so, we write Morning Pages rather than abandoning them. We force ourselves to undertake the levity of a small Artist Date. We make ourselves go for walks. Rather than trying to act big and strong, we allow ourselves to be small and convalescent.

Take pen in hand. Write a letter to God, taking care to be as small as you actually are. This is the time to write a letter that says, "Dear God. I need help to get my hair washed and get out of my pajamas. Please help me to clean up and get dressed and make my bed." Such an honest letter to God builds intimacy. We are no longer posing. By asking God to meet us exactly where we are, we are practicing compassion toward ourselves. Compassion, like humor, begins our healing.

I am a daylight atheist.

BRENDAN BEHAN

Focusing on the Positive

The tree beneath my writing window is now nearly fully in leaf. The leaves are bright green, fresh, filled with life. I live on the eleventh floor of an apartment building and the tree reaches nearly as high. I do not recognize its type. Its leaves are four-pointed and from a slight distance they are spatulate, like a maple's leaves. What matters to me about the tree is its very existence here in the heart of Manhattan.

When I need to dream, I look at that tree. Its leaves dance lightly in the evening breeze. A grackle hops limb to limb in its upper branches. The tree is a blessing, a gift from nature, a gentle wink from God: Yes, even amidst this concrete, I am still here. I need God to be here.

My friend Bernice tells me that in times of despair we cut ourselves off from God. God, she says, reaches us through small positive actions. If you want to find God, she suggests trying something concrete and affirmative. God might be found in brushing the dog. God might be found in scrubbing the sink. God might be found in doing a load of laundry. And, in my case, God might be found in typing.

"God does not live in the abstract," Bernice tells me. As a

To attempt the destruction of our passions is the height of folly. What a noble aim is that of the zealot who tortures himself like a madman in order to desire nothing, love nothing, feel nothing, and who, if he succeed, would end up a complete monster!

DENIS DIDEROT

Art is too serious to be taken seriously.

AD REINHARDT

Surely all art is the result of one's having been in danger, of having gone through an experience all the way to the end, where no-one can go any further.

RAINER MARIA RILKE

writer, I believe God lives in the tap-tapping of my typewriter keys, in the tiny bell that sounds when I reach the end of a line. God may live also in stacks of snowy white paper. I have a friend who swears God lives in her cleaning supplies. When she has a crisis of faith, she cleans house. When I have a crisis of faith, I go to the page.

Tonight I am at the page and it is calming to me. I reach for words and my reaching is a tiny prayer. "Find me here, God," I am praying. As if on cue, my little dog Tiger Lily lets out a long and gentle sigh. She is curled serenely on the end of my bed. Her breathing is deep and rhythmic. Animals breathe naturally as we are taught to breathe by meditators. Perhaps this is why it is so calming to touch the muzzle of a cab horse, to smell its hay-sweet breath. The horses queue up at the southern end of Central Park. As taxis whirl past them, honking and rushed, the horses stand drowsily, waiting for the cluck of the reins. We, too, need to wait and rest, alert to the cluck of our God. God knows and loves our animal selves.

A friend of mine says that she meditates by stroking Kellie, her cat. "I know it isn't formal. I know it isn't how most people do it, but I swear that for me it works," April says. When she strokes her cat, she reaches the spiritual realms of a larger world. "God brought us together," April says of her pet, a rescue cat. "We were meant to be."

Every night, in a monastery, the monks make prayerful rounds. There is the same feeling of Godly duty in the dog-walking rounds of my neighbors. Each night, between nine and eleven, the owners come out with their dogs. In my building alone, there are two gay little Westies, a silky golden retriever, a fine brindled boxer, a giant chocolate brown Chesapeake Bay retriever, and above all Rovie, a squat dark-coated pit bull who has three people walking her each in their turn.

If Tiger Lily knows I am her servant, she wisely does not let on. Instead she flatters me with a wild greeting whenever I come in the door. "Thank God you're home," says her bounding leap as she does a quick spin in the air. Bernice is right, I think; God is in the concrete facts of our life. The leap of a young dog is a joyous prayer.

Divining Rod

When joy is elusive, we must actively seek it out. We must put ourselves with people and things that bring us delight. Sometimes, when we are at our most depressed, it can be difficult to even recall the joys in life. It is for this reason, that one more time we must take pen in hand. Turning to the page, number from one to fifty. Now list fifty things which you love.

For example: raspberries, kittens, red-winged blackbirds, brown-eyed Susans, hazelnut lattes, kalamata olives, oil paints, *The New Yorker*, fall leaves, blackberries, West Highland terriers, fantail goldfish, good tweed cloth, parakeets, African violets, New York pizza, real whipped cream, calico cats, window boxes, gargoyles, stained-glass windows . . .

Using your list of fifty items as a resource list, plan a week in which you allow your self to be near what you love. You may take yourself to an aquarium store to visit goldfish. You might buy yourself a pint of raspberries or a hazelnut latte. On your walk, you might keep a special eye turned for good window boxes or calico cats. An African violet is not an expensive purchase and it repays the expenditure with lasting beauty. As your list will quickly show you, there are many small ways in which we can fill our lives with those things that bring us happiness.

One does not become enlightened by imagining figures of light, but by making the darkness conscious.

CARL JUNG

The Bagel Scrap

It is a cool gray day. There is a light breeze that holds a trace of moisture. It looks like we are going to have a rain. The red-brick town houses below my writing-room window are somber. Earlier in the day, I saw an optimistic sunbather stretching out a towel on a rooftop but then the day turned damp and the sunbather got discouraged. Now the roof is empty. A few pigeons perch on its cornice. A few more wheel in flight heading toward the park.

This morning, on our way into the park, Tiger Lily snatched up a scrap of bagel. There was no getting it away from her. She was fierce in holding on. She gripped that bagel as tightly as an old man chaws a cigar. She had exactly what she wanted. On her turn in the park there was no chasing squirrels, no mock attacks on passing dogs. She had one thought only, that bagel, and everything else passed her by in a blur.

He who fights with monsters might take care lest he become a monster. And if you gaze for long into an abyss, the abyss gazes also into you.

FRIEDRICH NIETZSCHE

When we have an obsessive fear, we hold on to it like Tiger Lily and her bagel. We cling to the thought with a diehard intensity, nothing can pry us loose. It is a mantra we repeat to ourselves, "I am afraid that X is going to happen." Afraid of X, we fail to notice Y. We are fixated and, in our fixation, we feel trapped.

We are never trapped. There are always choices. We do have freedom of will and movement and we can exercise them. We can find a small way to move forward and pry open the jaws of our trap. It is a question of being open-minded, but when our mind is trained on the bagel scrap, nothing can help us. This is when we must learn to let go and let God. But how do we do that?

For me, this is where the tool of walking comes into play. It is difficult to walk and keep our mind trained on the bagel scrap of fear. We may start off, like Tiger Lily, focused on our obsession, but soon enough other thoughts will start to nudge loose our grip. We see the cat in the window, calico and plump. We see the pair of matched pugs coming toward us, the Korean grocer's buckets full of gently budding pussy willows. The window dressing has been changed in the thrift shop. Tiny things catch our attention and tiny changes begin to happen along our neural pathways. We have something to chew over besides our bagel. In a moment of distraction, we drop the scrap.

What happens when we drop the scrap? We may have a moment of free-floating panic. We may dive wildly to our feet looking for another scrap to hold on to. Freedom is disorienting. What do we do when we have so many choices? This is where the walk helps us out again. If we just start moving, a footfall at a time, a footfall at a time we will be led. First we notice the calico cat. Then we think perhaps we would like to have a cat. If not a cat, something else plump and comforting. A needlepoint pillow, for example. It does not purr but it does sit on your lap. Little by little, as we walk, we can identify what it is that we are missing. For me, in the city, it is often "nature." If I get to the park, that yearning begins to be soothed. Walking out, I hear what it is I am missing.

So much of being sane and happy begins with the doing of things that are sane and happy. This means that we must train ourselves to think small rather than large. We become frightened because we have "big decisions" to make. But big decisions can be made gently, a small step at a time. But again, notice that word in there—"step." Walking leads us a step at a time. Walking gives us a gentle path. We are talked to as we walk. We hear guidance. It comes from within us and from the world around us. Walking is a potent form of prayer. "Guide me, show me," we pray as we walk, and as we walk we are guided and we are shown.

Walking in the park today, Tiger Lily got distracted and dropped her scrap of bagel. Suddenly she was straining at the leash, happily in pursuit of a provocative squirrel. Suddenly she was yapping, tugging at the lead. She desperately wanted to intimidate a black-and-white Jack Russell terrier named Hannah.

"She was born in Ireland," Hannah's owner cheerily reported.

We cannot change anything until we accept it. Condemnation does not liberate, it oppresses.

CARL JUNG

Talent develops in quiet places, character in the full current of human life.

JOHANN WOLFGANG
VON GOETHE

"She's beautiful."

"I think so."

"Hannah is a rough-coated Jack," Hannah's owner volunteered.

"Tiger is a cocker spaniel with a tail," I reported back.

Not needing names or formal introductions, the two dogs crouched in play.

Tiger Lily, a blond-and-white beauty herself, leapt and pirouetted at leash end. She was all dramatic posturing, all bravura and show. "Just let me at her," her body language seemed to say. I loosened the leash. With nothing to fight against, Tiger Lily suddenly wagged her tail. She stepped forward and sniffed Hannah's nose. No longer clutching her bagel scrap, she found herself making a friend.

Against the assault of laughter, nothing can stand.

MARK TWAIN

Divining Rod

The task I propose now requires a little bit of planning and extra soupçon of effort. I am asking you not only to take a walk but to take a walk at an unusual time for you. Break your routine and enjoy the sense of adventure it immediately brings to you. Allow yourself at least one half hour.

You might want to get up early and get out to explore your neighborhood while your neighbors are still sleeping in. You might want to take a leisurely after-dinner stroll while your neighbors are tucked safely indoors. By venturing out at an odd time, you will experience a more vivid focus. You might catch the morning light streaming through the park. You might spot the crescent moon just as it clears the skyline, a snowy-white sickle against a cobalt sky. One more time, you are being urged to experience yourself as a character. Your thoughts and perceptions are interesting. What do you notice that is new and interesting to you in your habitual habitat?

We do not see things as they are. We see them as we are.

THE TALMUD

CHECK-IN

1. **How many days this week did you do your Morning Pages?** If you skipped a day, why did you skip it? How was the experience of writing them for you? Are you experiencing more clarity? A wider range of emotions? A greater sense of detachment, purpose, and calm? Did anything surprise you? Is there a "repeating" issue asking to be dealt with?

2. **Did you do your Artist Date this week?** Did you note an improved sense of well-being? What did you do and how did it feel? Remember, Artist Dates can be difficult and you may need to coax yourself into taking them.

3. **Did you get out on your Weekly Walk?** How did that feel? What emotions or insights surfaced for you? Were you able to walk more than once? What did your walk do for your optimism and sense of perspective?

4. **Were there any other issues this week that felt significant to you in your self-discovery?** Describe them.

Uncovering a Sense of Resolve

All creativity requires grounded action. There is nothing airy-fairy about the artist's world. It requires good husbandry. Making art requires that we put our shoulder to the wheel. Action is the key to success. In this week's tasks, you will focus on small actions that lead to a larger unfolding. Just as a bucket is filled a drop at a time, so too a creative life develops by the smallest acts. One more time, you will invite the Great Creator's aid on your behalf. You may experience a sense of heightened autonomy as you undertake long-postponed endeavors.

Savoring

It is a beautiful day, clear, cool, and sunny, but I find myself caught in self-questioning, missing the day at hand. It is so easy to become caught in the mind, in the weighing of invisible variables: Should I have? Was I right to? Am I doing the right thing? We become like Prufrock, wondering if we dare to wear our trousers rolled. I am determined to "have" the day.

Life unfurls a day at a time. It is full of situations that will resolve themselves if we give them enough time and give God a chance to get his hand in. The trick is not to panic. The trick is not to overreact. Life unfolds one day at a time, and we must let it. This is the discipline I have set for myself.

My phone rang earlier today and it was a friend of mine calling in, frantic. She outlined the "jumps" ahead of her in the

Birds sing after a storm; why shouldn't people feel as free to delight in whatever remains to them?

ROSE FITZGERALD KENNEDY

*The wildest colts can make
the best horses.*

PLUTARCH

month and it was several jumps too many and all of them hard. I suggested she might want to try simplifying things a little. My advice fell on two deaf ears. She was much too busy to think about having the day she was having. She was far ahead in the days that were coming up. Jumping ahead, she was wild with anxiety.

It is so easy to rush ahead into fear and panic. It is so easy to miss the beauty that awaits us in the here and now. The tiniest things can bring joy. Just this morning, as I walked my dog in the park, I came upon a family taking a photograph. We were in the part of the park where cherry blossoms make a pink canopy overhead, some boughs hanging down so far they nearly touch the ground. As I passed, a mother had urged her child to stay balanced on a tree stump. He balanced gingerly, arms out to the side to keep things steady. "Now how about a smile," the mother urged. Sure enough a brave three-cornered smile lit the child's face and there he was, a buoyant six-year-old caught forever in a soft pink cloud. "What a great photo," I called out.

So much of life is like taking a photograph. We must pause to catch the moment and savor our delight. Savoring the moment is a learned art, and it is an art that must be practiced to be perfected. The mother must notice the pink blossoms and think to bring her camera. Her child is growing up, growing up daily, and the seasons of his life will come only once. This spring Sunday is worth capturing.

This week my daughter came in from California for a brief visit. For two days in a row, we ate lunch together in the tiny Greek diner on the corner of my block. Then we strolled arm in arm through the neighborhood. Three blocks up and one block over we came upon Claremont Riding Academy. It is an old brownstone filled with horses. When my daughter was four, she took riding lessons there. Now she is much older, old enough to have a four-year-old herself, and we stood hip to hip watching a lesson together, recalling the past. My daughter patted my hand.

"You were a little bit littler," I told her as we watched the young rider urge her mount around the arena.

"I don't think my feet quite reached the stirrups," my daughter recalled.

"I am so glad I taught you to ride," I told her. That was something I had done right.

"It's one of my great joys," she whispered back, her voice throaty with emotion. The young rider cued a trot, posting up and down.

Ride the horse in the direction that it's going.

Werner Erhard

I thought of a photograph that I cherish of my daughter and me. She is two years old and I am thirty-one. She is atop a small spotted pony. I walk beside her, guiding her mount. She wears a brave tricornered smile just like the little boy's in the park. In both photos, the one I cherish and the one I saw taken, there is a poignant mixture of safety and excitement. I think it is always a mixture of safety and excitement that we are after.

As an artist, it does me good to have the safety of the Morning Pages that I write daily. There is a steadiness to the Pages. They "mother" me. It also does me good to take an Artist Date, a small soupçon of adventure, a tiny act of daring, like piloting a pony or balancing on the stump of a tree. I do not need a big adventure, just the smallest something will do. When I manage it, I feel my heart tug upward, making its own tricornered smile.

Divining Rod

A friend of mine is a very fine novelist. She fills her books with small details that are garnered on her daily walks. She is always alert for some telling detail, a freshly seen "something" that will bring the reader pleasure.

No matter where we live, no matter how drab our surroundings, there is always magic to be seen. I live eleven stories up overlooking a city landscape and yet my apartment is on the flight path for large birds headed to the park. If I am alert, I can see a hawk, a heron, a flock of Canadian geese. Outside my window is a rusting fire escape. On rainy days, it is hung with silvery drops. On dry days, it is the frequent landing spot for a matched pair of blue jays.

Take pen in hand. Number from one to five. Pretend you are a novelist and that your own neighborhood is the setting for your current book. List five delights of your own locale. You might want to single out the Greek diner or the newsstand. You might mention the stands of chicory poking up near the mailboxes. Allow yourself to see your world as an interested stranger might see it.

He is well paid that is well satisfied.

WILLIAM SHAKESPEARE

Feelings Aren't Facts

It is balmy today and glorious. The fruit trees in Central Park are in full and joyous bloom. Tiny pink petals float through the air. Families are out, kites in tow, and the adults are childlike themselves, running the kites back and forth. "Daddy, give me a turn!" The daffodils and jonquils are spent now. Dandelions already laze across the grass. Friends are out in pairs, ambling through the park. At the gate on West Eighty-sixth Street, I bump into a happily married couple I know who love to run together. They are dressed in brief shorts and shirts. Their smiles are contagious. "How are you doing?" the wife wants to know. "Everything good?" In the face of their sunny optimism, it seems niggardly to confess the truth.

And what is the truth? I have been having a hard time of it. I have been washed over by fear and anxiety. I have been having trouble sleeping and the city, New York, New York, has seemed huge to me and frightening. I have had what might be called a negative week. I have had the companionship of Nigel, my inner critic, who has busily told me that I am a foolish woman and that my dreams will come to naught. When I talked with my older friend Bernice, she accurately said I was on an emotional binge, what I call a "dry drunk." I have felt that way, not sober enough, unable to see the beauty and hope all around me, instead caught up in feelings of despair.

"Feelings aren't facts," I have lectured myself. Again and again my Morning Pages have urged me to keep things simple. I now dread going to bed, knowing that I will lie awake while my fears parade past me dressed in their most ghoulish and convincing garb. Negativity seems to cling to me these days like a cloud of cheap perfume. "Just don't drink," I remind myself. "You can live through another breakdown if you just don't drink." Each day passed sober is a small victory. Each day edges me slightly back from the abyss. At the corner newsstand, I try to not glance at the day's dire headlines. Must all the news be bad news? It seems that way.

I am not sophisticated enough to take in cynicism and shrug it off. I do not know how to be hip. I do not know how to be "with-it." At times, I think I am simply not grown up enough. I do not know how to listen to bad news and bounce back brightly. I tell a woman that I am frightened that I am one more time sliding toward a breakdown, and she replies, "This city has driven many people to madness." What am I to say to that? "Thanks a lot"? It is as though she has just given me a small but decisive shove toward what I think of as the brink.

Bernice tells me that the way back into sober thinking is through thinking small. "Get tiny," she advises. "Find small actions and take them. God lives in the concrete actions not in the abstract. Wash your hair."

And so I wash my hair, which does look better and clean and glossy. I clean the top of my bedroom bureau. I make my bed. Each small action restores a sense of optimism and with opti-

Everything has its wonders, even darkness and silence, and I learn, whatever state I may be in, therein to be content.

HELEN KELLER

I'm grateful for computers and photocopiers. I appreciate where we've come from.

JULIAN SIMON

mism comes hope. I hope I will turn the corner soon and be back to having a sense of equilibrium. I hope I will begin to see the many small beauties that fill my world. I hope I will be able to shake off the drama of comments that come floating my way. I need a way to just edge through the afternoon. I am, after all, here. Here is where I need to find some beauty. Here is where I need to find some faith. I live a block from Central Park. It has beauty. And there are many other things that have beauty as well if I am just willing, as Bernice says, to get tiny, not large. A block up Columbus Avenue from my apartment there is a good plant store. It is filled with beauty. Out on a brief Artist Date this week, I stopped in the plant store. I bought a bouquet of sweet williams and a small potted African violet. I have the violet set up on my dining-room table. Its delicate tissue paper blooms are vibrant and deep. Its velvety dark green leaves are covered with the softest fur. The plant is beautiful.

"Write a poem to your little plant," Bernice tells me. "Put a festive cloth over your computer." She is urging me to get playful.

When I get playful, I have again a childlike faith and that faith tells me that I can edge ahead. "Think little, get little, be little," I urge myself. Big things are accomplished by many, many tiny strokes. If you cannot right now take in the big picture, try taking in the little picture. Try to just do the next right thing. And what is the next right thing?

So many memories come flooding back to me. As I lie in bed, not sleeping, I have a hit parade of thoughts that all turn toward the dramatic. I remember being sick before and how very frightened it made me. If I am to avoid becoming sick again, I need to cling to the simplest of thoughts, "Just don't drink, just don't kill yourself from despair." One more time I just need to put in time, to go forward a crumb at a time. I have been here before and survived it. I will be able to survive this, too. My humor will return and with humor will come strength.

Gardens start with seeds. Seeds are tiny and look like nothing much. And yet, it is from seeds that we get blooms and from blooms that we get hope. Hope is what tells us that if we just keep going a day at a time we will be led. Hope is what tells us that there is always a tiny something that is possible, some place for God to meet us.

Divining Rod

Spiritual seekers speak of the "dark night of the soul." It is an inexplicable period of black despondency that steals over us for no apparent reason. I am in one now. Prone to breakdowns, I tend to experience dark nights as a regular, if unwelcome, occurrence. Over the years, grappling with both my alcoholism and my depressions, I have had to learn many self-protective measures. I have a need for all of them. And for friends like Bernice who can gently remind me how to use them.

It is a truism of 12-step programs to say, "You cannot think your way into right action but you can act your way in to right thinking." Faced with despair, small actions do hold the antidote. We can train ourselves to act in our own behalf.

Take pen in hand. Number from one to ten. List ten small actions that you could take which would make you feel better. For example, "I could get a good haircut." Or, "I could polish my shoes." Or, "I could sort my receipt pot." Or, "I could clean my refrigerator." If you are depressed, most of these small tasks will still seem beyond your reach. Choose the smallest and least threatening and execute that.

He who is contented is rich.

Lao Tse

Rain

Today is a wet, gray day. The rooftops of the brownstones beneath my writing window are slick and wet, shiny silver and black. Today there are no intrepid sunbathers. Everyone is tucked indoors waiting for the storm to pass. Even the birds are in hiding, nestled under the brownstones' eaves, tucked away in high tree branches. No one wants to get wet—or any wetter than they are. It is a day of limited adventures.

Despite the wet, I will head over to Central Park. The dogs will like it there, once they get over their initial squeamishness at the weather. We will make a loop near the reservoir, underneath the fragrant pink trees. There is much to be said for dailiness, for braving the elements in the name of "routine." Life is made of small sweetnesses, and they come to us when we are willing to be little, instead of big.

What do I mean by being willing to be little? I mean that on a gray day we count the beauty of the raindrops hanging from the fire escape railing. We listen for the song of birds even though those birds are out of sight. A gray day is a good day to polish a pair of shoes, to put new laces in your sneakers, to run a damp cloth along the window ledges cleaning up the grime. On a gray day, we are like children and perhaps it is a good day to act like them.

In a tall bookcase just off of my writing room, I keep a row of children's books. I have books on fish, on Africa, on trains and, today's book, a book on birds. Written to perhaps a twelve-year-old's level, these books are just the kind you might use in grammar school to give a report. With the rain slicking the windows, I turn the pages slowly. I learn that the smallest bird weighs only 0.5 ounces while the largest bird weighs 275 pounds.

Curled in a large leather reading chair with a lamp lit against the afternoon gloom, I learn that birds have hollow bones supported by interior struts. A pigeon's skeleton is so light, it weighs only one-twentieth of the weight of the bird. In order to assure

My crown is called content, a crown that seldom kings enjoy.

WILLIAM SHAKESPEARE

I am not an adventurer by choice but by fate.

VINCENT VAN GOGH

a pigeon of a quick escape from danger, the wing muscles are very powerful, counting for a full third of the bird's weight. Strong wing muscles enable the pigeon to take off rapidly and to accelerate swiftly to a speed of up to fifty miles per hour. The pigeon is built for daring escapes from danger.

By way of contrast, the peregrine falcon embodies danger. Able to dive at the rate of 175 miles per hour, it bags its quarry by knocking it to the ground with the force of its impact and slashing it with its talons. The northern reaches of Central Park make an urban home for the peregrine falcon. Birders haunt the park, tramping through forested areas and creeping up to wetlands. They carry binoculars and often a Sibley field guide. They speak in excited whispers, jotting down their sightings of the day. To my eye, the birders themselves are an exotic species.

The silvery day is starting to lighten. The gray mist shrouding tall buildings is starting to thin. While water drops still cling to the fire escape railings, no new droplets are forming. We have had the rain we are going to have and by late afternoon, the day may begin to clear and brighten. The dogs are eager now to get outdoors to the park.

Sometimes we must play the sleuth with ourselves, asking ourselves what makes us eager. We must follow our noses and allow ourselves to pursue curiosities. We must edge our way toward the wetlands, careful not to startle the birds that we seek. It is good to sneak up on an enthusiasm. Let us say we have an interest in Paris, as I recently did. We might begin by searching the Internet to find a guidebook on Paris. We might order the book. Next, we might try our hand at language. Prior to our Parisian trip, Emma and I studied French with the Pimsleur Method. We queued up CD's and listened carefully, responding to the cues that said, "Where is the hotel?" and "I would like to eat dinner with you at nine." Although there were a disconcerting number of ways to order wine, I practiced my lessons faithfully. Eventually, thankfully, I learned how to decline a glass of wine. As a sober alcoholic I was interested in being able to say "No." And say "No" I did all through the journey that was our

Do you not see how necessary a world of pains and troubles is to school an intelligence and make it a soul?

JOHN KEATS

Every time a child says, "I don't believe in fairies," there's a fairy somewhere that falls down dead.

SIR JAMES M. BARRIE

next step. *"Non, merci, merci bien,"* I managed to say, declining red wine, white, and pink.

Before our trip, still anticipating it, we began learning foods we would encounter. We learned that hot chocolate was *chocolat chaud*. We learned that a ham and cheese crepe was *jambon et fromage*. It was thrilling once we made it to Paris, to put our newly won knowledge to the test. I ordered a crepe from a stand at the flank of the Eiffel Tower. In a cozy bistro I ordered a raspberry soufflé and declined the dessert crepe made with Grand Marnier. Each morning, for breakfast, I would order a *café crème*. That, and a *pain chocolat*. It was delicious being a beginner in the language, making my way a syllable at a time. It was nearly forty years since I had studied French in high school. After all that time, stray phrases would come swimming back.

The afternoon has cleared. I have taken "the girls" out to the park. The weather reminds me of Paris, luminous and soft, lightly misting. As I pass the benches lining the westward walk, I hear a dog owner calling to his dog, *"Fifi. Ici. Ici, Fifi."* Fifi, a cream-colored dog with a sweet face, crosses obediently to her owner's side. *"Bonjour,"* I say as I lead my charges from the park.

Beauty is truth, truth beauty.

JOHN KEATS

Divining Rod

We speak of having a "childlike wonder" without realizing the cue that is contained in the phrase. It actually gives directions for an action plan. To awaken our sense of wonder—a necessary ingredient in all creativity—we must be willing to be childlike. We have heard this before in spiritual matters. Christ told us that in order to have faith we must "become as little children." Since creativity is a matter of faith, becoming childlike can help us in our creative endeavors. We must learn to explore with openness and curiosity. What better place to do this than a children's bookstore?

Set aside one full hour. Take yourself to a good children's bookstore. Allow yourself the delicious luxury of browsing. Chances are that many books will pique your interest. There are books on cars, trains, and butterflies. There are books on birds, reptiles, and dinosaurs. There are books on Indians and books on India. Do not be too adult to be enticed. What is more fun than a picture book on dogs or cats or horses? Or maybe you want to know how an automobile engine works?

A children's book on Magellan set me off on a year's worth of writing about the great mariner. As scholars will tell you, Magellan is a very adult subject but the children's books on his adventure fired my imagination more than the worthy biographies that bore his name.

Remember that too much information can dampen the imagination. You can always explore a topic at more depth if you wish, but children's books are an ideal place for starting off.

He must pull out his own eyes and see no creature, before he can say, he sees no God; he must be no man, and quench his reasonable soul, before he can say to himself, there is no God.

JOHN DONNE

The Stubbornness of Dreams

A friend of mine is suffering from a depression. She worked for a long time to manifest a dream and the dream seems to have gone glimmering. She is at a loss as to the next action to take. She feels adrift without her dream to moor her. Who is she if she doesn't have a dream?

"I admire people who don't give up," she says. "I admire people who keep on going despite the odds." Her gentle voice is sorrowful.

"Maybe you just need to resolve to be one of those people,"

I tell her. I am telling her what I tell myself: Act your way into right thinking.

"I'd like to be," she says. She sounds weary, small and sad.

"Just do the simple things," I tell her. "Set up a gentle grid and stick to it. Go back to basics." I urge her to write Morning Pages, to take Artist Dates, to go for walks. I tell her that optimism will come seeping back—this is what I have been telling myself and I do believe it. I am in a black period, a bleak time, but I believe that such time will pass. I tell my friend exactly what it is I myself most need to hear.

Dreams come to us from a divine source. If we follow them, they lead us back to a divine source. When we work toward our dreams, we are working toward our God. In reaching for guidance about our dreams, we are reaching toward God. Our dreams are not futile. They do not spring from our egos. They have their roots in our souls. My friend is right to fear the destruction of her dream. Dreams must be guarded like children. Like children, they must be nurtured and soothed.

As an artist, it can be very difficult to sort through destructive criticism. When we receive feedback that is vague or simply way off the mark, it can be hard to have the resilience necessary to spring back. In my friend's case, the "no's" she has been receiving around her dream are particularly frustrating because she knows that the work she has done is good. She has had support and encouragement from two estimable authorities—people who, unfortunately, are not in the position to offer concrete help. "Your show is good," they have told her. "Keep on keeping on."

What my friend needs is the gift of healing. Her beleaguered heart must find some way to mend. I have said to her that she should try walking. Walking has a way of drawing pain to scale. Walking has a way of giving us perspective. My friend laughs. She does walk. Walking has made her dreams feel only more painfully real.

"I walked all the way home from Times Square," my friend countered. "The more I walked, the stronger became my dream."

Art is only a means to life, to the life more abundant. . . . In becoming an end, it defeats itself.

HENRY MILLER

"Well, then. I guess you can't give up," I tell her.

A step at a time we are led forward and sometimes those steps are literal. On the strength of her dream, my friend must one more time take action. Praying for guidance, she was told to push forward. To be an artist, one needs a good dose of stubbornness. We need a mulish side that refuses to be bullied or cowed. "I will win out," some obstinate voice in us must be insisting. "There has to be a way," is the mantra we must chant.

Many times, success comes through unseen doorways. When conventional routes have been exhausted, success steps forward wearing an eccentric cloak. How many times do breaks come to us through sources as unlikely as "my dentist's cousin"? How often do we find that we are led through a maze of lucky breaks and coincidence? Embracing her dream again, my friend is about to step into the maze. "Dear God, show me," must be her prayer.

Another friend of mine is a minister. He warns against depending on one source for our well-being. "God has a thousand ways to meet you," he says. "Do not look for someone else to give your dream permission to go forward," he warns. "When you make one person or place the source of your lucky break, you are denying the power of God who can work from many corners." Trust God and look for leadings, he advises.

The world of publishing is filled with stories of best-selling authors who became that way by first publishing themselves. A publisher I know laughs ruefully over these stories. "There's more than a grain of truth in them," he says. "Very often a book will be turned down 'everywhere' only to have the author self-publish, driving his book from store to store and ending up with a whopping success."

To be an artist, we must be willing to be Don Quixote, to tilt at a few windmills, to look foolish to others and even to ourselves. Every artist carries within him an Inner Dreamer. The dreamer might be called "the Believer," the part of us that is willing to go forward on faith. Every artist carries, too, an Inner Censor, the skeptical part that might be called "the Devil," the part that tells us the game is over, that we might as well quit.

Every production of an artist should be the expression of an adventure of his soul.

W. SOMERSET MAUGHAM

*If a man does not keep pace
with his companions, perhaps it
is because he hears a different
drummer. Let him step to the
music which he hears, however
measured or far away.*

HENRY DAVID THOREAU

The Devil is clever and it comes at us from many quarters. It always asks us to deny the power of God. One of the chief forms the Devil takes is an urge on our part toward self-sufficiency. We count on ourselves and stop counting on a Higher Power. We feel that we ought to be able to figure things out and when we cannot, we conclude that we are phonies, has-beens, crazy. The Devil finds our Achilles' heel and comes at us through that. Let us say we are worried about money. The Devil will tell us that we will soon be homeless. Let us say we are worried about prestige. The Devil will rehearse for us our future bad reviews. Say we are an expert at some area of knowledge. The Devil will tell us that all our expertise matters nothing. It will say we have no answers when our answers lie right before us but we are too blind with fear to see them and pick them up. For me, the Devil is a form of drunkenness. I have alcoholism not alcoholwasm. The Devil comes at me saying, "What's the use? Poor me. Poor me. Pour me a drink."

Help is all around us. Help is at every hand. Help is just waiting to meet and greet us. We are the ones who insist there is no help. Our hearts are closed to the many gentle forms of help that are offered to our suffering souls. What we are after, all that we need, is a sip of water. Our challenge is finding water when we are in a spiritual drought. We need the gentle draught of encouragement, the water of spiritual truth. "There is a God," we need to hear. "You are cared for," we need to believe.

Divining Rod

You have already practiced writing a humble letter to God, perhaps more than one. You have experienced the grace that comes from spiritual candor. There is something very healing in telling God exactly where it hurts and why. It is a relief to get our despondency off our chest. The exercise I am now asking you to undertake requires some further open-mindedness. I am asking you to imagine an answered prayer.

Set aside an hour's quiet time. Take pen in hand and write God a letter about anything and everything that is currently bothering you. Write for as long as a half hour, then stop. Now take your pen to page a second time. This time listen for an answer and write a letter from God back to you. In your fondest hopes and dreams, what compassionate response does God have to your yearnings? Allow your imagination to guide you. Comfort and soothe yourself as you wish that God would. Listen to your deepest intuitions about the solutions and perspectives that God has to offer. There is a wise being within you that deserves to be listened to. The "still, small voice" does speak to us all.

What is art: It is the response of man's creative Soul to the call of the Real.

RABINDRANATH TAGORE

CHECK-IN

1. **How many days this week did you do your Morning Pages?** If you skipped a day, why did you skip it? How was the experience of writing them for you? Are you experiencing more clarity? A wider range of emotions? A greater sense of detachment, purpose, and calm? Did anything surprise you? Is there a "repeating" issue asking to be dealt with?

2. **Did you do your Artist Date this week?** Did you note an improved sense of well-being? What did you do and how did it feel? Remember, Artist Dates can be difficult and you may need to coax yourself into taking them.

The artist's object is to make things not as nature makes them, but as she would make them.

RAPHAEL

3. **Did you get out on your Weekly Walk?** How did that feel? What emotions or insights surfaced for you? Were you able to walk more than once? What did your walk do for your optimism and sense of perspective?

4. **Were there any other issues this week that felt significant to you in your self-discovery?** Describe them.

Uncovering a Sense of Resilience

Most of us have little sense of our true strength. The essays and tasks of this week ask you to focus on your personal resiliency. By focusing on your available resources, you will see that you do indeed have sufficient fuel for your journey. Your spiritual well will not run dry if you take the time and care to replenish it by self-loving actions. At midpoint in the course, your spiritual connection to the Great Creator both deepens and becomes ever more personal, revealing to you perhaps previously unsuspected inner strength.

Support

This morning, I paid a visit to Therese, an older woman who lives in a snug apartment a few blocks south. Therese radiates a sharp, incisive intelligence. She is nobody's fool.

"The problem so many of us have is self-sufficiency," Therese said. "We fall into depending on ourselves instead of God and then we wonder why we feel so alone. We cut ourselves off and then we feel isolated. You know, we really are not alone."

Therese knows whereof she speaks. She is herself a walking example of what can be done with the power of God. A low-bottom alcoholic, she has been restored to sobriety and sanity. Once a helpless drunk, she now helps others.

"I am having a hard time writing," I tell Therese. "Words are not coming to me easily. I feel inarticulate."

Our real blessings often appear to us in the shape of pains, losses, and disappointments.

JOSEPH ADDISON

Two things make a story. The net and the air that falls through the net.

PABLO NERUDA

"Sometimes it is good to be inarticulate," Therese answers back. "When we are dealing with deeper layers of the psyche, we don't always have a line of glib chatter. Occasionally, being struck speechless is good."

"But I make my living with words," I protest, even though I can feel the truth of what Therese has said to me. I find myself wondering what it would be like to be wordless for a while, simply living, existing in the flow of life like a satiny gray river rock, washed over by the flow.

"You are filled with self-centered fears," Therese tells me. One more time her blunt words seem to accurately name the precise condition I have found myself facing.

I am filled with self-centered fears. I am worried about drinking, about running out of money, ending up homeless, wandering the streets like the many lost souls I see on my rounds in Manhattan. Fight it as I will, my imagination has snagged on the negative. I have a recurrent dream, one in which my daughter is four years old and I am wandering the streets of New York with no place for us to live. It is nighttime and there is no place safe for us to rest.

"It's just a nightmare," I tell myself. "It's just a dream."

And yet I am afraid that the dream will become a reality. I know that I can make it one by simply picking up a drink and allowing the drink to lead the way.

Therese is talking again. "You need to share how you are feeling," she says. "You need to let it out."

"Therese," I tell her. "I am supposed to have answers. I am twenty-eight years without a drink. People look to me for answers—and today I have none. I need help."

"You need support," Therese rephrases it.

Once again, her words accurately name an inner state I lacked words for. I am shaken to the core and I need to feel a sense of divine guidance. I have been craving the help and security of other people. They say that alcoholism is the disease of isolation. I certainly have it. One more time, I need to reach out.

Divining Rod

At our most alone feeling, most of us still number several friends and supporters on whom we could count. Miserable and despondent, we nonetheless have more resources for help than we are able at the moment to see or access. When our despair tells us that we are isolated and without help, cut off from God and from all human understanding, the truth is that most of us do have friends who understand us—if we give them the chance. It is a lie of the mind that we are alone and friendless. We do have allies. The trick to identifying such allies lies in making a list of our resources when we are not sad and beset. Try your hand at this now.

You have already made a list of five people who are encouraging to you and your art. Turn to that list again and see if there are any among them who could be counted upon for more generalized emotional support. In all likelihood, you will find several. Choose one. When you have made your selection, call, write, or e-mail your friend. Explain that you are reaching out, that you are not always so needy but just at the moment you could use some cheering up. Allow yourself to express some vulnerability, to reveal a peek behind the upbeat surface you work so hard to maintain.

When your friend responds to your contact, take time to check in with yourself about exactly how their response makes you feel. You are in a sorting process, seeking to find friends with whom you can be small as well as large. Some of our friends prefer us only when we are doing well. Others, those with broader emotional keyboards, are able to take us in in whatever condition we come to them. (Be alert to avoid in the future those friends who are shaming to you

Think before you speak is criticism's motto; speak before you think is creation's.

E. M. FORSTER

*Give what you have. To
someone else it may be better
than you dare to think.*

HENRY WADSWORTH
LONGFELLOW

about your feelings of vulnerability. We may "know" bet-ter but be unable to "do" better at being upbeat.) You are looking for friends who can take you just as you are.

"You sound tired," such a friend might say to you. "Are you sure you aren't a little under the weather? Maybe you should ease up a little bit." Support for our human selves can go a long way toward easing our pan-icked sense of isolation. Friends, above all, are friendly. They do not shame us or urge us back to the treadmill when we are suffering from burnout. Friends encourage us to be flexible and kind toward ourselves. They are friends not only to the work but to the worker. Allow yourself to experience their support.

Discernment

The day today is bright but chill, very, very chill. The wind from the west is sharp and needling. People walk clutching their coats and jackets. What happened to spring? Wasn't it just a day or so ago that we were rushing forward into summer? This new, colder weather seems like a betrayal.

Out in the park, pale, pink cherry blossoms shiver in the breeze. A flowering plum looks nearly purple with the cold. Still, it is a pretty day and a few landscape artists have set up easels un-der the bouffant cherry trees. One painter balances her water in a small green cup. She is working in watercolor and she is paint-ing a miniature, each delicate stroke following on the next.

This afternoon, I got a letter from Rhonda. She was writing to say she had received a copy of my latest book and she was en-joying it. Her letter came on pretty stationery. Her writing added more whimsical hearts and flowers. She was looking for-ward, she said, to our summer's walks. Rhonda is used to my returning to New Mexico every spring. I am used to it, too, and her letter caused me to wince with sorrow.

"Oh, dear," I think to myself. "No walking with Rhonda. No long hikes up El Salto Road past the buffalo and llamas." No, this summer will be more domesticated. My strolls will be around the perimeter of the reservoir and sometimes south to Central Park's small lake, the rowing pond. If I am lucky, and if I go at odd hours, the park will not be too crowded and there will be flora and fauna to spot.

If I am lucky, I will be able to muster optimism. I will be able to stick to my gentle grid of walks. This summer is an experiment, an attempt to forestall danger. Last summer in New Mexico I was struck suddenly and savagely fragile. A breakdown loomed. Far from doctors, diagnosed by telephone, the only solution was to take strong doses of medication and make the long drive back to Manhattan and to relative safety. In Manhattan, doctors are at hand. Friends are nearby who have seen me through rough patches before. In New Mexico, there is only beauty and fear. No, this year is not a year for New Mexico. It is a year to make the most of the wildness and beauty I can find in Manhattan.

Just yesterday, Emma reported that she had spotted something big. "I don't think it was an eagle, but it was very, very large. Its head was brown, not white, and it had thick feathers fluffing out its legs."

To my ear, it sounded worth a jaunt to the park to try spotting this creature. It could be a peregrine falcon or some species of hawk. I could take my birding binoculars and hope for a good glimpse of it. It is not the same as a day's jaunt on the Rio Grande with eagles soaring overhead. It is a tamer, smaller adventure, but it will do.

As I work to bring myself back into balance, I must turn to the tiny things I can do each day to muster a sense of optimism. I wake and curl in a large leather chair to write Morning Pages. I say my prayers. I read some of Ernest Holmes's writings. I go to the computer and work. After I work, I take myself on a small adventure.

When you cease to make a contribution, you begin to die.

Eleanor Roosevelt

If I can stop one heart from breaking, I shall not live in vain.

EMILY DICKINSON

With Tiger Lily by my side and the birding binoculars around my neck, I head over to the park. I am looking for Emma's large bird. What I find, instead, are a plethora of robins and one beautiful red-winged blackbird. Later in the day, back at my computer, I glance out the window just in time to catch sight of a heron flying past. My late father loved herons, and I have two Audubon prints of herons framed in my living room. Spotting the high-flying bird, headed to Central Park and the small lake where it makes its home, seems auspicious to me. I am ready to see good omens.

On a roof garden across the avenue from my building, two large fake owls stand sentinel. They are there to ward off pigeons, their stiff silhouettes signaling, "Danger. Enemy territory." The pigeons give the garden a wide berth.

As artists, we, too, must learn who and what to give a wide berth. We must steer clear, if we can, of people who dampen our enthusiasms, who cut short our flights of fancy. Like the sharp-taloned owl, a sharp tongue goaded by cynicism can quickly tear our optimism to shreds. We are resilient but delicate. We must be alert.

As artists, we must be vigilant. We cannot control everyone around us, but we can learn whose company is good for us and whose company causes us to shrivel and shrink. As we work to set new boundaries, we will provoke some anger and some resentment. When we say "Hands off!" there will be those who take a quick final pinch.

It is the perilous truth that many of the people who talk to us as artists do not know how to talk to us as artists. They mean well but even their well-meaning does not undo the damage they inflict, almost in passing. In America, we are taught how to take things apart, not how to build them. In our school system we learn how to criticize, not construct. As a result, people know how to weigh in with what is wrong but without balancing it with comments about what is right. The artist, hearing only the criticism, begins to shut down. Valid points may be made, but they are made over the artist's nearly dead body. "Oh, what's the use?" A certain sullen stubbornness may set in, "I am not changing anything." Here again is where friends can help us to parse out the criticism that is tough but useful.

In my experience, artists do want valid criticism. We feel a sense of excitement and a willingness to work when a piece of criticism hits the mark and we intuitively feel it will make our work better. Instead of "Ouch!" we register, "Ah ha!" and the creative wheels start to turn as our engine kicks over and we begin "fixing" something—almost whether we want to or not. Sometimes, however, it can take a friend's translation to help us hear criticism accurately. "Maybe he's really saying X," the friend might suggest, giving us a slightly more neutral way to view a set of remarks. Equally, a friend might say, "Oh, Julia, he's way off the mark, just ignore him," which is easier said than done but is possible to do with the help of your friends.

When I was a young writer, I lived in an apartment behind the Washington Zoo. Every morning as I woke up and every night as twilight fell, I would hear the roar of wild animals vying to be heard over the sound of traffic. There were lions and tigers and bears—many, many bears. And so it happened that I wrote my early short stories to an exotic accompaniment. The animals were always present, an odd, primal sound track eclipsing the hubbub of the city. They were at once comforting and terrifying.

Judy Bachrach was my best girlfriend in those days, and she was both comforting and terrifying, too. Another young writer, she had firm opinions about all I wrote. We both wrote for *The Washington Post*. She was that exalted creature, a staff writer. I was a lowly copy aide who freelanced for the paper on the side. Judy was tall and willowy with a striking resemblance to young Lauren Bacall. She was my primary cheerleader and hardest critic. "You can't publish this one," she said of one short story, "it will ruin your career."

The fact that I had no *career* at the time did not faze Judy. She believed in me and my work and my future career was a certainty to her. She—and I—must protect it, she felt. I put the short story in a bottom drawer. I never did publish it. I went on to write other stories, stories that could pass muster with Judy

He does good to himself who does good to his friend.

Erasmus

and not damage my career. All of us need our Judy's, friends vigilant enough to tell us when the work wobbles, which it sometimes will. These friends are our sentinel owls and we can use them to protect our creative gardens.

Divining Rod

My friend Julianna McCarthy has taught me a parlor game that I believe all artists should learn to play. The game is called "Who Would You Take to the War?" It asks you to survey your friendships and assess them in terms to their health to your well-being and goals. Most of us, looking over our friendships, will discover that we do not have too many friends whom we could take to the war but that we do have some.

A friend that I would take to the war would need to be someone who is able to keep his head and objectivity when the going gets tough. I have such a friend in my believing mirror Ed Towle. Shrewd and longsighted, he keeps his emotions at bay while he parses out the best course of action. I can depend on him both for humor and for realism. If I tell him an emotional story, he puts it in the framework of the "big picture." Ed is a friend I could take to the war.

I could not take my friend Felice to the war. She is prone to drama. She would encourage me to overreact to the first signs of trouble. Felice would encourage my own fears to step too far forward. No, Felice could not be depended upon to keep her head.

My friend Julianna, the inventor of the game, is someone I could take to war. Hardheaded and yet compassionate, she always has an eye on the bottom line, drawing things to scale. If I call her with a manufactured misery,

The bravest sight in the world is to see a great man struggling against adversity.

SENECA

Talk that does not end in any kind of action is better suppressed altogether.

THOMAS CARLYLE

she will snap, "You're doing fine, given that you should have been dead years ago." She is referring of course to my alcoholism and the fact that every day sober is a win. And yet, if I phone her with a legitimate misery, Julianna is quick with compassion. She says, "Life is hard and what you're going through is hard." Her empathy always makes me feel better.

Take pen in hand. Survey your friendships for those people whom you could take to the war. List their names and the qualities that would make them invaluable. This is an exercise in discernment.

Advice is what we ask for when we already know the answer but wish we didn't.

ERICA JONG

Healing

The sun is playing peekaboo. When it is out, the day is warm. When it is hiding behind a cloud, the day is cool. Kids are out in shirtsleeves and shorts on their skateboards. Adults clutch their thin jackets closer to their bodies. The fur on a fluffy collie ruffles in the wind. At the entrance to the park, mock orange is now blooming. The maple trees are coming into leaf. The flowering fruit trees, apple and plum and cherry, are white, purple, and pink according to their nature. Spring is at hand, advancing daily, but the warm weather is still fractious.

This afternoon, I talked on the phone with Bernice who lives in Boulder, Colorado. "It's snowing very hard here," she said. "Of course that is good because we've suffered a drought. There's an inch on the ground here but in the mountains it is really building up."

Bernice and I talk on the phone once weekly. I depend on Bernice for her wisdom and her humor. She listens to my life and offers wisdom from a decade further on the path.

Today, I told Bernice that I still was feeling shaky, that New York was feeling overwhelming to me, and that I was longing to

I have learned more about love, selflessness, and human understanding in this great adventure in the world of AIDS than I ever did in the cut-throat, competitive world in which I spent my life.

ANTHONY PERKINS

Beauty is as relative as light and dark.

PAUL KLEE

be in New Mexico, where the long vistas draw things to scale. I needed a reality check. Wasn't I just as close to a breakdown here as I had been last year in New Mexico?

"No. And you're sounding better than you have been," Bernice responded. "But you're not out of the woods yet. I think you are grieving. I believe your losses around your art have rattled you to the core. For a while, you need to keep a very narrow focus. Remember what I've told you. You need to get tiny."

"Get tiny" is good advice for how to inch forward. In 12-step lingo, we are told to "do the next right thing." When we suffer a loss around our art, we need to find some small positive action by which we can go ahead. Discouraged as I am about *The Medium at Large,* I might still listen through that show to remind myself that it is good, no matter how its reception might feel. Sometimes the action is an action in the outer world—mail the poem off one more time. Sometimes, however, the action needs to be in our inner world. We may need to write a nursery rhyme to comfort our inner creative youngster. We may need to do a piece of doggerel to help us get to the other side.

When I suffered a bad review in the Sunday *New York Times*— the only bad review I got on an otherwise well-liked book, *The Dark Room*—I had to write a scrap of poetry to get myself out of the doldrums. And so I wrote a poem at my wrongheaded reviewer:

If you don't believe in God, all you have to believe in is decency . . . Decency is very good. Better decent than indecent. But I don't think it's enough.

HAROLD MACMILLAN

This little poem goes out to Bill Kent
Who must feel awful the way that he spent
His time critiquing Carl Jung
Instead of on the book I'd done.

Writing the little poem gave me a naughty sense of power. It made me feel that one more time I had an impish sense of play. It is a sense of play that tells us we have things in healthy perspective. It is when life feels deadly earnest that we blow things out of all proportion. With the rim of the glass looming, I have to watch that tendency right now. I sometimes think that self-pity is the dominant, distinguishing characteristic of my alcoholism. If my periodic depressions are biochemical events, they must be fought with every tool I have at hand, both medically and spiritually. But when I am teetering on the brink, the temptations to self-pity seem fiendishly persuasive.

This afternoon, I was interviewed by a woman from a large Canadian magazine. "How does it feel," she wanted to know, "to be pigeonholed as a 'Self-Help' writer?" The question went straight to one of my worst creative fears, that I would always be known first and foremost as a teacher and that the level of my craft as an artist would never be allowed to shine. I told the woman frankly that I couldn't afford to think about how I was perceived. "That's a drink for me," I explained. "All I need to do is start thinking about how I am not appreciated and never will be and it becomes, 'Poor me, poor me, pour me a drink.'"

I explained to the woman that my need to stay sober was actually my greatest teacher. All of the stratagems I have learned to apply to the artist's life come straight out of the toolkits I have acquired to maintain my sobriety. When Bernice says, "Get tiny," I hear, "Oh, yes, one day at a time." When Bernice urges me to make small lists and execute them, I think, "Ah, yes, just do the next right thing. Follow first things first."

At the moment, I am shaky. I have no "I" to write from. My ego feels shattered and with it my prose style. I look at older books that I have written and I wonder at the writing style and the wisdom contained within them. "Where did that wisdom go?" I wonder. "What happened to my syntax?"

It is a Friday night in Manhattan. Couples stroll Columbus Avenue, arm in arm. The Chase Bank on the corner is doing a brisk ATM business and nowhere, in any of the faces that I see, do I see a trace of my lost syntax. People are busy. People are happy and my missing syntax is my own sad little secret. I leave the young lovers to the street below and I come upstairs to write. Bernice has estimated that it will take me several weeks longer before I will be back in my stride and writing well. She thinks, as do I, that I need the benefit of a simple routine, a dull

We artists are indestructible; even in a prison or in a concentration camp, I would be almighty in my own world of art, even if I had to paint my pictures with my wet tongue on the dusty floor of my cell.

Pablo Picasso

and daily life, for my psyche to settle back down again. For my part, I long to burrow into my routine. If it cannot be a summer of long walks in Taos, let it be a summer of long walks in Manhattan. I need to stretch my legs and my imagination. I need to find healing and health.

If sex and creativity are often seen by dictators as subversive activities, it's because they lead to the knowledge that you own your own body (and with it your own voice), and that's the most revolutionary insight of all.

ERICA JONG

Divining Rod

The monasteries of the great world religions run on ritualized schedules. The gong sounds and the monks are called to worship. Their days are fruitfully divided according to regular activities. In our own more secular lives, we are the ones who must set in place our rituals and our rounds. Morning Pages give us a way to begin our days. A midday walk finds our souls stretching as well as our bodies. Winding down to bedtime, it is healing to have a regular evening ritual. In this way, we can begin our day and end our day with a spiritual contact.

Some students have found that simply listing the five beauties of the day places them in a mood of gratitude and receptivity. Just before sleep, they often feel a sense of conscious contact with the Divine. It is in this mood of openness and acceptance that I ask you to undertake an experiment.

Take pen in hand. Remembering that God is the Great Listener, write a simple prayer. (You have done this before when you were feeling shaky. Now try it on a "regular" night.) You might tell God about the day that you have just had. You might revisit your dreams or disappointments. You might ask for guidance, to be awoken the next day with a clear sense of God's will for you. Some evening prayers are prayers of gratitude. Some are prayers of petition. It matters less what you say than that you say it. The evening prayer is a time for candor. Think of this interval as being like a nightly chat between fond lovers. Show God your secret heart.

Soldiering On

It is May Day. The weather is cooperating, sunny and breezy and seventy degrees. In the park, picnickers abound. In the pinetum, a pine grove just off the Great Lawn, there are two picnic tables laden with cakes and sodas and a bevy of young children weaving a merry dance with the streamers from a maypole held aloft by a quickly tiring adult.

At Turtle Pond, the turtles have emerged from their winter's hibernation below the ice-locked pond. The pond is a shimmering surface broken only by the wake of paddling ducks. The turtles bask on rocks and logs, soaking up the sun's warmth after their long winter's chill. On the dock that juts out into the water, parents stand with their young offspring, peering through the railings.

Patience is the companion of wisdom.

St. Augustine of Hippo

"See, there's a turtle!" they say, pointing to the shell of a lounging turtle. The turtles look like so many silvery river rocks. They are hard to see against the shore.

"I see one," a triumphant and precocious five-year-old trumpets. He points to where a slow-moving turtle is lurching into the water.

"Yes, well, there are lots of them," his father advises. "Can you see the rest?"

"No." Now the child's voice is petulant. "I want ice cream."

A vendor has set up shop nearby, poised for just such an eventuality. The vendor's wagon offers pretzels, hot dogs, "Froze-ade" and, yes, ice cream.

"Want a pretzel?" The father is trying to dodge a sugar high.

*Hasten slowly and you will
soon reach your destination.*

MILAREPA

"No, I want ice cream."

"What kind of ice cream do you have?"

The vendor waves a hand at a large sign which enumerates a dozen or more ice-cream treats.

"I see." The parent sounds testy now. A sugar high lies ahead. The child stands on one foot. Is it bathroom time as well?

"What kind do you want? Orange? Rainbow? Vanilla?"

"Rainbow." The child points a stubby finger at the rainbow pop.

And so, rainbow it is. The child grabs eagerly at the garish concoction, a swirled mass of pink, orange, lime green, and white.

"Is it good? Are you happy?" The parent sounds a little beleaguered. I flash a look at his left hand: no ring. Another divorced father, trying to make the best of his weekend visitation rights. Seeing his child once a week is far from perfect, but he is making do the best he can.

Also making do the best he can is the German shepherd who now paddles toward us, front paws striding the ground, back paws hitched aloft in a bicycle contraption. German shepherds are prone to hip problems and clearly this dog's owner was unwilling to put his dog down.

"Here we go. This way, Max," the owner urges, backpedaling in his running gear to keep pace with his dog. Max trots briskly ahead. He is used to the contraption that makes his life possible.

The divorced father and Max's owner have in common a rugged resilience. They both work to make the best of a difficult situation. They both refuse to be counted out by the hand fate has dealt them. They both reach inward and discover there some steadying reserves.

By breaking our life down into daily bites, we all have far more strength than we may realize. It is possible to make the best of a difficult situation "one day at a time." It is a discipline that we must set for ourselves, the narrowing of life's scope to a manageable amount.

Just for today, we are able to do the best we can with our child. Just for today, we can get our dog out for an outing. Just for today, we can soldier on.

As an artist, soldiering on is often what is called for. We may not be able to see any opening, any sure path for our work to follow. "What's the use?" our Inner Critic may hiss. "It's all going to come to nothing anyhow." The hiss of the Inner Critic is the voice of the Devil. It urges us always to despair, to seeing not the progress we have made but the far distance we have yet to travel. "It's hopeless," the Inner Critic announces, dismissing our dreams with a swoop of one hand.

But it is not hopeless. If we are willing to soldier on, there are bright days ahead of us as well as dark. If we muster the courage to continue, there is hope that we might succeed. We need to focus on the possible positive. We need to count on ourselves and on a benevolent larger power that wishes us well. How do we do that?

Writing Morning Pages moves us past the negative chatter of our own minds. We put the chatter on the page and emerge inwardly into a quiet oasis. "Easy does it," we tell ourselves and listen with an inner ear cocked to see what may bubble up in the form of guidance. Quite often, the guidance that comes to us is firm, quiet, and gentle. Just for today, we may have no answer to the larger questions of life but we will have answers to many of the smaller ones.

In art the best is good enough.

JOHANN WOLFGANG
VON GOETHE

As we acquire more knowledge, things do not become more comprehensible, but more mysterious.

ALBERT SCHWEITZER

Divining Rod

In times of sorrow and malcontent, walking lends us a sense of overview and perspective. Although we may walk out with our own problems, we quickly encounter the world. We may walk out feeling alone and trapped but we soon sense that we are all in this together—"this" being the shared soup of human experience. The tool I ask you to use next requires you to reach for a larger perspective.

Teach yourself to work in uncertainty.

BERNARD MALAMUD

Take pen to page and allow your fingers to do a little walking. Number from one to five. List five circumstances in which you did not get what you wanted, where you felt thwarted and denied. Looking over your list, search out the silver lining that came from each denial. There is always some good that comes from sorrow, some grace that comes from difficulty, some opportunity that comes when one door closes and another opens. You may want to ask a blunt question on the page. "What possible good could come of this?" Ask the question and then listen for the answer. It will often surprise you. In searching for some good that came from my terrible breakdowns, I saw that I had been rendered more compassionate. My breakdowns had given me empathy for the fears and terrors of others.

Having rounded up your disappointments onto the page, having searched for the unexpected blessing that they held, I now ask you to take a longish walk, holding loosely in mind what you have discovered. Allow yourself time enough to slow down and allow the world to speak to you again of its beauties and its glories. What you are after here is a sense of tranquillity. As you walk, you may find your melancholy tinged by acceptance.

CHECK-IN

1. **How many days this week did you do your Morning Pages?** If you skipped a day, why did you skip it? How was the experience of writing them for you? Are you experiencing more clarity? A wider range of emotions? A greater sense

of detachment, purpose, and calm? Did anything surprise you? Is there a "repeating" issue asking to be dealt with?

2. **Did you do your Artist Date this week?** Did you note an improved sense of well-being? What did you do and how did it feel? Remember, Artist Dates can be difficult and you may need to coax yourself into taking them.

3. **Did you get out on your Weekly Walk?** How did that feel? What emotions or insights surfaced for you? Were you able to walk more than once? What did your walk do for your optimism and sense of perspective?

4. **Were there any other issues this week that felt significant to you in your self-discovery?** Describe them.

Nobody, not even the poet,
holds the secret of the world.

FEDERICO GARCIA LORCA

Uncovering a Sense of Truth

Each of us bears within us an inner compass, a sort of spiritual dowsing wand. When our actions match our values, this compass points true north. This week you are asked to focus on personal grounding. As you plan and execute rituals that both soothe and enliven you, your compass will become more steady. Reaching out to others is another means by which we gauge our own position. As we extend ourselves in empathy toward our friends, we experience ourselves as generous and compassionate.

Change

This morning, though a chill, gray and drizzly day, Tiger Lily and Charlotte went for their annual physicals at Westside Veterinary Clinic. The clinic is a cheerless place with heavily barred windows. It could stand in as a methadone clinic. There is the same air of desperation. In the waiting room, a small Havanese dog yapped repeatedly from the depths of a Louis Vuitton carrying case. A sprightly looking Lhasa apso sat chipper and alert on the lap of its weeping owner.

"He's doing much, much better," the owner managed to gasp between mournful sniffles. "But he's fifteen years old. How old are your dogs?"

"Tiger Lily is five," I indicated the cocker spaniel who was eyeing the little Lhasa aggressively. "Charlotte is four," I nodded toward the Westie.

Artistic growth is, more than it is anything else, a refining of the sense of truthfulness. The stupid believe that to be truthful is easy; only the artist, the great artist, knows how difficult it is.

WILLA CATHER

"Oh, well then. They're young," sniffled the Lhasa's owner.

In the examining room with the kindly lady veterinarian, Charlotte was seized by a bout of shivers. She stood on the silver, metallic examining table and shook with fear. Tiger Lily by way of contrast, snarled and lunged. She was having none of it, the gentle poking and prodding. The nurse handed me a muzzle and asked me to slip it on. "Perhaps she won't bite you," she said doubtfully. I managed to slide the muzzle into place and with a quick yank by the nurse, it was secured. Tiger Lily has never had a bad vet experience so just why she becomes so aggressive is a very good question. The lady veterinarian explained her view.

"We have dogs who have had multiple operations begging to come inside for a treat as they walk past," she said, with a chuckle. "And then we have dogs like Tiger Lily who have once had a shot and have learned from that they want never to come back."

The vet found all the stances endearing. She could empathize with Charlotte's trembling and with Tiger Lily's fit of rage.

As artists, when we encounter change, we often react as the dogs do. No matter that the change is "for our own good," change is still change and it is hard for us.

This morning my phone rang and it was a young writer-director on the brink of signing a deal. "I just don't trust them," she complained of her newly acquired partners. "And I can't tell if my red flags are accurate, my stuff or just the process. I guess the bottom line is that I am about to be in business with some possibly questionable characters but the good news is, I am about to be in business."

When we strive to undertake a creative partnership, cold feet abound. We find ourselves questioning our prospective partners and our own ability to size them up. What we are dealing with, of course, is the question of control. When we have no partners, we are squarely blocked. We may be frustrated by that, but we do not feel out of control. We feel safe and even a little smug: we always knew the odds were stacked against us.

When the odds start to shift, when the dominoes are falling

in the right direction, we can suddenly feel out of control. Where before we knew how we felt—frustrated—now we feel something worse—vulnerable. And we hate to feel vulnerable. Once more our dreams have been nudged awake. Once more our dreams have the capacity to break our hearts.

No matter that the change we are undergoing is a change for the positive. Like Tiger Lily, we snap and bite. Like Charlotte, we quiver and shake. As we are moved forward, we yearn for the safety of where we have been. We become paranoid, seeing shadows every place. Our new benefactors seem like predators.

"You know how well I take good news," the young writer-director jokes to me.

"I think you need to do some daily things," I say. "You need to cling to whatever aspects of your old life you are able to."

"I could write Morning Pages, I suppose. I could have lunch with an old friend."

"That sounds like a very good start."

When we are rickety, Morning Pages lend us stability. They miniaturize the terrors that we are walking through. They bring life back down to the possible: Exactly what can we do, today?

Taken in a daily bite, most change, however extreme, can be metabolized. Our Pages give us time and place to get used to change. "I am afraid," we write and then, a few sentences on, "I need to remember to buy kitty litter."

When we remember that we have a daily life, we begin to find our grounding. The kitty litter must still be bought whether or not we suddenly have a million-dollar deal. That upstairs toilet needs to be repaired and that is a matter of some urgency. Morning Pages tell us to call the plumber.

It is our job, faced with impending change, to continue to husband the life that we have got. It is our job to buy the kitty litter, call the plumber, keep our hand moving across the page.

"Maybe they are not such monsters," the Morning Pages might suggest, pausing to consider our friend's potential colleagues again once she has vented a little. "Maybe they are doing the best they can and trying as hard as they know how."

Truth is such a rare thing,
it is delightful to tell it.

EMILY DICKINSON

Morning Pages allow us to take a longer view. They give us the ballast necessary to stay balanced. Coupled with a longish walk, Morning Pages give us much needed detachment. The Pages raise an issue and the walk helps to resolve it. We might walk out thinking, "Good Lord, I do not trust these people," only to think, after walking on it, "Perhaps I should try trusting a little, perhaps I am the one at fault."

By the time I was paying the vet bill, Tiger Lily was happily chewing on a small dog treat. Her nerves had calmed down. She was no longer in enemy territory. So, too, when we give ourselves the benefit of time to adjust, we may find the world is not the hostile place we take it to be.

You could not step twice into the same rivers; for other waters are ever flowing onto you.

HERACLITIS

Divining Rod

When we are fatigued or overstressed from too much change, we frequently view the world as a hostile place. We brace ourselves for the shock of impending doom. We gird ourselves against the worst. But what if the best is about to happen? What if, despite our fears, we are being handed a resounding success? Are we ready to face that eventuality as well?

Change for the better is still change, and so we need to ready ourselves for the good that comes our way as well as the bad. As always, it is the grounding of our lives with regular routines that makes it possible to handle any eventuality. Morning Pages are one such grounding rod. Walks are another. Artist Dates are a third. In times of sudden or extreme change, however, we may require additional measures to yield us a sense of safety.

We "sense" change like animals and sometimes the most comforting rituals we can undertake are those that speak to our animal natures. My collaborator Emma Lively gets manicures whenever her nerves become too much for her to handle. You can be certain that on the day when we have a critical backer's audition, she will find time to nip out for new nail polish. My friend Sonia, a six-sensory person, works to stay in touch with her other five senses. She favors long hot soaks. For myself, I make a huge pot of homemade vegetable soup. My friend Linda bakes bread.

Take pen to page. List five rituals that are sensory and can move you to a sense of safety and expansion. For example, you may want to burn a stick of savory incense. You may light a scented candle. You may buy fresh flowers. When you are stressed, you need to woo yourself a little. It might be the night for a nice dinner out—or the night for a nice dinner in. Allow yourself the touch of luxury: good bath salts, a new hairbrush, a fresh change of sheets. The psyche speaks in symbols. Tell yourself symbolically that you will be fine.

The Eyes Have It

This afternoon I went to the eye doctor. My doctor is a kind and amiable man who chatted to me about his dozen trips to Paris and his love for that city and the French people. "You could go for a month and not begin to scratch all there is to do there. Did you get up to Sacre Coeur? I love the side streets filled with artists and the many houses where famous artists have lived."

"Yes. I got to Sacre Coeur," I murmured. The doctor was talking as he worked and I was now squinting uneasily at an eye chart that was still blurred. What did Paris have to do with my eyes?

"Number one or number two—which one is clearer?" he asked.

Change alone is unchanging.
HERACLITIS

"Number two, I guess."

"Ah, yes." He sounded satisfied as though his hunch were being ratified. "Now, try it again. Number one or number two?"

"This time number one."

"Ah, really." Did he sound dismayed?

"Yes." I was not about to be distracted.

"We stayed last time not far from the Trocadero. Did you get over there?" Now he was affixing a reading chart. I could read it all.

"Yes, but not for long." We were still on the Trocadero.

"The gardens are magnificent." He sounded wistful.

"Yes. They are." I had loved the gardens.

"April in Paris. Flowers abloom." The doctor sighed.

"Yes." I sighed too. It had been beautiful.

"Which is clearer now? Number one or number two?"

"Number two." The doctor was fine-tuning things now. As he revealed his enthusiasms to me, my doctor swam suddenly into focus, no longer just a technician.

I have a friend, April, who is open to all whom she meets. In the Greek diner, she knows the name of the owner's wife and the ages of their children. On the street, she greets the homeless man by name. "We're both human beings. We both see each other and recognize each other. Why not know each other's names?" she asks.

Henry Miller advised artists to take an interest in life. By all accounts a lively man, as outgoing as April, he remained open to the end of his long life to new people and new experiences. They were the stuff of his art. He set a fine example.

As artists, we run a risk of staleness if we close ourselves off to fresh experience. Each day must remain an exploratory expedition. We must remain tourists on our home terrain. We must hold on to a sense of adventure. To do this, we must keep our curiosity alive and gently feed it. Walking, the world moves toward us at a manageable rate. We are able to take in the new flowers at the green grocer's, the fresh plantings in a window box. We are able to see that a Turkish restaurant has displaced the

If we want everything to remain as it is, it will become necessary for everything to change.

GIUSEPPE TOMASI
DI LAMPEDUSA

pricey French one two blocks from home. We are able to see and admire a silky long-haired lady dachshund who eddies at her owner's feet while she buys a tabloid from the corner newsstand.

Walking, a city becomes a series of linked neighborhoods, each one a manageable size when taken by itself. Every few blocks, there must be a corner deli, a dry cleaner, a frame shop, a copy shop, a shoe repair shop, a florist's. Each neighborhood has the same human needs. There must be a grocery store, a butcher's shop, perhaps a corner stand selling fresh fruits and vegetables. Each neighborhood must be central to itself, self-sufficient, a tiny world.

While he was testing my distance vision, my eye doctor talked about the neighborhoods he and his wife had explored in Paris. "There is a tiny little book of walking tours. We got through perhaps half of them," he said.

Clicking the proper lenses into a contraption that balanced on my nose, the doctor continued. He had been to Paris perhaps a dozen times, starting back in the sixties. He believed the French to be hospitable to women, most especially to attractive women. They were hospitable, too, to anyone who tried to speak their language.

"Well, we tried," I told the doctor. "We spoke French whenever we could, but so many of them spoke English!"

"Ah, yes. That's true," the doctor allowed.

I noticed the doctor's age then—middle-aged, perhaps five years younger than myself. His eyes were bright behind tiny glasses. His beard was chic. I imagined him in Paris, ordering a croissant and a chocolat chaud. No wonder he loved to go.

"My wife won't go back there," he suddenly volunteered. "She doesn't like their attitude about Iraq and she's afraid, too, of terrorists. My wife is a very determined woman. She has her views." He sounded doleful and slightly henpecked.

Remembering his wife and her attitudes, the doctor abruptly became all business. "I am altering your prescription slightly in both eyes," he said. "You will call me if you have any trouble." I promised that I would.

Wisdom lies neither in fixity nor in change, but in the dialectic between the two.

OCTAVIO PAZ

You must be the change you wish to see in the world.

MAHATMA GANDHI

Leaving the eye doctor, I blink for a moment in the bright afternoon's sun. Talking about Paris, I have suddenly "seen" the man who has served me for several years in dutiful anonymity. My eye doctor suddenly has an "I" to speak from. I am sorry that his wife hates Paris. I hope they will be able to work it out.

If you compare yourself with others, you may become vain or bitter, for always there will be greater and lesser persons than yourself.

MAX EHRMANN

Divining Rod

Most of us lead lives of hurried contacts. We rush forward pell-mell and do not take the time necessary to savor life and its occupants. Faces are familiar to us but names go unmentioned. Our regular waiter at the diner goes nameless. We are too busy to "get into it." And yet, getting into it is what we crave and deny ourselves.

Take pen in hand. List five people with whom you have regular yet anonymous contact. On a New York corner there may be a news vendor and a fruit vendor where you make daily purchases without breaking a stranger's careful decorum. In the suburbs, you may go routinely to the same car wash. Your dental hygienist may be another friendly yet nameless face. Your server at Starbucks might be the same every morning. Survey your regular rounds and make a list of those you see but do not let yourself "know."

From your list of anonymous contacts, select one to explore slightly further. Introduce yourself to your corner vendor. Ask that waiter his name. The next time you are riding an elevator with a familiar but nameless face, break the silence and give your own name. Say, "I see you all the time. I thought I might introduce myself." Do the same at the office water cooler. Extend yourself—and your world—by just a bit.

Connecting

The day is cool, breezy, and sunny. On the loop around the reservoir, the cherry blossoms are just past their height. Pink petals are carried on the breeze. Pink petals make a thick carpet underfoot. Soon, the blossoms will be gone and the pink confetti we walk through will turn to brown. Just for today, however, the footing is festive. Just for today the runners tread a pink cloud. Spirits are high. Everyone senses that the beauty of the day is fleeting. There are quicksilver smiles and shouted out comments: "Isn't it something?" Yes, it is something.

Jealousy is all the fun you think they had.

ERICA JONG

Laboring along the north loop, an oversized Akita trudges after its owner. His coat is moth-eaten, half winter, half summer, shed out in spots, deeply furred in others. Another week of warmish weather, another week of grooming from master, and he will be sleek and summer-fit. Just for today, his dignified face looks disgruntled, as if he is saying, "Imagine. A dog of my dignity looking like this!"

In a cordoned-off area just at the water's northernmost tip, a small forest of soon-to-be-planted trees stand with their roots bound in burlap. High in the branches of one of them, keeping an eye on us all, perches a peregrine falcon, motionless except for the alert swivel of its head. Nothing escapes its notice, certainly not Emma and me, two blond women with small, fancy dogs in tow.

"What do you think?" Emma asks. "Do we look like a case of dogs matching their owners?"

"I suppose we do," I answer. Emma's platinum do matches her Westie's crest of bangs. My Veronica Lake waves match my cocker spaniel's silky ears.

Rounding the reservoir's tip, heading back south, we come upon another set of cherry trees, this one creating a pink tunnel, arching over a well-worn trail. The boughs of the trees sweep nearly to the ground.

"I must remember to bring out my camera," Emma says.

"Yes. The blossoms will be gone soon."

This year I am not going back to my beloved New Mexico for the summer. I will not witness the short-lived glory of wild roses flushing pink along El Salto Road, perfuming the air with their heady scent. This summer my flora and fauna will be more domesticated than the bison and llamas I spot back home in Taos. I have seen buffalo as moth-eaten as this morning's Akita. I have seen eagles standing sentinel like this morning's falcon.

"Do not compare. Enjoy." I abjure myself. Although it is less wild than the beauties I am accustomed to, there is great beauty to be found in Central Park. There are, for example, London plane trees, great dappled citizens with wide-spreading boughs.

"Bloom where you are planted," I lecture myself. I must work to open my eyes to the beauty all around me. It takes discipline to find the glory hidden in these concrete canyons. When a snowy dove dives past my writing-room window, its flight declares, "Beauty is everywhere."

As artists, we must be alert. We must savor the glory of each passing moment. We must notice the parade that passes us by. At the corner newsstand, the vendor is a flirt. He has a flashing smile and a wink for the women who stop to buy today's *New York Post*.

At the Greek diner on the corner, George, the kindly waiter, has a saint's compassion for us all. "Menu tonight?" he asks, not wanting to insult the regulars who know what they will eat. "Water? Coffee? Iced tea?" George doesn't want your thirst to go unslaked. When you tell him, "Spanakopita," he acts delighted, as if you have made the wisest of choices—and perhaps you have. The spinach filling is light and fluffy. The Greek salad that comes on the side is tangy and crisp. George serves you deftly, alert to your every need.

"I got sober in that coffee shop," declares a friend of mine. "I lived there my first year because I couldn't cook without thinking of drinking. I knew everyone in the place and they knew me. I was this young and crazy somebody. They nursed me through my early sobriety. They really did."

To cure jealousy is to see it for what it is, a dissatisfaction with self.

JOAN DIDION

Just beneath the surface of New York there is kindness and caring. Just beyond the bustle of the crowd, there is time enough to connect. As artists—and as people—we must connect. We must take the extra beat necessary to notice that the newsstand vendor is flirting again and deserves a smile. A silky, long-haired Yorkshire terrier sniffs inquisitively at your ankles while the vendor makes change.

The ideal has many names and beauty is but one of them.

W. Somerset Maugham

"Beautiful dog," you take time to murmur. The owner preens, "I think so." There is a flash of connection, another fine filament in the web of connections that holds us all.

Divining Rod

Our lives are far-flung. Friends and relatives live in distant cities. We make contact by phone and e-mail but it is not the same as living close at hand. How can we draw closer? How can we make more connection? Ben, a young musician, who recently studied for a year in France, now lives in Manhattan. He has a small digital camera and he keeps in contact with his French friends by sending them New York images over the Internet. His friends are grateful and intrigued. One of them is so enticed, she is planning a trip to see his life firsthand.

Beauty is one of the rare things that do not lead to doubt of God.

Jean Anouilh

The postcard is a more old-fashioned way to say, "I was here but I was thinking of you there." Using either a digital photo or a postcard, contact one of your distant beloved. Remember that "seeing is believing." Find an image that speaks to you of your life and one that you believe will speak to them. Take the time and trouble to assure them of your ongoing connection. In reaching out to others, we remind ourselves that we, too, are beloved and missed.

Keeping On

Steadily and loudly since nine a.m. there has been hammering coming from the apartment above me. The hammer blows are rhythmic and dull except when they crescendo. They crescendo often.

Life in Manhattan is a series of accommodations. At night, walking the dogs, you must weave between people busily talking on cell phones. On trash days, you must pick your way past plastic bags filled with garbage. Now, when the high level of noise is a pollutant, you must remember, "People have a right to renovate," and they don't mean to be noisy, they just are.

My writing-room window looks out across five rows of brownstones. I see when my neighbors take to their rooftops hoping to catch a few rays. I see when someone goes all the way to the roof just to smoke a cigarette unperturbed. On a day like today, a dull, gray day, there is no one either sunbathing or smoking. Today is one of those just-to-be-gotten-through days. Even the vendor at the corner newsstand, normally an inveterate flirt, is subdued. Today is a day just for keeping on.

So often in a creative career, the magic that is required is quite simply the courage to go on. Singers must sing their scales. Actors must learn their monologues. Writers like myself must spend time at the keys. We would like a break in the weather. We would like a break, period, but the breaks, if they come, will not come today. Today is about keeping on.

Divining Rod

Sometimes we need credit for a job well done, even if there is no one at hand to offer us their praise. We must learn to praise ourselves, to take pride in our abilities to keep on keeping on.

Take pen in hand. List five things at which you have persevered.

It is very important not to become hard. The artist must always have one skin too few in comparison to other people, so you feel the slightest wind.

Shusha Guppy

Fear of Success

Yesterday I got a phone call from the young writer-director. The news was good, but still difficult. It looked as though a script of hers had made it through a series of hurdles and was now okayed for a September shoot. "It actually looks like I have a go picture," said the quavering voice over the telephone. There was no elation.

"It's good your picture is a go."

"Yes. I suppose so." The doubt in her voice asked, "Is it?"

We are used to soldiering on. We are accustomed to doing our work against the odds and against the tide. When the tide turns, when the odds are suddenly in our favor, we need to find our sea legs. We have become comfortable, sitting on the sidelines, critiquing the game. Now, suddenly, we are being asked to play it. The pitch is coming across the plate and it is our turn at bat.

In making the transition from bystander to player, it helps if we take with us some of our daily routines. Morning Pages will still serve us very well. They have been useful lo these many months at fielding our complaints, let them do service now at fielding our fears. Chief among these fears, of course, is "What if I am not any good?" "What if I have fooled everybody?" "What if I am an imposter and I am just about to show it?"

Artists are the monks of the bourgeois state.

Cesare Pavese

Morning Pages do not talk back, but they do give us a place to ventilate. They do give us one way to keep grounded. They do give us the privacy we crave and the intimacy we need to spit out what it is that is troubling us now, just when we "should" be grateful.

Now that the stakes are real, we do well to steal away for a head-clearing walk. A footfall at a time, the walk will also ground us. We can walk our way out of paranoia and into perspective.

"If the contracts vet out, then I am officially in preproduction," the writer-director marveled. "It all feels so fast."

On the days when we are just soldiering on, it seems impossible that any project could come to fruition too fast. Haven't we already been waiting "forever"? But breaks, when they come, seem to come just as we can barely handle them. The young writer-director has been working two years toward the goal of a go picture. Now that the light is green, the terrain seems threatening.

For good and evil, man is a free creative spirit.

JOYCE CARY

It is difficult when we are constricted by fear to allow ourselves the expansion of an Artist Date, and yet this is the very medicine we need. On an Artist Date we sense that we are part of a larger world. In this larger world, our dreams and ambitions have their place.

"I need to find a horse," confessed the writer-director. "I need to take some Artist Dates where I can just stroke a velvety nose."

I told the writer-director that her self-diagnosis sounded accurate. What she needed was a dose of regular life. "Find a horse to pet or a dog to walk. Find something that soothes and comforts you."

"I think I'll do that. What's that noise?"

I explained about the renovation. A former New Yorker, the writer-director hooted with laughter. "Gee. I guess there are worse things than suddenly having a million-dollar deal." When we got off the phone, the hammering mysteriously stopped.

Divining Rod

When we are faced with a heady change, there is warning in that word "heady." There is nothing like a success to bring on a misery-inducing bout of self-centered fears. To enjoy our triumph, we must not feel that it isolates us from our peers. A long sought accomplishment can be very alienating. Who are we now? Who can understand us? (More people than we think.) Despite our newly won victory, we must connect to those we love. In other words, we must move from our heads back into our hearts.

One more time, consult your list of friends. Who among them is going through a hard time? That is the person you need to talk with now—and not so much to talk as to listen. You need a strong dose of regular life and that is what your troubled friend offers you. Rather than calling with dramatic tales of your new triumph and the fears that it raises for you, call with an agenda of empathy. Say, simply, "I have been wondering how you are?" Coax from your friend the details of life-at-the-moment. Lose yourself in the play by play that greets your ear. It is grounding to listen to the cares and concerns of others. As you reach out to them, you also reach within yourself. Your heady fears diminish, replaced again by the reminder that we are all in "this" together.

Nothing great was ever achieved without enthusiasm.

Ralph Waldo Emerson

CHECK-IN

1. **How many days this week did you do your Morning Pages?** If you skipped a day, why did you skip it? How was the experience of writing them for you? Are you experienc-

ing more clarity? A wider range of emotions? A greater sense of detachment, purpose, and calm? Did anything surprise you? Is there a "repeating" issue asking to be dealt with?

2. **Did you do your Artist Date this week?** Did you note an improved sense of well-being? What did you do and how did it feel? Remember, Artist Dates can be difficult and you may need to coax yourself into taking them.

3. **Did you get out on your Weekly Walk?** How did that feel? What emotions or insights surfaced for you? Were you able to walk more than once? What did your walk do for your optimism and sense of perspective?

4. **Were there any other issues this week that felt significant to you in your self-discovery?** Describe them.

All rising to a great place is by a winding stair.

FRANCIS BACON

Uncovering a Sense of Perspective

Creativity requires that we focus on both the large and the small, the grand and the particular. Remember, the Grand Canyon was carved a drop at a time. This week's essays and tasks concern expansion. You are asked to imagine yourself larger and more surefooted than you may feel yourself to be. You are asked to focus on ways in which you can increase your conscious contact with the Great Artist. It is by feeling yourself connected to a larger Something that God can work through you. You are seeking to forge an artist-to-artist bond with your Creator.

Seasons

The cherry blossoms are spent. The trees that were bouffant pink clouds are now softly misted with green. The showy blooms are gone for another year. Spring moves toward summer. The London plane trees are the last to reveal their leaves, but even they are unfurling. Dandelions laze across the lawns and some have already passed into fluff. The joggers turn out earlier now to avoid the heat. Today simmers.

When we are incubating something creatively, we, too, follow a cycle of seasons. We begin locked in winter, when we look and feel devoid of ideas, although the ideas are there for us, simply dormant. Our wintry hearts lurch toward spring and suddenly an idea puts out a hopeful bud. The idea may be as fes-

Books are the bees which carry the quickening pollen from one to another mind.

JAMES RUSSELL LOWELL

There is properly no history, only biography.

RALPH WALDO EMERSON

tive as the buoyant pink cherry blossoms. It may be as determined as the forsythia flaring bravely into bloom. Make no mistake, our idea is bright and indisputable. We blossom as the landscape does. And then what happens? As surely as the seasons turn, our brightly budded ideas must now ripen and mature. Spring turns the corner into summer. Showy pink and gold give way to industrious green. Now come the long days of labor. We must work to bring forth the fruit of what we have envisioned.

Last night, in Los Angeles, there was a reading done of a play of mine, *Love in the DMZ*. This morning, I got the first of several feedback calls. The play was brilliant, the first caller said, but perhaps too demanding, perhaps a little long. She couldn't tell me exactly where, or how, but the play needed some pruning. I had to consider the attention span of the audience. Could I see my way clear to making some changes?

I waited for caller number two. This time, there was no talk of cutting. The play had played and played well, this caller believed. It was a timely play, set in the Vietnam era but echoing our misgivings about involvement with Iraq. This play had a future, the caller assured me. What were my intentions for the piece? How could it go forward?

Although I didn't say this to my callers, I had been waiting a long time to find a proper unfolding for this play. It was a piece of work that I had completed and then been unable to harvest. There had been no one waiting to pluck the play from the vine. It had lain in the field, ripe and ready, but no one had taken it to heart. I was delighted by the wave of interest in it now.

Each of us is in charge of cultivating our own talent. We have ideas that we are charged with bringing to fruition. Some of us remain locked in winter, unable to go forward because we doubt the strength of our ideas. Others of us make it to spring, shooting forward with rapid growth but unable to bring things to fulfillment, unable to put in the heavy labor necessary to cultivate our crop. Still others, myself included here, bring work all the way to completion but lack the resolution and bravado necessary to sell the work that we have done. A critical failure of nerve at the last moment causes us to doubt the worthiness of projects we have birthed. Novels go into desk drawers. Plays languish on shelves. The pumpkin rots on the vine.

How can we go forward from here? What is necessary to successfully harvest the fruits of our labors? We must believe, first of all, in the worth of our brainchildren. We must not abandon them. We must keep them a priority. Faced with rejection, we must keep trying. At root, it comes back to being a matter of faith. We must see our work as divine in origin. We must believe there is a divine path of goodness ahead in its unfolding. When we are rejected, we must ask, "What next?" and not, "Why me?"

There is always a way to move forward. We may be blinded at times by our own belief in conventions. We may say, "I cannot go forward without a producer," or "I cannot go forward without a director," but the truth is that God is both a producer and a director and often we can move forward if we are willing, one more time, to trust a wing and a prayer.

Many playwrights have moved ahead by renting a venue and raising their own money for a production. Worried lest these "vanity" productions be exactly that, we fail to see that if we want others to believe in us we must first be totally committed to ourselves. If creativity is an act of faith, we must move out on faith and be willing to take action to make our dreams into concrete reality. Independent films are often made on a shoestring. Where does the faith, the sheer chutzpah, come from to take such an action? It can, and often does come, from prayer.

Experience is the name everyone gives to their mistakes.

Oscar Wilde

"God, grant me the serenity to accept the things I cannot change, courage to change the things I can, and wisdom to know the difference" 12-steppers are taught to pray. This prayer has value for us all. Very often we accept "no" for an answer where courage might tell us to look for a different way forward.

Left to my own devices, I am far too easily discouraged. This flaw in my own creative makeup is why I see so clearly that a lack of faith is often the sticking point. All too often our lack of faith is a personal matter. While we can easily muster belief in other peoples' projects, it is in our very own that we lack tenacity.

"What would I be willing to do for someone I love?" we might ask ourselves. The answer may surprise us. We may find that we are willing to rent a venue for the play written by a beloved. We might discover we have the daring to self-publish. We might rent a space for a dance recital or organize a gallery space for a group show. There are many things we might do.

Willing to go to bat for others, we must become willing to go to bat for ourselves. We must become willing to put cash on the barrelhead. When I directed my feature film, *God's Will,* I bankrolled the production with monies I received writing for *Miami Vice.* I could have put that money in the bank, saving it for a rainy day. Instead I placed a bet on myself and my talent. I look back on that film with satisfaction. The harvest was worth the labor.

We are born believing. A man bears beliefs as a tree bears apples.

RALPH WALDO EMERSON

Divining Rod

You are asked to write rapidly to evade your Censor. Take pen in hand. Number from one to ten. Very quickly fill in the blank ten times. "If it weren't so risky, I would try_____."

Now number from one to five. Fill in the blanks again. "If it weren't so conceited, I would try_____."

A third time, go to the page. Number again from one to five. Fill in the blanks. "If it weren't so expensive, I would try_____."

The responses to these questions should give you a portrait of your fears and the ways that they keep you crippled. Scanning your lists, select one risk that seems possible to take. Take one concrete step in its direction.

Ebb and Flow

The pink blossoms are gone from underfoot and overhead. The cherry trees are anonymous citizens now clothed in green. There are few flowering trees and bushes left, chiefly mock orange. For the most part, the trees are garbed in green as spring gives way to summer. At the westernmost reach of the reservoir, a man is schooling a Burmese mountain dog puppy. The puppy is not much of a learner, splay-footed and cuddly, flopping to the grass wanting to wrestle. On the cinder bridle path, adult dogs trot past the puppy busily resisting its blandishments. One German shepherd, a recent puppy itself, bounds closer in a playful crouch. "No, no," its master carols out and the dog, chastened, goes back to a dutiful trot. For Tiger Lily, my cocker spaniel, the puppy is irresistible. She leaps toward it, growling with bravado. The puppy scampers a retreat.

It is not the language of painters, but the language of nature which one should listen to.

VINCENT VAN GOGH

So much of a creative life is knowing when to go forward and when to retreat. So much of winning through in the long haul boils down to knowing when to push forward and when to hang back. There is wisdom to working on having multiple projects simultaneously so that a "no" on one can send you back to work on another. At the moment, my collaborator Emma and I are back at work on *Magellan*. The news—or lack of news—around our musical *The Medium at Large* was too daunting to push forward there.

So much of the feedback we get as artists is heartless or simply thoughtless. Our last round on *The Medium at Large* qualified as both. "You're really onto something with the idea of guidance from the afterworld," one producer's feedback began. "And you've got some really good music. But the story about two sisters . . . well, it's just too narrow. You need to tell a different story." Listening politely to this advice, we did not run from the room shrieking, "Our lives are overrun by idiots!" But we felt that way.

We didn't choose to throw away our whole show based on

this feedback but we did decide the time had come for us to let the world spin a few times before we pushed forward again. Here is what happened when we stopped trying. Another producer unexpectedly stepped forward. This time there was no talk of throwing away our whole story line. This time the elements seemed more right. "I would like to help you," this producer said. We listened eagerly. We were more than ready to be helped.

But we were also balanced. While taking time out from submissions on *The Medium at Large,* we had put ourselves back to work on *Magellan.* I had written new music for the opening. We had restructured the opening sequence. We had made the show more lean and focused. With the ballast of *Magellan* to help us hold steady, we were ready to take in more feedback on *The Medium at Large.*

In the first days following our backer's audition, our friend Bruce Pomahac had advised us to start to work again at something creative. "You girls are lucky you have multiple projects. That's what's going to save you," he said. Bruce reminded us of the story about director Hal Prince, the way he always schedules a meeting about a new project for the morning after he opens a show.

"What you are after is stamina," Bruce reminded us. And stamina is exactly what it felt like we were exercising the first time we tried to work again in the wake of our disappointment. Fortunately, synchronicity was at hand. The precise place we needed to enter Magellan's story was the point at which he was the most discouraged and disheartened. Scooping the inner creative barrel, we did not have far to look for inspiration.

Once we accept that creativity is a spiritual act, it doesn't seem like such a far jump to expect such synchronicity to be at hand. There is a benevolent Something that is kindly toward ourselves and our art. The Great Creator is an artist and loves other artists. The Divine does play a hand in what it is we are making. We can consciously choose to invite divine participation. We can ask for and receive divine help and guidance.

Art, like nature, has her monsters, things of bestial shape and with hideous voices.

OSCAR WILDE

We do not need to feel that our dreams and God's will for us are at opposite ends of the table. We can consider the possibility that our dreams come from God and that God has a plan for their proper unfolding. When we seek daily spiritual guidance, we are guided toward the next step forward for our art. Sometimes the step is very small. Sometimes the step is, "Wait. Not now." Sometimes the step is, "Work on something else for a while." When we are open to Divine Guidance, we will receive it. It will come to us as the hunch, the inkling, the itch. It will come to us as timely conversations with others. It will come to us in many ways—but it will come to us.

We are not alone and unpartnered in our desire to make art. Art is an act of expansion and faith. We are the children of an expansive power that interacts with us when we act on faith. When we are open to good things, good things come to us. Sometimes, in order for something good to happen, something apparently bad must happen first. This is when we are asked to have faith. This is when we are required to search for the silver lining. "Bad" feedback on a project helps us to know and appreciate "good" feedback on a project. A "no" from person A allows us to receive a "yes" from person B. We are always being brought along. Our dreams may feel thwarted when in reality they are being tempered. We are being shaped to fit a divine purpose. We can cooperate or we can resist.

Last night, on my final night of teaching down in SoHo, I received a letter from one of the members of my class. "I am very well connected in the theater world and I would love to help you with *The Medium at Large,*" the letter ran. "If it seems appropriate to you, please contact me."

Emma and I read the letter, laughing to ourselves. We had so despaired of finding help and here was the very help we were needing right under our very noses. We couldn't wait to place the call.

Art is a vast, ancient, interconnected web-work.

CAMILLE PAGLIA

Divining Rod

When we become clear about what it is we need and hope for, help comes to hand. Clarity triggers manifestation. A lack of clarity prevents our good from coming to us. Very often, when we feel cut off from helping resources, it is because we have prematurely closed a door that needs to be reopened. We have decided, for example, that writers' workshops are not for us—when that is the next step necessary to move forward the play that we have been working on. We must be willing, one more time, to be a beginner. We must ask, "What venture could I take if my ego would just allow it?"

In order to move ahead creatively, we must be flexible. We must open our minds to the opportunities that abound around us. Before we say, "I would never," we need to ask, "What can I be humble enough to try?" Humility opens the door to diversity. Our help can come to us from any quarter.

Take pen in hand. Number from one to five. List five things you could be willing to try if you were open-minded.

There is nothing stable in the world; uproar is your only music.

JOHN KEATS

Companionship

We are midway through May and the weather is rapturous. Today is a day to swoon for. Baby carriages are out in droves, their bonnets tipped back so that little citizens can catch the sun. It's a workday but you would barely know it to see the park. It is crowded with joggers playing hooky. The reservoir is hip to hip with revelers in the day. On my block, a boxer dog and a Pomeranian make each other's acquaintance with courtesy and barely throttled eagerness. The snow-white Samoyed bobs a near curtsy to a handsome rottweiler. Out for their morning walk, Tiger Lily and Charlotte lurch the length of their leashes, wriggling merrily at the approach of a Harlequin Great Dane. On a day like today, high spirits are the rule. Manhattan is a friendly village.

This morning, I walked over to see my friend Therese. She greeted me warmly, her face still flushed from her own trip to the gym. "Make yourself comfortable," she said, showing me to a loveseat. "Something to drink?"

"I'm fine," I told her. "It's such a beautiful day." Sitting in Therese's comfortable sitting room, I felt a flush of well-being. Perhaps, just perhaps, I thought, I may be coming somewhat back on the beam. Therese seemed to sense this.

"Do you have a sense of companionship?" Therese wanted to know. "Do you sense as you are working that a higher force is working with you?"

"On my good days," I told her.

"You know you can talk to God as a friend," she continued, her eyes gently twinkling. "You do not need to be alone. You can reach out."

"I try to do that," I answered. Therese was teaching me what I knew but what had seemed to be beyond my reach in my dark times.

"Conscious contact isn't a feeling," Therese went on. "It's a decision on our part to be in touch. We must make the effort, but if we do, God is there."

"I believe that," I said. And I do. In my dark night of the soul, I could not feel the comfort of my beliefs but I still had them. Every Wednesday night as I taught a classroom full of seekers, I would speak the good news of our spiritual connection even if at the moment I couldn't feel it. I might have been at the edge of the abyss emotionally but I knew there was a great invisible net waiting to catch me. Even if I couldn't see the net, I knew it was there. This was my experience, strength, and hope.

As a sober alcoholic, I was taught not to drink "five minutes

Music is the mediator between the spiritual and the sensual life.

Ludwig van Beethoven

before the miracle." I was taught to just hold on, that the dark night of the soul would pass if I just didn't drink. I was taught that my sobriety was a power of example. That each day that I managed to live without a drink was something to be proud of. And so, talking with Therese, I reiterated my determination not to drink.

"The liquor stores are pulsating at me," I complained. "They are whispering my name and I hate that." I told Therese that I was working with a newly sober alcoholic, that I was trying to teach her what I had been taught.

"You're a very sober lady," Therese told me. "You work hard at your sobriety. You really try to stay in the solution."

"The solution, as you call it, is the truth," I told Therese. "Despair is the great lie, and I should know better than to believe it." Just at the moment, despair felt at a safe remove. I could one more time feel myself connecting emotionally to the comfort of what I knew. My sobriety and my creativity were both safeguarded by a Higher Power.

As artists, we are ever companioned by the Great Artist. We are being nudged ever so gently forward, urged to continue making what it is that we make. There is no moment at which we are alone, even though our mythology makes much of artists as loners. We are not loners—certainly not spiritually. There is a higher octave that is always available to us. We need only to keep one ear cocked. There it is: the still, small voice. It comes to us as the hunch or the inkling. It comes to us as the lucky guess. It comes to us in all times at all places. We are never unpartnered, never solitary although we may, to the casual eye, make our art "alone."

We can forget that we have such accompaniment available. We can cut ourselves off from the sunlight of the Spirit. We can work at working so relentlessly that the joy of working leaves us. We can enter a dark time, as I have recently. We can lose heart and as we do, our losses multiply.

We can forget to ask for inspiration. We can convince ourselves that we need to draw upon our own stores of inspiration.

Wishing to be friends is quick work, but friendship is a slow-ripening fruit.

ARISTOTLE

We can scoop at our hearts until they are as hollow as empty gourds. What happens if we work this way? We become desperate and desolate. We become hardened and disheartened. We forget that there is a Great Creator and that we are its creations, intended to be creative ourselves. Forgetting the proper order of things, forgetting that there is a divine plan of goodness for us and our work, we can strain ourselves striving for "more." And is there ever enough? When we compare ourselves to others rather than to ourselves, we come up lacking. There is always someone who has achieved more of what we desire. Sick at heart, truly soul sick, we forget to count our blessings. We may not even see that we have any to count. The glorious day, the friendly nods of strangers, all these pass us by unnoted. We are bent on achieving our aims. We are blinded to all around us.

And what happens when for a moment we remember?

When we remember that we are partnered, an ease enters our work. We begin to write more freely. We begin to paint with an inspired brush. Something or Someone larger than ourselves is striving to enter the world through us. We are the portal, the entryway, the gate. Through us great things come to pass. We are the conduits of a higher will. We are "humble" in the words of Piet Mondrian, essentially a "channel." When we cooperate, we feel a sense of right action, an ease.

Cooperating with a Higher Power, rather than striving to conquer, we find ourselves carried along by the tide of what we are creating. There is an energy flow that moves us forward. There is a propulsion to what it is we would create. It is as though all the plays, stories, songs, dances, paintings, and sculptures have a life of their own. They are our brainchildren and they actively seek birth through us. We are merely the doorway through which they enter the world. We open our hearts to what wishes to be born. We are receptive and what we receive is miraculous.

Any painter will tell you of time "lost" at the easel. A dancer will speak of being "lost" in the dance. Writers become absorbed

Tell me thy company and I'll tell thee what thou art.

MIGUEL DE CERVANTES

Friendship ought to be a gratuitous joy, like the joys afforded by art.

SIMONE WEIL

and immersed and lose track of what it is they are writing. True artists become pawns and the hand that moves them is Art itself.

This morning Therese wondered if I had ever felt exalted, if I ever felt a submersion of self in the work that I create.

"On my good days," I answered her. "When I am in a dark time, I can remember my connection to God, but I cannot feel it."

We can elect to remember that we are partnered. We can ask a divine force to work through us. We can request the ability to erase ourselves as the conscious architects of what we create. We can strive to serve by what we make and, in that quality of service, we can attain a degree of egoless anonymity that is the midwife of good work.

"So you lose your sense of self?" Therese asked.

"Yes, the self becomes absorbed by something larger."

"I've had that experience when I'm helping someone," Therese volunteered.

"Yes. It's the experience of being in service to something other than our ego."

Therese goes to the gym and loses herself in the rhythm of her body. As artists we can lose ourselves in the rhythm of our souls. We can make what seems to want to be made. We can approach our day's work with a childlike glee. When we remember that there is a Great Creator we can begin to experience ourselves as children.

We can begin by thinking, "Something larger and grander than I made all that I see." We can look then at the boxer and the Pomeranian. We can look at the Harlequin Great Dane as it gaily sidesteps its tiny attackers, Tiger Lily and Charlotte. Even taking just this small survey of dogs, we can see the hand of something marvelous. Who made that rottweiler with its placid dignity? Who invented the feisty dachshund, so certain of its own number-one ranking in the world? Clearly there is Something or Someone at work who has great imagination and verve. This great Something waits to befriend us. We need only speak the word: help me.

And so I pray as I pass through my difficult passage. I lie in bed at night, awake with my fears, and I try to remember what I know. I know that God is good. I can ask that good God for mercy. I can pray:

> Help me to become more teachable. Help me to become more open. Help me to see your face in every face; your hand in every hand. Give me a child's delight in the world that you have fashioned. Help me to know that I can work with you and play with you to fashion the world still further. Give me a sense of your power and your majesty. Give me a graceful heart that acknowledges the Great Maker in all that has been made. Help me to know that I am an artist companioned by the Great Artist. Allow me to make my inventions as part of a greater whole.
>
> Help me to feel companioned always. Help me to make all days, good days. Help me to create knowing that in fact I cocreate. Help me to be small that I may be a part of Something very large. We are midway through May and the weather is rapturous. Help me to revel in its God-made delight.

"Yes, on my good days I feel companioned," I told Therese.

It's not what you look at that matters, it's what you see.

HENRY DAVID THOREAU

Divining Rod

All of us pass through periods when we do not feel companioned. We feel cut adrift, lost at sea, friendless, isolated, and alone. What has happened? As Therese warned, we fall prey to self-sufficiency. We unconsciously try to go it alone without God's help and aid. Because our human resources are always limited, we sooner or later reach a wall. We are brought up short by our own feelings

*The possible's slow fuse is lit
by the imagination.*

EMILY DICKINSON

of lack. At such times, we must reach out both to God and to others who can hold a lantern to our path. In such times, I seek out Bernice or Therese, Julie or Ed or Sonia or Larry or Libby or Elberta. When I feel really bankrupt, I seek out all of them. "Help me," I ask. "Put me in your prayers." My friends are believers. I want to be reminded there is a God.

Take pen in hand. Consciously draw to mind some of the dark nights of the soul that you have already survived. What did you do to help yourself through these bleak periods? What were your stratagems for making it through? How did you seek God? Or did God seem to seek you?

Number from one to five. List five things you could do to improve your conscious contact. For example, take more walks, read spiritual reading at bedtime, ask one of your friends to pray for you, make it a practice to write out a daily prayer. Choose one action and execute it. Remember that "conscious contact" is a decision and one you can make at any time.

Do a Little

The wind in the trees whispers secrets. The park has long green corridors hushed by the overarching trees. The weather is "perfect" yet another day. On the bridle path, horses are absent but pigeons pick their way among the hoof prints. Tiny finches dart amid the mock orange. A huge heron suddenly crosses the sky. It is headed south to the wilder "lake" where it makes its home. All along the trail, songbirds pipe from the bushes. Last night's heavy rain stands glistening in puddles. It's a good day for walking.

Tiger Lily and Charlotte take to the cinder bridle path. When a pigeon strays too close, Tiger Lily gives chase. Charlotte is too busy with the smells and sights to be bothered. Walking toward us comes a lady with two small poodles, one underfoot and one cradled in her arms.

"Charlotte, do you want to be that spoiled?" Emma asks. She confesses to having once carried Charlotte around the reservoir: "She was doing a lot of Westie position, balking, and so I had to drag her forward. I finally couldn't stand it anymore."

Just last night, a handsome stranger stopped Emma on the street. "Do you know why it is that Westies do that dragging thing?" he asked. "I once had two of them and they both did it."

"Maybe they're just stubborn," Emma replied.

Charlotte is now demonstrating her brakes-on "Westie position." There is no apparent reason for it. "Charlotte, come on," Emma begs.

As artists, our creative progress is also characterized by stubborn legs. It is for this reason that we do best to go forward slowly and steadily. There will be days when we are working uphill, tugging at our artist for cooperation. Not all days will be filled with eager forward motion. Our artist is willful.

If we hew to a course of "easy does it," we will do best. If we set our jumps too high, we may take them one day and fail miserably the next. Better to set modest jumps, jumps we can navigate even on the days our artists are acting up.

Things won are done; joy's soul lies in the doing.

WILLIAM SHAKESPEARE

In order to succeed as an artist we must have two well-developed functions: our artist and its trainer. The trainer is steady and adult. It keeps its eye on the course and the long run. It coaxes, wheedles, begs, cajoles, and occasionally disciplines our artist which, Westie-like, proceeds in spurts and sometimes not at all.

The trick is setting the jumps low enough that our artist can be lured into action. If I am writing nonfiction, I set my goal at a modest three pages. Almost anyone can write three pages of something and my artist knows that. On days that it digs in its heels and refuses to budge, I can drag it, kicking and screaming, for three pages. On most days, when it sprints ahead, three pages are easy. And the same kinds of goals can be set in all of the arts.

A musician might set a goal of playing for fifteen minutes. Some days, that is an eternity, but most days, it is over in a blink. A dancer might set a certain set of warm-up exercises. An actor might tackle a monologue; a singer, a song.

If we set our jumps low enough, our artist can be lured into cooperation. It helps to think of our artist as an inner youngster, one susceptible to bribes. The promise of a treat can often induce a bout of good behavior. Our artist does best coaxed and cajoled. "If you write three pages, then you can talk with Sonia," I might promise, knowing that Sonia is one of my artist's favorite adults because she, too, is playful. "Write for three pages and then you can go for a walk," I might wheedle.

There are those who feel an artist should be treated with more dignity. In my experience, dignity doesn't go very far. Emma jokes that she was once told of her Westie, Charlotte, "I am afraid we can't do much with a terrier, ma'am." The same can be said of artists, "I am afraid we can't do much with an artist, ma'am." This is why artists are so frustrating to nonartists. It is not that we set out to be rebellious. It is simply a part of our nature. Sometimes it is a part of our nature despite our desires to the contrary. Ask any artist who has been suddenly derailed just when he has the most to lose—the director who is having trouble delivering film number two, the novelist who is having trouble delivering a follow-up to a promising debut.

The deed is all, the glory nothing.

JOHANN WOLFGANG
VON GOETHE

"Just do a little," is the medicine that most artists respond to. A novelist can manage to eke out a sentence or two. A singer can manage a set of scales. The whole trick is to think small, not large, although our adult "trainer" knows that all the smalls do add up to a large.

"You just write all the time, don't you?" a doctor recently exclaimed to me.

"Yes," I told him, "I do. I have noticed that writers who try to take down time are often very unhappy. Writers simply need to write and if we do it just a little at a time, it does add up."

"It does add up" is the phrase that everything boils down to. Whether we are talking about writing, singing, dancing, or acting. Whether we are talking about sculpting, designing, sewing, or cooking. No matter what our art form is, if we just do a little of it, we will find that all of our littles add up. "Fifteen minutes at the easel and then you can have an ice cream" may not strike you as the most adult way to make art. It does, however, make art.

Divining Rod

You will need to set aside an hour and take yourself out to a café or coffee shop where you can write unimpeded. Order a good cup of tea or perhaps a cappuccino and take your pen to the page. You are asked to write a letter to your artist from your trainer.

This letter will look at your life with objectivity, talking with you about the ways in which your care of your artist could be improved. You might find, for example, that your trainer thinks you set your jumps too high. You may be urged to lower your daily quota so that you will not be too discouraged to try to meet it.

Your trainer may want to help you dismantle your perfectionist. Or tell you need more Artist Dates. Or that you could benefit from joining a writers' support group, something that you have heretofore scorned.

Your trainer has your best interests at heart and may come up with actions that move you out of your comfort zone. You might be told to join an online Artist's Way group—or start one in your neighborhood. Your trainer might think you are falling short on your walks or are not really using your list of believing mirrors. Alternatively, your trainer might feel that you are doing better than you think. You might be urged to write a positive inventory.

Adapt yourself to the things among which your lot has been cast, and love sincerely the fellow creatures with whom destiny has ordained that you shall live.

MARCUS AURELIUS

Checking in with your trainer is a tool that you may wish to repeat at regular intervals. My trainer tells me when I have let my piano practice slide or when I am procrastinating on a script. Like many of us, I may wish for an outer mentor but having an inner mentor can be enough.

It is only with the heart that one can see rightly; what is essential is invisible to the eye.

ANTOINE DE SAINT EXUPÉRY

CHECK-IN

1. **How many days this week did you do your Morning Pages?** If you skipped a day, why did you skip it? How was the experience of writing them for you? Are you experiencing more clarity? A wider range of emotions? A greater sense of detachment, purpose, and calm? Did anything surprise you? Is there a "repeating" issue asking to be dealt with?

2. **Did you do your Artist Date this week?** Did you note an improved sense of well-being? What did you do and how did it feel? Remember, Artist Dates can be difficult and you may need to coax yourself into taking them.

3. **Did you get out on your Weekly Walk?** How did that feel? What emotions or insights surfaced for you? Were you able to walk more than once? What did your walk do for your optimism and sense of perspective?

4. **Were there any other issues this week that felt significant to you in your self-discovery?** Describe them.

Uncovering a Sense of Safety

Contrary to our mythology, creativity is not a dangerous pursuit. The creative flow is both normal and healthy. We have the safety net of both our friends and our Creator to fall back on. Our trepidations fade as we focus on the many positive resources available to us. As we "count coup," enumerating for ourselves our creative accomplishments, we see that more accomplishment is possible. Focused on small actions on our own behalf, we experience a sense of ourselves as our own friend and comrade.

Risk

The sky was a dark, coppery green. Raindrops the size of dimes pelted down. It was a tropical deluge—and this was midtown Manhattan, mid-May. Emma and I stood underneath a theater marquis watching as the rain created torrents on the street. We were on Forty-second Street. We had just seen *Twentieth Century* starring Alec Baldwin and Anne Heche. We were elated.

"They were good, weren't they?" Emma exclaimed. "I could almost go see the show one more time just to watch the direction." The snappy direction was by Walter Bobbie of *Chicago* fame. Physical comedy abounded. Performances went over the top and stayed there, taking the audience's spirits right along with them.

"He did such great things with his hands," I said. "I hadn't expected him to be funny physically."

When you go in search of honey you must expect to be stung by bees.

KENNETH KAUNDA

"Yes, but he certainly was."

"Wasn't he, though?"

Twentieth Century is a play about theater people. Baldwin plays a larger-than-life impresario, down on his luck. Heche plays the leading lady he created. At no time did Baldwin or Heche seem like Hollywood actors, unused to life on the stage. They both seized the stage as if born to it. They leaned into Bobbie's boisterous direction. When they finally went for a clinch, it was a humdinger, a good case of chemistry requited. You could almost feel their actorly glee knowing that they were pushing the envelope, pulling out stops and gears that no one knew were there.

The play was the thing and "play" was what they were doing. The actors' high spirits leapt across the footlights. Theirs were big, risky performances. The joy of the show was that no one was playing it safe.

In order to grow as artists, we must be willing to risk. We must try to do something more and larger than what we have done before. We cannot continue indefinitely to replicate the successes of our past.

There are some risks that we cannot avoid taking. These adventures whisper to the heart, "Wouldn't it be fun to try . . . ?" and don't let up until they are fulfilled. Careers are made by following the star of what our heart calls us to do. This means we may fly in the face of safety and convention. An actor like Baldwin moves from tragedy to comedy. He does not rest on the dignity of his darkly brilliant performances in films like *The Cooler*. He takes a chance the best may be yet to come.

Great careers are characterized by great risks. It takes courage to jettison the mantle of what we have done well for the chance to grab at the cape of what we might do even better.

Robert De Niro has crafted a career filled with brave choices. Known for the stark intensity of his dramatic work, he has insisted that he also can do comedy. His audience was at first reluctant to take the leap of faith with him: "Robert De Niro in a comedy?" But De Niro persisted and the audience eventually

Yes, art is dangerous. Where it is chaste, it is not art.

PABLO PICASSO

followed. Now a Robert De Niro comedy can be a must-see ticket. *Analyze That* followed the success of *Analyze This*. It took courage for De Niro to insist on playing comedy.

How do we know when a risk is right for us? We must learn to listen to the heart and not the head. The head is always full of second thoughts and second-guessing. It will arrive at a thousand reasons that we should not risk. "Why, you'll look like a fool," the head will start in. "Everyone knows you and respects you for doing X. If you try Y, you'll never get away with it." Then the heart enters, "Come on. Lighten up. What's the worst thing that can happen? You fail. Wouldn't you like yourself better for failing at trying than you would like yourself for playing it safe?"

We cannot play it safe and expand as artists at the same time. We must risk expanding our territory—and we will survive if we are shot down for it. There are certain risks that come with pursuing an artistic career. All artists working in public run the risk of bad—even patently unfair—reviews. Even Baldwin and Heche, for all the fun they are having, are having it in the face of mixed reviews. It is for this reason that our reward must lie in the risk itself, in the self-esteem we feel for undertaking it. Looking back on our careers, we may have rueful laughter at the chances that we took, but we will not have regrets.

If you don't risk anything, you risk even more.

ERICA JONG

Divining Rod

Many times we do not want to take a risk with our creativity because we want a guarantee of a positive outcome. This is very American of us. We think that risks have to be large and noteworthy. We want a "product" to show for our process. We want a payoff in terms of our career. In order to free up our creativity, we need to be able to do some creativity for free, that is, with no guaranteed

You aim for what you want and if you don't get it, you don't get it, but if you don't aim, you don't get anything.

FRANCINE PROSE

outcome. We need to practice some creativity that is not goal-oriented. Put simply, we need to let ourselves play.

Take pen in hand. Number from one to ten. List ten tiny creative actions that you could take that have no bearing on getting ahead in the world. (These actions are often things you tell yourself you are "too busy" to do.) For example, you might manicure your nails bright red; you might sit at the piano and noodle for ten minutes; you might write a short poem; you might do your mending; you might paint the inside of your closet chartreuse; you might sketch your boyfriend; you might bake a colleague a birthday cake; you might send a postcard to your ailing aunt; you might brush the dog; you might make a collage; or you might bake a batch of chocolate-chip cookies or mix up some Jell-O.

None of these risks is earth-shattering, but they are sufficient to shatter your "boredom" or depression. An intellectual friend of mine scornfully calls such risks, "Martha Stewart risks." He has forgotten the joy that can come from practicing a hobby or handicraft. He has forgotten, too, that small risks train us to take larger ones. Think of your tiny risks as a form of self-training. You are learning to say, "Yes, I can" instead of "No, I can't."

Reviews

It is mid-May and the temperatures are in the mideighties. Summer is not yet here, but it is already upon us. Yesterday's torrential storm leaves today's simmering puddles. Yesterday's risks, well taken, leave today's self-respect.

It takes courage to be an artist. The part of us that creates is youthful and vulnerable. We make our art with high hopes.

While we may not make our art with reviews in mind, they are always lurking. It is an artist's job to survive reviews and live to work another day.

I have a friend, actress Julianna McCarthy, who says that good reviews are as dangerous to an actor as bad reviews. She warns that if something is singled out for praise, an actor may end up trying to play that something, with the result that his performance becomes hopelessly skewed.

"If you're going to believe your good reviews," Julianna warns, "then you have to also believe your bad reviews." It's better not to believe any reviews and to try to work for the sake of the work.

"What is it with friends always wanting to make sure you know about reviews?" wonders another friend of mine. She tries not to read reviews, positive or negative, until the run of a show is safely over with.

Actors are not the only ones who run the risk of spoiling their work by taking in reviews. Writers, too, suffer from undergoing the review process. Seldom are the reviews accurate in helping an artist to improve his work. When they are, when the critical arrow actually hits the mark, most artists respond with excitement, "Ah hah! This is how I can make the work better!"

Making the work better is the true goal of most artists. We have, at heart, a purity of intention that gets lost in the reviewing process. We are out to make something that can stand on its own as worthy and this often gets lost in the shuffle of the marketplace. As celebrity increases, so does vulnerability to the reviewing process. As fame enters the equation, judgment—good judgment—seems to leave. The artists now finds himself reviewed not as an artist but as a media phenomenon.

Artists at all levels run the risk of reviews. Small-town press can be just as hurtful as a bad review in *The New York Times*. At bottom, reviews often focus on what is lacking and not on what has been accomplished. It is as though critics carry in their heads an imaginary movie, book, play, or painting, against which the actual work is measured and found wanting. And it does not matter how popular an artist may be—in fact, popularity seems to increase the

Only those that risk going too far can possibly find out how far one can go.

T. S. ELIOT

There is no happiness except in the realization that we have accomplished something.

HENRY FORD

*Too many people overvalue
what they are not and
undervalue what they are.*

MALCOLM FORBES

incidence of unfair reviews. There is almost a spoilsport aspect to reviewing that insists on pulling the feathers off.

Yesterday I went to visit a famous writer. The writer lives in a sprawling sun-filled apartment overlooking Central Park. A full room was set aside to hold the writer's first editions. Everything about the place spoke of success. "I've had only one *New York Times* review," the writer told me. "That was two years ago and it was so mean that my friends advised me not to read it—which I haven't." This writer is so successful that new books debut at number one on *The New York Times* bestseller list.

"A book launch is like a NASA launch," the writer continued. "They will call me and say, 'We're going for the seventh. There's a two-day window between Grisham and Clancy. We're aiming for that.' I just let them aim where they see fit. My job has to be writing the books, not marketing them."

As artists it is our difficult job to do the work for the work's sake and to retain a healthy level of detachment from sales. This is easier said than done. I recently spoke with a best-selling author who was at her wit's end regarding her latest book. "They just dumped it into the stores. There was no thought, no publicity, nothing to help the book along. It was sink or swim and good luck to you."

We may put years of work into a project that a reviewer dismisses in a few quick paragraphs. Reviews now often come graded like grammar-school papers. A film that was three years in the making may garner a scanty two stars. An album that was five years in the writing may get three stars if the artist is lucky. It is very rare to see a full four-star review. That takes a generosity of spirit that critics are hard put to come by. As artists, how do we survive such stinginess?

Work is the best antidote for savaged work. If we are engaged in making something new, we are less invested in the reception of something old. If we remember to keep our own counsel—"How did *I* like the work?"—then we are less likely to be blown apart by the judgment of others. Having a healthy forum of before, during, and after friends is also an enormous help. We

*None think the great unhappy
but the great.*

EDWARD YOUNG

need those who love us and our work for the long haul and not for a hot-off-the-presses pick or pan.

It pays to remember that the reviewing process is historically misguided and often unfair. Wonderful work, work that has stood the test of time, was often savaged when it first appeared. The artist had to muster inhuman amounts of fortitude to keep going in the face of such discouragement—and yet, artists have kept going. We are stronger than we think.

"My success has to lie with my readers and not with my reviewers," the best-selling author concluded. "I need to go to my desk excited by what I have to share. It's up to me to try to retain some optimism and to do so in the face of tough reviews. I need to ask myself, 'Do people enjoy my books?' 'Do I enjoy making them?' If both answers are 'Yes,' then I am doing all right no matter what the critics say. And you know what? I am doing all right."

Envy is a kind of praise.

John Gay

Divining Rod

As working artists we deserve credit for sheer courage. We need to applaud ourselves for having the fortitude to continue making our art. Every scrap of art that we make deserves our encouragement. In addition to our believing mirrors, we ourselves need to cheer our progress. In Native American terms, this is called "counting coup." To 12-steppers it is called "taking a positive inventory."

Take pen in hand. Number from one to five. Enumerate five creative accomplishments. (These may have been included on your list of things you were proud of.) For example: I learned how to work with gouache; I wrote a one-act play; I learned a new monologue; I did a basic jazz dance course; I made my own Halloween costume.

No theoretician, no writer on art, however interesting he or she might be, could be as interesting as Picasso. A good writer on art may give you an insight to Picasso, but, after all, Picasso was there first.

David Hockney

Remember, a statue has never been set up in honor of a critic!

Jean Sibelius

In listing your accomplishments, allow yourself to look at process and not product. Even if it hasn't sold yet, you deserve credit for having written that romantic novel. Although you are still looking for a proper venue, you deserve points for having written a one-man show. Remember it is the making of art, not the reception of your art that makes you an artist. Van Gogh and Gauguin were both outcasts. Beethoven's later work was a century ahead of his time. Respect lies in the doing. Focus on that.

Receptivity

The tree beneath my writing-room window is a mystery to me. It has four-cornered leaves and large yellow flowers that are gold to the swarms of yellow jackets that feed and cruise and feed again amid its branches. This is the first summer that I have stayed on in New York rather than going on out to Taos, New Mexico. It is the first season when the tree has become a part of my story. I write at an IBM Selectric typewriter set on a small Chinese desk, up against a large window. The bees come to the window. They are large yellow jackets and they soar menacingly close. I remind myself that there is a pane of glass between them and me. I am grateful for the window.

Very often in our creative lives we can feel ourselves in jeopardy. We may have a sudden and debilitating doubt that our work will continue to be supported by the Universe. We may have been earning a living so far, but that's so far—our fear says—and so far is no guarantee of tomorrow. Rather than trust that there is an unseen but benevolent web gently holding us in our place, we often panic and act like we have gotten where we have gotten entirely on our own. Panicked that we do not know

A critic is a man who knows the way but can't drive the car.

Kenneth Tynan

how to go forward further, we flail in midair, caught between our fears and our projections.

But there is a benevolent web that holds us gently in our place. There *is* a larger power that wishes us well. We are led well and carefully. In order to be led further, we need only to ask for help. Help is always available to us. We need to open ourselves up. We need to be receptive.

For some of us, it is difficult to be receptive. We are used to self-propulsion and self-will. We count on ourselves and only on ourselves. When the chips fall our way, we do not thank a benevolent God, we thank our "lucky" stars.

The problem with depending on our luck is that luck is capricious. Our good luck can always change. Today we may be the darling of the gods and tomorrow we may be wailing at the gate, begging to be admitted one more time to paradise. How much better if there is something reliable on which we may build. How much better if there is a benevolent Something that is not capricious. To find such a Something, we need only look to the natural world. In God's world, the sun rises and the sun sets. The seasons appear each in their turn. Trees bud and bear leaves and flowers. Fruit grows heavy on the bough. There is a time of harvest.

It is our ego that tells us that we stand apart from nature. It is our ego that says we alone can force our growth. When we pray to be a part of the great unfolding plan, we are relieved of the burden of strategizing. We are relieved of the need to plot, to plan, to project. Each day we will be given what we need for that day. When we must act, we will have the clear knowledge of how it is we are to act. We will be guided. We will be shown. Is this a delusional fantasy?

Artists, when they speak candidly, almost always speak about higher forces. We may call it Guidance. We may call it Fate. We may call it Destiny or the Muse. Whatever we call it, it is the hand of a higher power at play in our lives. Artists will talk humbly about lucky breaks, about happening to be in the right place at the right time. We will speak of being led person to person, hand

It is the weak and confused who worship the pseudo-simplicities of brutal directness.

MARSHALL McLUHAN

to hand. There is an invisible guiding force present in all of these transactions. Our destiny unfolds within a larger plan. When we set our hand to our work, something larger than us works through us. We sense that Something. Some of us call it God.

"When I write, I communicate with a greater Something," a writer friend of mine explains. "I am working at my plot but Something is working on me and through me. There is a truth that I am intended to express."

The truth that we are intended to express is that we are all larger than we know. We are part of a grand design. There is room for our expansion. The Universe falls in with worthy plans. As we strive to grow larger and more expansive, the Universe seeks to expand through us. When we reach for support, the support is there. Our expansion is planned for, even counted upon. If we do not expand, the Universe cannot expand. If we thwart our true nature, we also thwart God's.

And yet, all of us go through times when we doubt our capacity to expand. All of us go through times when we feel the Universe to be unsafe, when we are frightened about what will become of us. I have been weathering just such a time. In times such as these, we turn, sick at heart, to prayer. "God, I believe. Help my disbelief," we pray, asking to be shown again how to trust. Our very prayers seem empty, based on an intimacy we no longer feel.

"I have a very intense, very meaningful relationship with God that comes and goes," one man jokes, kidding on the square. It is his experience that faith does not stay comfortable, that he is asked, again and again, to expand his faith beyond his comfort zone.

"It's not that I don't believe in God," he says. "It's just that sometimes I do not experience the relief of my belief. At times God feels like a fact of life to me and at other times God feels like a theory. During my theoretical times, I must act 'as if.' I must say to myself, '*If* I believed in a benevolent God, how would I act now?' and then I must act that way. Eventually, comfort returns."

"Faith will come back to you," another friend always assures

Man is least himself when he talks in his own person. Give him a mask and he will tell you the truth.

OSCAR WILDE

me. "And then it will disappear again." I have had times of faith—even years of faith—but now my faith has gone glimmering. I know from experience that it will return again if I can simply keep on "faithfully" keeping on. It is ironic that I am one more time asked to grow larger by growing smaller. As Bernice advises, I must get tiny in order to be connected to the larger order. And so, on a sleepless night, I must pray, "Help me, God." And then I must lie there, knowing that I am in fact being helped.

Our relationship with God appears to be tidal. Sometimes it is at high tide, full of power and glory. Other times it is at low ebb, barely visible. Always, it is in the act of making art that contact again can be felt.

"I think of painting as prayer and meditation," one painter tells me. "I go to the canvas and I empty myself of me. I ask to paint and then I surrender control. I may take the first stroke but the strokes thereafter follow one upon the other with me hurrying along in obedience trying to paint what comes next. Time disappears when I am painting. I am hollowed out, empty of anything but a kind of listening. I have my skills but my skills are in service of something larger. That larger Something may be some sort of ideal. I paint toward that perfection. Reaching for perfection, I am reaching for God."

Whether we call it reaching for God or reaching for the Muse, there is a humility to be found in the making of art. We strive to make what wants to be made. We open ourselves to inspiration and as we do so, we are led. We do not always *feel* that we are being led. We must affirm it in the face of our own doubt. We must go forward acting "as if." When we are willing to do that, we get a sense of our place in the greater scheme of things.

"When I am procrastinating about my art, it always feels risky to me," says one writer. "I always think I will be dropped on my ear. I think, 'I cannot believe I am really going to spend another day doing that.' And then I start working and suddenly the world all around me begins to make sense again. It is as though by working at my art I am given faith in the proper unfolding of things."

To have great poets, there must be great audiences too.

WALT WHITMAN

An audience is never wrong. An individual member of it may be an imbecile, but a thousand imbeciles together in dark—that is critical genius.

BILLY WILDER

Divining Rod

You will need an hour's time and a notebook. Once again, seek out a space that feels sacred to you. It might be a church or synagogue. It might be a library or reading room. It could be a grove of trees. What is important is that the place hold a sense of the transcendent. Seat yourself comfortably. Do not turn immediately to your notebook. You are asked to sit quietly and see what thoughts and feelings come to you.

This is an exercise in receptivity. You are seeking to receive Guidance. Your Guidance may be diffuse—a sense of well-being—or it may be very particular. Try focusing on your breath or on something beautiful in your environment. Allow your everyday world to slip gently away. It may take a little while for you to become calm and quiet. Once your thoughts have slowed, deeper insights can swim to the fore. What thoughts come to you?

You have your notebook on your lap. You may wish to use it now to write a prayer—or to simply note the insights that you are receiving. What you "get" may be very simple: call your sister more often, remember to buy stamps, get yourself a good houseplant, let yourself buy some Joni Mitchell albums again. Alternatively, your Guidance might concern larger issues: "I really can't stay in this job."

You might receive "marching orders" that pertain to any area of your life. What you take in may be a fleeting impression: "I am doing better than I think," or "I really need to change a few things." Listen closely to what it is that you receive. Record what you will need to jog your memory. You are simply checking in. You may wish to make a daily practice of such stolen quiet moments. Many of us find that a lunch hour can afford us a spare quarter hour. Some stu-

Lord I disbelieve—help thou my unbelief.

E. M. FORSTER

I do not believe . . . I know.

CARL JUNG

dents keep a special journal just for their quiet times. In that journal, they may use leading phrases to nudge themselves into greater introspection. They might write, "I wish" and complete the phrase twenty times. They might try, "I could try" and finish the phrase ten times. Alternatively, they might simply ask, "What do I need to know?" and record the answer that comes to them. You are seeking to "tag base" with a source of wisdom greater than your own.

Productivity

Question with boldness even the existence of God; because, if there be one, he must more approve of the homage of reason, than that of blind-folded fear.

THOMAS JEFFERSON

"It looks like a koi pond," my sister Libby has announced to me about her trout-covered kitchen table. "I have ordered a sheet of glass to protect it and I have signed it, which is fun." Over the phone line her voice bubbles with enthusiasm. She has had a very good time painting a school of trout just for fun. I picture her table in my mind's eye. I ask her to take some shots of it and e-mail me.

It has been fifteen years since my sister and I last lived in close proximity to each other. We have kept in touch by phone, e-mail, and mail. It is important to me that Libby be current with the events of my life. She is also a great inspiration to me and I like knowing just what portraits she has in process. What exactly is she painting in her studio on "Fairietale Farm"?

I like knowing that this month she is painting the tricky, thick coat of an elkhound. I like imagining the work she has done getting an aging thoroughbred exactly right. Long distance, I walk through the steps with her from the initial photo session through the client consultations, the decisions about size and medium that will be used. My sister works in colored pencils, watercolors, and oils. She especially loves oils.

When my sister is at work on a large oil, I can feel her concentration over the phone line. Always aware that for her client, the portrait represents a considerable cash outlay, Libby is determined to give good value and she does. Still, she is always on pins and needles waiting to see the client's response. She always has jitters before she delivers a commission. Do they like it? Yes!

Working full time as a portrait artist, it is relatively rare for her to indulge in creating something sheerly for the glee of creation. When she does, her joy leapfrogs over the phone line. Last year, she sculpted an eight-foot-tall poodle. It was kelly green and lit by Christmas bulbs.

"I had the poodle right in the middle of my kitchen. Guests would come by and go, 'Gee. I guess you're up to something.' I love being up to something. It gives me back a part of my artist identity. If I am too much the drone for hire, I stop respecting myself. It all starts feeling a little too corporate for me, I guess."

To the outside eye, there is nothing corporate about Libby's life unless it is the consistent productivity that she musters. At any given time, she may have as many as five portraits in varying stages of completion. Moving portrait to portrait keeps her from going stale and allows her to edge further along on each commission without freezing up.

"Like anyone, I get scared. I think, 'Is this one good enough?' Working on more than one work at a time allows me to postpone that block-inducing question. I just do a little more work each day on each commission and then I move on. It may be an eccentric way to work, but for me it is productive. I am never bored and I am seldom stymied. There is always a little more that can be done on something. You keep adding up those 'little mores' and you do get quite a bit accomplished."

Although she doesn't phrase it this way, I see that my sister has arranged her work life to keep her work fun for her. Each portrait offers its unique set of challenges. She must be true to her art, true to her own vision and yet accommodating, too, to the client's vision. Sometimes an angry jawline must be softened. Sometimes a waistline must be whittled in.

"My job is to paint not only what I see, but also how they see themselves," Libby explains. "I try to bear in mind that I am offering them a service. When I remember that, it keeps my ego out of it."

Working to keep her ego out of it, Libby finds that she is able to paint more freely. She is able to "listen" to each painting as it unfolds. She strives to be open to the painting that wants to happen, not just to the painting that she has planned. Some of her best works are what she describes as "happy accidents."

"I sometimes seem to stumble upon an idea that is better than the idea I had. I do believe that when we are open to it, we are led. I try to be available to whatever higher force is striving to work through me. I ask to be of service, and I ask for inspiration. My paintings are really my answered prayers."

God does not compel the will. Rather, He sets the will free so that it wills not otherwise than what God Himself wills.

MEISTER ECKHART

Divining Rod

In 12-step lingo, God is sometimes spoken of as "Good Orderly Direction." There is something about creating order that does put us in touch with a sense of the Divine. The task I ask you to do now is a humble one. Set aside one half hour and a stack of your mending.

Take needle and thread in hand and set to work. You may have buttons that need tightening; socks that have a hole. The seam on a pair of slacks may need some reinforcement. Quietly and calmly, allow yourself to work gently through your pile. Be alert for the sense of well-being that may steal over you. Be alert, too, for some flashes of creative inspiration. Needlework goads the imagination—think of the Brontë sisters hiding their

I decided that it was not wisdom that enabled poets to write their poetry, but a kind of instinct or inspiration, such as you find in seers and prophets who deliver all their sublime messages without knowing in the least what they mean.

SOCRATES

Art is an invention of aesthetics, which is in turn an invention of philosophers . . . What we call art is a game.

OCTAVIO PAZ

novels under their handiwork. Many novelists have found that needlepoint, crocheting, and knitting help them to stitch up their plots as well.

Prayer

It is hot and hazy in New York. In Chicago, it is cool and rainy. I know the Chicago weather because my friend Sonia lives there, and I am, by phone, a regular part of her Chicago household. I am, too, a part of my friend Elberta's household in New Mexico and my friend Ed Towle's household in Los Angeles. Here in New York, I am often lonely, wishing that my friends lived in the same city. But I am grateful to have friends, carefully collected and nurtured over the years.

"You are in my prayers twice each day," says my friend Larry, who lives in Taos, New Mexico, where I myself lived for ten years. As the sun comes up over the mountain ridge, Larry rises to pray and meditate. "I think of you every morning," he assures me. I, for one, am glad to be thought of.

"I wake up at five-thirty and you are at the top of my prayer list," declares my sister Libby who lives in Racine, Wisconsin. "I pray for you every single morning, chiefly the Our Father, but a prayer that you will feel well and work well during the day to come." Libby lives on a horse farm and light comes to her through a bank of pine trees bordering her farm. I am grateful to think that as the dawn comes so do prayers for my well-being. I myself wake up with a prayer not far from my consciousness. I get to the page for my three pages of morning writing and after my three pages, I pray. I ask that my day be in the care of God and that I be made into what God needs for me to be. The answer to that prayer seems most often to boil down to: Be a writer. And so, I come to the typewriter and I write.

In our modern world, prayer is seldom discussed as a viable part of living. It smacks a little of esoterica. In previous ages we had the great bells tolling across the countryside, marking the days into intervals of prayer. In modern life, no bells toll. Prayers are elected, not suggested by the very fabric of the day. Someone like Larry, who rises to pray and to meditate, is rare. Most of us find our day gets under way willy-nilly. We are out of bed and into the great maw of onrushing events without the buffer of prayer to gird us for the day's events.

Prayer is profoundly useful but we seldom see it as such. Instead it seems somewhat arcane, a dubious pastime of those with nothing better to do. In point of fact, prayer is intensely practical. It works like a routing system, sending divine energy just where it is needed. As artists, we can pray to be of service. We can ask that our work serve the greater whole. We can pray for practical things, too. We can pray for an inspiration, for the ability to do justice to a certain idea, for an acknowledgment of our work.

As artists, when we pray, we are joining a long tradition. Throughout the centuries, great art has been born of great humility. Although the Sistine Chapel was commissioned, Michelangelo sought to serve both his patron and his God. We, too, can seek to serve.

"I believe that when we are writing, we are communicating with something higher than ourselves," states one best-selling author. "Working at art is really an act of communion. When I write, I am praying. When I miss a day's writing, I, in effect, miss a day's prayer—and I feel it."

"I believe there are higher forces that we connect with when we work," the writer continues. "I have been writing for twenty years. That has given me a spiritual life. I believe that I am intended to write, that when I write, I open myself to Spirit."

When an artist is fully engaged in working, there is a self-forgetting that happens. The artist becomes absorbed in the service of the work that he is creating. The ego dissolves and the soul steps forward.

"I believe that I am guided," the writer speculates. "I believe

No artist is ahead of his time. He is his time, it's just that others are behind the times.

MARTHA GRAHAM

He neither serves nor rules, he transmits. His position is humble and the beauty at the crown is not his own. He is merely a channel.

PAUL KLEE

that I am a conduit for God to put forward some truth. At times I am frightened. I feel that what I am writing or saying is uncomfortable, and yet I feel guided that it is what I am intended to say. I do my best simply to cooperate. I am not saying I am without fear, but rather that I try to set fear to one side."

When Larry and Libby pray for me, they pray that I, too, may set aside my fear and do what it is God would have me do with my day. They are praying that my personality might be malleable, teachable by the Great Teacher. I have come to depend upon their prayers. Many days, I ask for them.

"I don't feel very good about what I am trying to write. Can you stick me in the prayer pot for some inspiration?" I might ask my sister. With Libby praying for me from her studio in Racine, Wisconsin, I sit down to write at my desk in New York, New York.

There is an uncanny Something that kicks in as the result of prayer. I may find myself at my desk, writing for longer hours than is my usual wont. I may find myself writing with greater candor, risking a self-revelation that I might normally have eschewed. Days when I am being prayed for, I find myself more willing to keep myself at the typewriter. I find myself cocking an inner ear for what it is that I am trying to write and then writing it out with more fluidity. I do not know that I would say my style improves as a result of prayer, but my willingness to write and therefore have a style improves. Writing would seem to be a secular activity and yet it benefits from spiritual aid.

"I think that when we deal with Spirit, we are dealing in the realm of archetypes," posits a renowned editor. "It is as though there is an ideal book that is striving to come forward and the writer and the editor are both in service of this larger and better Something. In a sense, a book tells you what it wants to be. Perhaps the best books are the ones where the players are the most obedient to the book's demands."

"I pray for you to be willing to write what wants to be written," says my sister. As a painter herself, she is familiar with a piece of art having its own imperious sense of where it wants to

The product of the artist has become less important than the fact of the artist.

DAVID MAMET

When you pray for anyone you tend to modify your personal attitude toward him.

NORMAN VINCENT PEALE

go. "There are days when you write what I seem to need to hear. Is that because I am the one praying? I sometimes wonder."

"Wonder" seems to be at the heart of inspiration. We receive a small, inner prompt and although we wonder where it could be taking us, we obediently follow. In that sense, the writing seems to move one step ahead of a writer. We write not to display what we think but to discover what we think. More is always being revealed to us as we are open to higher input.

"I don't know about the word 'higher,'" a writer friend of mine interjects. "I think all people are guided always. I don't think artists have a lock on it. I just think that our guidance results in something tangible on the page or on the stage or on the easel, whereas for other people guidance may result in something more ephemeral, say a shift in direction or emphasis. My point is that inspiration is a very daily and matter-of-fact phenomenon. Artists simply have something to show for it. Our art can easily seem to be inspired. But we're all inspired when you come down to it."

If we are all inspired, perhaps prayer gives us the consciousness of that inspiration. If the universe is ready at all times to guide and mentor us, perhaps we can be more or less open to such tutelage.

The sun rises over brownstones and Central Park. Before it has arched very high in its course, prayers have been sent up for my benefit. I am grateful to be the recipient of such prayers. They are like added lanterns on my path so that when my own prayer goes up, "Lord, show me what you would have me do," there is already illumination of the task at hand. I pray daily, "God, grant me the serenity to accept the things I cannot change," and among those things I cannot change is the fact that I am a writer. And so, prayers said, I write.

I write at a small Chinese desk. I look out over the brownstones and I hope that God will send me words. Sometimes words come to me in a rush. I am grateful for such times. Other days, I know that I am to write and I do write but it is without comfort and ease. Those days, I feel myself dependent on grace and that grace is something that I ask for and my friends ask for for me.

He must pull out his own eyes and see no creature before he can say he sees no God.

JOHN DONNE

On the mornings after I have spent a sleepless night, it is harder to write. I go to the page already weary. "Help me," I pray. "Please help me." Help then comes to me in the form of a small thought, a notion really of how it is that I might go forward. Sometimes I feel that my very thoughts limp and that I am lame following after them. At times like this, I must remind myself that prayers have been said and that my job is simply to trust, to take down what appears to be next. Sometimes I look out my window at the rooftops as though answered prayers might materialize there, like Santa Claus with a fully laden sleigh. I pray and I write. The gift is being given the words to do so, however haltingly. "Help me now," I pray. Then I must trust as help comes.

I searched for God and found only myself. I searched for myself and found only God.

SUFI PROVERB

I have no objection to churches so long as they do not interfere with God's work.

BROOKS ATKINSON

Divining Rod

Prayer is always an exercise in open-mindedness. You could think of it as a scientific experiment: if I pray (action), what will happen (response)? Although we may give lip service to the idea that God is all seeing and all knowing, there are usually areas about which we do not pray. We may, for example, consider our finances too worldly a concern to involve God. And yet, those students who have experimented with financial prayers report that they have received very useful financial guidance.

Take pen in hand. Number from one to twenty. List twenty topics—people, places, and things—about which you could pray. Your prayers may range from the tiny, "Help me to find some good-looking stamps," to the large, "Help me to know how to help my sister through her husband's death." Be alert for areas that you do not pray about. Is your need for a new haircut fuel for prayer? Is your diet, or your willingness to exercise? Some students make a regular practice of prayer after their Morning Pages. Others report great comfort from an evening ritual. The time you pray matters less than that you do find the time to pray. Consider your list a preliminary prayer.

CHECK-IN

1. **How many days this week did you do your Morning Pages?** If you skipped a day, why did you skip it? How was the experience of writing them for you? Are you experiencing more clarity? A wider range of emotions? A greater sense of detachment, purpose, and calm? Did anything surprise you? Is there a "repeating" issue asking to be dealt with?

2. **Did you do your Artist Date this week?** Did you note an improved sense of well-being? What did you do and how did it feel? Remember, Artist Dates can be difficult and you may need to coax yourself into taking them.

3. **Did you get out on your Weekly Walk?** How did that feel? What emotions or insights surfaced for you? Were you able to walk more than once? What did your walk do for your optimism and sense of perspective?

4. **Were there any other issues this week that felt significant to you in your self-discovery?** Describe them.

Good art is a form of prayer. It's a way to say what is not sayable.

FREDERICK BUSCH

Uncovering a Sense of Discipline

Nowhere is the phrase "Easy does it" more useful than in the pursuit of our creative endeavors. Small and gentle daily actions build upon themselves to make large accomplishments. A novel is written a page at a time. A painting proceeds brushstroke by brushstroke. By thinking small, we are able to become large. As we exercise our creative gifts, we experience the joy of artistic rigor. Like athletes, we keep ourselves in training. Our daily laps build stamina.

Twenty Minutes

The sky is pewter. Heavy drops hang from the fire escape. Down on the streets umbrellas are folded under arms. The sun pulses behind the clouds, threatening to break through the over cast. The news from Wisconsin is rain, rain, and more rain. As usual, we have inherited their used weather.

The bird of paradise alights only on the hand that does not grasp.

JOHN BERRY

This morning's e-mail included photographs of my sister Libby's trout-pond kitchen table. The trout are beautiful, mixing with each other, swirling to the surface. The table, viewed at a glance, does look like a koi pond. It will be fun taking meals atop those fish.

Trying to take in the idea of something "fun," I feel myself straining. I am still caught in the undertow of depression and "fun" remains largely theoretical to me. When I talk on the phone to my sister, I must work to be really present and accounted for in the conversation. Libby chats brightly and I must force myself to listen to her and not to the undercurrent of despair that is still my constant sound track. I must set a discipline for myself, a mental fence to contain my negativity. "Try to be positive," I lecture myself. "Try to show up and be of service. Take an interest in other people, not just in your own dilemma."

Last night, my friend Sonia phoned in from Chicago. She was overtired, overworked, and frustrated. She has a book to write and no window in her schedule in which to write it. She longs for an empty savannah of time. I don't think she's going to get it, and so I urge her to fly at the page in the minutes to spare that she has got. "Just start where you are," I tell her. "Put down something and then we will go from there."

I say, "we," because I am functioning as a believing mirror for Sonia's writing career. I see her books as finished and successful. When she has doubt, she needs only check in with me to know that the books are a reality and not a "mere" dream. This is Sonia's eighth book. Sooner or later, her identity as a working writer will catch up to her. At this point, she still regards each book as a fluke, something she is lucky to be able to pull off.

"I am going to try to write page one," she announces. She will wedge that page in between readings, teaching, and interviews. "This is supposed to be a small book. I ought to be able to do that, right?"

"Let's take this book a page at a time," I tell her.

Nobody wakes up to suddenly find themselves a best-selling author, a Tony Award–winning director, a Pulitzer Prize–winning playwright. Successful careers in the arts develop one step at a time. Books are written a page at a time. So are plays. A songwriting career unfolds song by song. An acting career involves each day's immersion in that craft. When we keep our sights trained on the small and doable, we are able to do the large and unthinkable. It is all a matter of breaking things down to a day-by-day practice: What can I manage today?

It is rare to have a day without twenty minutes to spare in it. That twenty minutes is enough to get down one page. It is

I like trees because they seem more resigned to the way they have to live than other things do.

WILLA CATHER

enough to get to the keyboard. It is enough to run through a monologue. Ideally, we want more than twenty minutes and we often get that, too, but I have found that twenty minutes is the minimum time we need and that is nearly always available to us.

"But Julia," Sonia says to me, "in twenty minutes I will barely get started."

"My point precisely. You will get started. Getting started is what you need."

"Yes, I guess that's true," Sonia concludes reluctantly. "Right now I am writing in my head."

"Well, give it twenty minutes and try writing on the page," I advise her.

"Oh, all right. But it's just one of your cheap tricks."

I believe in cheap tricks. I believe in whatever makes you more productive. This means that I believe in twenty-minute windows where we hurl ourselves at the page. These are the creative equivalent of sexual quickies—another practice that isn't perfect but is still very good.

"Imagine that you are a famished lover," I tell Sonia. "You only have twenty minutes to see your beloved. Would you take it?"

"Of course I would," Sonia laughs.

"Well then . . ."

When we are hungering for our art, we are like famished lovers. We yearn for contact and even the smallest amount, while it leaves us craving more, still gives us the will to go on. Yesterday, I got to the piano for twenty minutes. I played through a little bit of *Magellan* and then I just fooled around. When I got up from the keys, my phone rang. It was a director with an interest in *Magellan*. He wanted to set a meeting time. Was I amenable to that? Because I had just tagged base with the project, I felt in synch with it. I was able to schedule a meeting and promise myself a few more miniature piano dates before the meeting. My relationship to music is a lot like Sonia's to writing: although I have written a great deal of music, I still consider it a fluke. I have to take my career as a musician in tiny little bites. A day at a time, a note at a time, it is possible.

The trick is to make time— not to steal it—and produce fiction.

Bernard Malamud

When we are focused on the possible, we are able to ignore the probable. We are able to set aside that tricky question of odds. The odds stacked against us as an artist immediately lessen if we are in fact doing our work. The odds of publishing a novel are a hell of a lot higher if you have written a novel. In other words, when we can focus on what it is we are doing, then what it is we could do becomes a logical progression and not a wild fantasy.

Just at the moment, I am writing this book and I am working on *Magellan.* I work on the book daily. My habits as a writer are long-standing. I must nudge myself to extend the same courtesy to my music. It, too, can benefit from a gentle, "Easy Does It" approach. I touch the keys and Magellan sets to sea. He reaches for the wind, I reach for the next spate of notes. Outside, the sun breaks through the clouds.

Divining Rod

For one week, you are asked to spend twenty minutes daily on your art. Set a timer. It's "only" twenty minutes. Practice the piano. Work with your voice tape. Go to the page and write on that novel. Gesso a canvas and start to paint. Twenty minutes is not a long time. We all have twenty minutes if we look for them. Survey your day. When can you best squeeze them in?

You may find that you need the additional support of a believing mirror in order to pin yourself down about work. Go to your list of encouraging friends and select one as a colleague. Pick up the phone and explain that you will be working twenty minutes daily and that you need someplace to check in. When I am rewriting *Magellan,* I check in daily with my friend Daisy Press, an opera singer. "Hi, Daisy," my message might run. "I am just about to go to the keys." I find it is very grounding to call Daisy. Once I have actually committed to her, I don't seem to be so prone to wriggle out of my commitment. After all, it is "only" twenty minutes.

The Courage to Create

Outside the window, on Columbus Avenue, a siren whirls past. It is closely followed by another. For a moment, conversation is difficult. Then quiet returns, or relative quiet, and I am able to hear what my companion, Daisy, is saying.

Kindness is in our power, even when fondness is not.

SAMUEL JOHNSON

"For me music is ecstatic," she says. "When I am singing well, I feel myself to be in complete communion with God. It's like nothing else. There is an intense connection."

"I know what you mean," I counter. "When I go to the piano and write music, I, too, feel connected to God. I have a sense of expansion. It is unlike the feeling I get any other way."

We are seated in a small Greek diner. The waiter knows me well. He offers me a bowl of soup and a cup of chamomile tea. My opera singer companion orders peppermint. It is late on a gilded evening and we are talking about the connection between God and our work. We both find God through music. This spooks us a little.

"So has your guidance been telling you that right now it is all about music?" Daisy nudges. She encourages my music.

"It told me I needed to spend time at the keys. That if I wanted to learn piano, I had to simply put in time. It frightens me to sit at the keys. I don't want to feel all that I feel."

"I know what you mean. When you sit at the keys you feel everything."

"I may not be ready to feel everything."

"No," she says, laughing. "Neither am I."

The waiter refills our tea water. We sit for a moment in companionable silence. We both admit after a minute that we are avoiding our work. It simply feels too daunting. Somehow talking about it seems to swing open a door of willingness.

"I think I could call your machine and say that I was going to go to the piano," I volunteer.

"I could call your machine and tell it that I am about to sit down and write some music."

"Would you be writing in the morning or in the afternoon?"

"I don't know but I will write. How about you?"

"Me, too."

And so, just like that it is settled between us. I will return to work again on *Magellan* and my companion will start working on music composition for the first time. A virtuoso singer, a fine soprano, she has always yearned to compose. Now she will give it a try. All it took was having a believing mirror. All it took was the willingness to allow ourselves to be helped. Wherever two or more are joined together . . .

So often as artists the blocks that we feel to be ours alone can be dissolved by being shared. We have the opportunity to help one another and when we are willing to take it, great things can come to pass.

So much of making art is like running a marathon. We may have to run the race ourselves but it is tremendously helpful to have friends who can cheer us on.

"You are doing better than you think," Sonia might tell me. "You may not like what you are writing but you *are* writing. You are showing up at the page despite your resistance, and that speaks volumes. Why do we talk so little about artists needing courage?"

The courage to create is a courage to make something out of what we are feeling. Out of the swirl of emotions comes some cogent form of expression. It may be a daub of paint. It may be a poem. It may be a few measures of music. Whatever it is, it is the distillate of our human personality. We seek to express what it is that wants to be expressed through us. And sometimes that expression is not comfortable. Our ego will tell us it's not good enough and neither are we.

This afternoon, I got a phone call from an estimable writer. She is at the beginning of a new book and it is fighting her. "I found myself saying to myself, 'Start over.' But then I thought, 'No, don't do that. Try to trust.' I don't always think we are the best judge of what it is that is trying to come through us. I think sometimes we are very harsh. We cannot see the beauty that we create. I have written books that struck me as flat and without grace only to have those very books be the ones that people write to me about years later."

I think we have to admit that we do not own our art. It owns us. I think the sooner we admit that and try to relinquish control, the better off we are. For some reason, God has chosen some of us to write and we have little to do with it. I believe all people are creative, and that I have been given this form as my own. I have to try to set my ego aside and stop letting it vote on everything that I do. The ego's votes are so often incorrect. If only I could remember that.

Sitting in the homely booth at the Greek diner, making a plan to check in around our art, my companion and I are working to outmaneuver our egos. We are reaching for humility, which is always the way to outsmart a stubborn block. "I am willing to make bad art" allows us to make art, and often very good art at that. Tomorrow I will phone my friend and then I will sit down at the keys.

You can only perceive real beauty in a person as they get older.

Anouk Aimée

Divining Rod

When we are reaching for inspiration, we do well to reach first for humility. Very often a prayer to be of service will clear the channel and allow you to access your creative guidance. When we are focused on ourselves, on our need to be brilliant or original, we often constrict the flow of our art. How often, when we seek to help someone else, do good ideas flood us?

Take pen in hand. Number from one to five. List five ways in which you could use your talents to be of service. ("God, please let this work of mine be of service," you might ask.) When we try to be of service, our very syntax clears up. We begin to be clear and plain-spoken. When we ask to be of service, we are moved to feelings of generosity. We have a sense of largesse as we prepare to give something away. Rather than feeling pinched, we find ourselves feeling expansive. This brings us a sense of freedom and work flows more easily.

I don't believe in aging. I believe in forever altering one's aspect to the sun. Hence my optimism.

VIRGINIA WOOLF

Resigning as Author

At the piano this morning, I began piecing together the new opening for *Magellan*. The music must reflect a stormy night at sea, thirteen months into the voyage. The sailors must be mutinous and Magellan must be resolute, determined to continue no matter what the cost. Seated at the keys, I hear scraps of melody. One theme argues with the next. I strive to get the tumult onto the page. I call out to Emma, "Can you hear this? What do you think?"

"I think that's good," Emma says.

I have been working on *Magellan* for more than six years. The initial melodies came to me in a rush, song upon song. I raced to get them down, hurrying along with tape recorder and crabbed notation, trying to make a record of what it is I heard. On the early *Magellan* tapes I have scraps of conversation in the background as the music overtook me again as I tried to grab a meal in a restaurant. I have one tape recorded as I was driving.

Again, the music was imperious and came flooding in with no respect for whatever else it was I was trying to do. Emma has been working on *Magellan* for three years now. Its melodies have come to haunt her as thoroughly as they have haunted me. Between the two of us, we have studied biographies of the great mariner and we have examined closely the diary of his scribe Antonio Pigafetta. There is a great story to be told and we are laboring to tell it. We have eighty-five pieces of music that must be shaped into a whole.

Yesterday I spoke with a writer who has just begun a new novel. The work is coming at her in a halting form. So she took herself on a walk, ears cocked, listening for the story to start unspooling. "The work comes through us. We don't control it," she marveled to me. "There's something bigger than we are that's up to something, I think." She is waiting for that larger Something to show itself to her.

Working on *Magellan,* I have often felt there was something larger than myself striving to be born. The music revealed itself without regard for me and my limitations. It wanted to sound a certain way. I could hear that sound and chase it on the page, but I could not really create it. It seemed to come to me fully formed. I was its servant not its master. It had its own ideas.

Allowing the work to move through us without impediment means resigning as its author. The work must be allowed to author itself, to take on the shapes and colors that it prefers. I can plan a sequence, but then I must surrender to how the sequence plans itself. This is what we mean by inspiration, the willingness to surrender to a higher octave, the finer vibration that the work itself might hold.

Painter Robert Motherwell claims that while he may take the beginning brushstroke on a painting, the brush itself takes stroke after stroke once it is launched. It is the same with music. It is the same with performance. There is something trying to be born through us and we do best when we are able to allow its passage.

Art requires that we relinquish control. It asks us to move out

People from a planet without flowers would think we must be mad with joy the whole time to have such things about us.

IRIS MURDOCH

Just as the creative artist is not allowed to choose, neither is he permitted to turn his back on anything: a single refusal and he is cast out of the state of grace and becomes sinful all the way through.

RAINER MARIA RILKE

on faith. In this regard, art itself is always one step ahead of the artist, calling us forward. Agnes de Mille summarizes the situation very well: "Living is a form of not being sure, not knowing what next or how. The moment you know how, you begin to die a little. The artist never entirely knows. We guess. We may be wrong, but we take leap after leap in the dark."

It takes humility to not know. It takes courage to remain teachable by our art. Yesterday, I got a letter from a novelist. She wrote to me, "Creations are our mirror. They don't go well when we're not going well. They don't have time for us when we don't have time for them. They are tired when we are, and the powder comes off their wings when we handle them too much. The relationship is delicate and fierce, and without it we are truly miserable. So we must do whatever it needs."

"We must do whatever it needs" requires that we be vigilant about nurturing our art. We must do what our art requires because, as the novelist noted, "without it we are truly miserable." And so, for me, I do Morning Pages, Weekly Walks, and Artist Dates. I try to be attentive to what it is that wants to be born. I go to the page or to the keys and I wait to hear what wants to come into being. I try to be both delicate and diligent. I try to be alert. Because my art moves through me, I try to make certain that the circuits are static-free and rested. I pray to be of service and to live one day at a time. Art is born moment by moment and day by day. I must be willing to go slowly because slow has its own velocity. "Easy does it" doesn't mean, "Oh, calm down." It means "easy accomplishes it."

Fighting my depression, I must also fight inertia. I need grace to put myself in motion. I must ask for that grace daily. "Take away my difficulties," I pray. "Please remove from me now every single defect of character that stands in the way of my usefulness to you and my fellows." It takes daily discipline to keep my creative commitments. It is good that I have Daisy, the young opera singer, to call about my music. It is good I have the novelist to talk to about my book. From each of them, the question is the same, "Did you work today?" Just for today, I am able to answer, "Yes."

Divining Rod

The ego's hold on us is tenacious. To test this out, try the simple tool of finishing the following phrase ten times. Ready? Write: "The reason I can't let God author my work is _____." You will discover that you do not trust God. You will discover that you do not trust yourself. This very line of questioning may make you mad.

Take pen in hand again—or better yet, use a magic marker. Devise for yourself a small sign that you can post clearly visible in your work area. The sign reads: "Okay, God. You take care of the quality. I will take care of the quantity."

There's a difference between invention and what comes from inside of a painter.

EDWARD HOPPER

Joy

On Eighty-ninth Street and Amsterdam, a sliding door moves to one side and two horses pick their way carefully out to the street. Their riders frown in concentration. This is the tricky part, getting their mounts from the stable, Claremont Riding Academy, safely out to the park. It entails a three-block ride through traffic. It is a triumph just getting to the park where the bridal trails await.

Once inside the park's leafy domain, a crisp chirrup and a slap of the reins sends the horses briskly trotting forward. Rentals are for an hour at a crack. An hour is long enough to make a circuit of the reservoir and a loop through the woods to the north. When my daughter was a toddler, I kept an Appaloosa horse at Claremont. I would hoist my daughter up with me double and pilot our way to the park. Many mornings found

The unconscious creates, the ego edits.

STANLEY KUNITZ

us circling the reservoir, competing with joggers for the bridle path's right of way.

Mornings nowadays, as I walk the reservoir with Tiger Lily in tow, I still see my tiny daughter in my mind's eye. My daughter is twenty-nine now and she has just bought herself a horse. Daily, on the phone coast to coast, I get the horse report.

"Horses" are Domenica's answer to the question, "What brings you joy?" My daughter has learned that she needs to have a daily dose of joy to help counterbalance any disappointments in her career. It is not easy vying for parts with other actresses. Domenica's horse, Velocity, loves her for herself alone. His welcoming whinny is always the same whether she is winning parts or losing them.

A horse might be a large item to juggle in an artist's attempt to find a balanced life. My friend Tracy, a quilt restoration expert, managed to keep a horse for many years. She still rides every Wednesday morning, setting out from Claremont just as dawn is breaking in the city streets.

Alison, on a more modest budget, has a rescued greyhound. Mornings find her in Central Park as well. Before nine, it is legal to run your dog off its leash and Alison's dog does love to run.

"I worried that I wouldn't be able to keep up with her," Alison confesses. "Before Zephyr entered my life, I was kind of a coach potato. I was always thinking, 'I really should get more exercise.' Now I do."

For Nelson, joy came in the form of a pair of Rollerblades. "Before I got my blades, I was always snorting in contempt. Someone would whirl past and I would think, 'Who does he think he is?' Now I know that owning a pair of blades makes you feel that you own the world. I should also add that I have dropped twenty pounds and that helps, too. Now I am that smug guy that you spot whizzing past. It's obnoxious, but I love it. I'm just plain happy."

Caroline made the transition to a more joyful life without benefit of a single purchase. "I always felt I lived in the city but

I wasn't really a part of it. I felt alienated, trapped on the outside. All of that changed when I began walking." For starters, Caroline got off of the subway one stop early and walked the remaining distance to her job. That felt so good to her, she began grabbing walks on her lunch hour. One balmy spring evening, she tried walking all the way home.

"Now I walk several miles daily. I traded in my purse for a good leather backpack. I didn't set out walking as a fitness program, but I could have. Within a week, I had dropped a pound or two. More than that, my attitude shifted. I began to really feel a part of the city. My alienation slipped away. I also noticed that walks were really great for brainstorming. Walking makes me smarter and, God knows, I am all for that."

Down on the deck below my writing-room window, my neighbor the sunbather has been joined by a lover. They lie entwined in each others arms as the afternoon slips lower and the day begins to cool. As five o'clock nears, the horses in the park are due back at Claremont. Their hooves clip-clop through the streets as they wind their way home. It is twilight and I have yet to get in my day's walk.

Fighting depression, I fight lethargy as well. I know that a walk will make me feel better and yet it is hard to stir the muscles necessary. "Help me be willing," I pray. "Please remove from me now whatever defects of character stand in the way of my usefulness."

As I so often do when I am feeling weak, I piggyback my energy onto another's. "Would you like to walk the reservoir loop?" I ask Emma. When she says, "Yes," I call to the dogs who are delighted to be getting out even late in the day as it is. We enter the park with an hour of daylight remaining. Out on the trail, I note that the evening joggers seem to be more serious than their daytime counterparts. Lean and committed, they glide through the dusk. Tiger Lily pirouettes at leash's end, straining after a stray squirrel. I laugh at her antics and feel then a brief surge of optimism, the reward for putting my body into motion, an answered prayer.

You must be unintimidated by your own thoughts because if you write with someone looking over your shoulder, you'll never write.

NIKKI GIOVANNI

Divining Rod

You have already made a list of things that you love. Now you are asked to make a list of ten actions that bring you joy. For example: making homemade vegetable soup, baking fruit pies, cooking a pot of rice pudding, getting my hair professionally conditioned. Your list may range from the homely to the grandiose. Choose an easily doable action and execute it. For the next week, try to take one joy-bringing action a day.

The 12-step program Arts Anonymous believes that for many of us, our resistance to making art is addictive. Like anorectics, we get high on deprivation. Not making art is habit-forming just as not eating is. This cycle must be broken and we can do this a day at a time. We can write our pages, make our Artist Dates, take our walks. We can call and enlist the support of our believing mirrors. It is sobering and grounding to take small creative actions. Allow your self the joy of such sober grounding.

When I am finishing a picture I hold some God-made object up to it—a rock, a flower, the branch of a tree or my hand—as a kind of final test. If the painting stands up to a thing that man cannot make, the painting is authentic.

MARC CHAGALL

Cycles

Art, that great undogmatized church.

ELLEN KEY

Today no sunbathers loll beneath my window. The day is cool and gray. It is Memorial Day and New York is calm and subdued. Yesterday, a bright and gala day, the park was filled with strollers picking their way past bathers who lay on blankets just adjacent to the cinder trails. Dogs bounded the lengths of their leashes, greeting one another with wagging tails. Tiger Lily and Charlotte, bonded to each other, pursued squirrels in tandem, tugging at their leashes and straining to be free. But that was yesterday. Today the dogs are content to stay indoors. They stretch out on the Oriental carpets, napping through the gray after-noon.

As artists, we, too, must learn to live within our seasons. We must learn when to expand and explore and when to nap our way through gray afternoons. There is a rhythm to creative life. It expands and then contracts. We must learn to move with it, listening to our psyches for what is required at any given time.

"Creations are like children. They pout and sulk," a famous writer recently told me. "If we neglect them they grow petu-lant. They want our attention."

Giving attention to our creations means learning to sense when it is that they need inflow and when it is that they need calm. When our lives become too frantic, our art retreats. It does not thrive on a life lived pell-mell.

I need calm and quiet if I am to work, but I need a certain amount of stimulation, too. It's really a juggling act. I must be a gatekeeper on the traffic in my life. Too much traffic and I grow overwhelmed. Too little and I grow stagnant. It's a balance that I am seeking and I must be attentive because my needs are always shifting.

One more time, my night was restless and sleep eluded me until two a.m. One more time, waking up tired, I found myself cloaked in pessimism, wreathed by despair. It was with effort that I prayed my morning prayers, asking to be rendered fit for the day ahead. I found myself thinking, "If I were feeling good, then what would I do?" It was from that thought that the no-tion of taking an Artist Date came to me. Manhattan is chock-full of adventures.

After a cup of coffee and Morning Pages, I took myself to the American Museum of Natural History. From October to May of every year, they have an exhibit of butterflies. "I let you in as a senior," the ticket taker told me. "You're not quite a se-nior, are you?"

"No, not quite." He waved me in.

The butterfly exhibit walks you through a great deal of in-formation, some of it very basic: there are 250,000 species of

Art is man's expression of his joy in labor.

WILLIAM MORRIS

Art—the one achievement of man which has made the long trip up from all fours seem well advised.

JAMES THURBER

what we think of as butterflies, but of those only 18,000 are genuine butterflies. The average lifespan of a butterfly is several weeks. In a carefully sealed-off hallway, laden with tropical plants, one hundred species of butterfly fluttered freely. There were orange striped butterflies, azure butterflies, and large velvety moths. Four museum employees, identified by their badges, stood ready to answer any questions. They talked freely even without questions.

Moths, I learned, are largely nocturnal. Butterflies woo and begin their mating dance midair. Vladimir Nabokov was a noted lepidopterist. A section from one of his scholarly treatises on butterflies made it into *Lolita*. In Africa, in the Dzanga-Sangha region, there are 950 species of butterfly, leaning heavily toward specimens that are aqua and cobalt. A glass specimen case showed a panoply of examples.

"We order perhaps a hundred different species," a worker told me. "We get them from butterfly farms who ship them to us in the pupa stage when they are easy to transport. Once they get to us, they hatch. They may mate while they are with us but we don't keep any host plants for their young. They live several weeks, unless they are a monarch or other migratory species. Those live up to nine months."

Wide-eyed children walk amidst the butterflies. "Don't be afraid if one lands on you," cautions a museum worker. "But don't try to touch them. If one lands on you, I will remove it." The children, oblivious to cautions, reach their plump hands toward the delicate creatures.

"Gentle, gentle," chides a mother.

"See how beautiful," entices a worker. "We put out special food for them and they like it very much."

Gently fluttering from floor to ceiling, the butterflies flit plant to plant and occasionally land on a visitor.

"Stay very still," coaches the worker. "Stay still and don't do anything sudden. I'll move our little friend along."

Artist Dates, like this one, fire the imagination. They spark whimsy. They encourage play. Since art is about "the play of ideas," Artist Dates feed our work. They gently replenish the inner well. Art is an image-using system and Artist Dates restock our supply of images. The softly folding brightly colored wings, like tiny stained-glass windows, may not be an image we will use directly but they feed our inner artist, awakening a sense of wonder.

The gray sky grows grayer still. No yellow jackets patrol the upper branches of the tree beneath my writing-room window. It is too cool for rooftop picnics. Holiday revelers stay indoors. Turned back upon myself, I leaf through a butterfly book, the booty of my recent Artist Date. As the gray day closes down to dusk, I let myself read.

Everybody's an artist. Everybody's God. It's just that they're inhibited.

YOKO ONO

Divining Rod

Art is transformational. We do not make it as therapy and yet it is profoundly therapeutic. As we work with our creativity tools—Morning Pages, Artist Dates, walks—we are ourselves worked on by the Great Creator. Many of the changes that are wrought are very subtle, so subtle we may let them pass without noticing. Now you are asked to take note.

Take pen in hand. You are asked to witness your own transformation. I will give you a brief list of questions to start you off. Have you reorganized your living space? Have you thrown anything away? Has your color sense shifted? Has your relationship to music shifted? Do you find yourself being more plainspoken? Have there been any shifts in your intimate relationship? Have you experienced any difference in your energy? Have you experienced a weight gain or weight loss? Have you relinquished—or seriously thought about relinquishing—any other "bad"

I saw the angel in the marble and carved until I set him free.

MICHELANGELO

God is beauty.

ST. FRANCIS OF ASSISI

habit? Are you conscious of having more choices in your daily life? Has your relationship to a Higher Power altered? Are you more comfortable with your spirituality? Is it more a fact of your everyday life?

As you write, many other changes may occur to you. You may exercise more or differently. Your sleep habits may have shifted. You might be remembering dreams with more clarity. You might have lost your taste for junk food. Be alert for all forms of transformation. You are your own butterfly. What further changes can you envision?

The outer world, with all its phenomena, is filled with divine splendor. But we must have experienced the divine within ourselves before we can hope to discover it within our environment.

RUDOLF STEINER

CHECK-IN

1. **How many days this week did you do your Morning Pages?** If you skipped a day, why did you skip it? How was the experience of writing them for you? Are you experiencing more clarity? A wider range of emotions? A greater sense of detachment, purpose, and calm? Did anything surprise you? Is there a "repeating" issue asking to be dealt with?
2. **Did you do your Artist Date this week?** Did you note an improved sense of well-being? What did you do and how did it feel? Remember, Artist Dates can be difficult and you may need to coax yourself into taking them.
3. **Did you get out on your Weekly Walk?** How did that feel? What emotions or insights surfaced for you? Were you able to walk more than once? What did your walk do for your optimism and sense of perspective?
4. **Were there any other issues this week that felt significant to you in your self-discovery?** Describe them.

Uncovering a Sense of Perseverance

We are stronger than we know. Like deep wells, we have a capacity for sustained creative action. Our lost dreams can come home to us. By now you are familiar with the use of creativity tools. This week asks you to recommit to continued self-nurturance. Remember, creativity flourishes in a place of safety and acceptance. Focus this week on creating a healthy environment for your inner artist.

Dreams

By the calendar, summer is here. Tell that to the weather, which is cool, gray, and dim. In the Midwest, it is raining. Those storms move toward us. The sky this afternoon is "threatening." By evening, it will deliver on its threat. Rain will come and with it thunder and lightning. Charlotte, Emma's little West Highland terrier, has recently developed a terror of storms. When the thunder starts, so will her shaking. She will shake and quake until the storm has spent itself. There is no consoling her. She knows the storm is bigger than we are and any words of consolation are just empty murmurings. "We are all right. We are fine," I can tell her, but she does not trust the fates. I cannot comfort her.

Trusting the fates is learned behavior for most of us. Like Charlotte, we shake in the face of forces greater than ourselves. And yet, as we suffer through storm after storm, it becomes apparent that our fears do nothing to make it better. The gods do not demand our fears as bribes for our survival. Our fears are just

All writing is dreaming.

JORGE LUIS BORGES

needless suffering. We may as well elect to have faith. We may as well choose to be optimists. We can and do survive our storms. "This will pass, " I tell myself of my recent emotional turbulence.

For artists, optimism is a great advantage. It is too easy to buy into pessimism, to romance the many odds so clearly stacked against us. It is easy to give in and to give up. It is easy to declare ourselves beaten and to resign ourselves to a life of "if only's." But is it really so easy to let dreams die? Dreams are hardy. They are stubborn as weeds. We may think we have uprooted our dreams only to have a dream push upward again, daring us, one more time, to believe in the unbelievable. As long as a dream lives, so does a chance of its manifesting. We can cooperate with our dreams or we can fight them. Our dreams are tenacious. They don't just fade away.

Every time we make a piece of art, we dream of its coming to a fruitful maturity. We write the book in the hopes that it will be published. We paint the picture in hopes that it will be seen. Recently, I wrote a novel that has been making the rounds and "nearly" but not quite selling. My agent has finally given the novel back to me. "Something must be missing," she has said. "But I do not know quite what."

If I want the novel to live—and I do—then I must do the work necessary to help it. I have given the novel to four select readers. I have asked them all to look for ways in which the book could be better. I have read the book myself, searching for the same elusive something. All of us are like detectives, sleuthing to make the book better. Now my ego doesn't like any of this. My ego wants to say the book is fine the way it is and that the editors who are not buying it lack vision. Barring that, my ego would like to pack the book away, give up on it, give it a gentle burial in a bottom desk drawer and go on to other work. But that is not what is called for. What is called for is faith. Faith enough to work further. Faith enough to invest more. Faith enough to risk again. Dreams demand that we have faith in them. If they are brave enough to live, we must be brave enough to assist them. We must one more time try on their behalf. And so I spend my

I can imagine myself on my death-bed, spent utterly with lust to touch the next world, like a boy asking for his first kiss from a woman.

ALEISTER CROWLEY

evenings reading my novel. I press my friends into service to help me improve.

"I don't see any big something to change," I complain to one friend.

"Maybe there is no one big something. Maybe what you are looking at is a series of tiny tweaks. Maybe there is no one monster scene to be rewritten. Maybe you just need to improve many places just a little bit. Tiny shifts in tone may be your answer."

"Oh, no. I hate that!"

My friend clucks a little in sympathy. She is herself a writer and she knows the difficulty of what she is asking me to do.

My literary agent calls me on the phone. She sounds cautious, as if she may have just phoned up someone as volatile as a hand grenade.

"I just want to know how it is going," she says cautiously. "I am wondering if you have found anything to change yet or if you are still looking."

"Still looking," I tell her. "Although I have read the book again and I am now in the process of making a detailed outline. My readers are all finishing up this week."

"Well, good. I just wanted to see if you were okay."

"I'm okay."

I want to explain to her that I am like Charlotte, the little dog. I am shaking and quaking faced with changes I do not know quite how to make. I am certain that this round of work will be the storm that does me in and so I quaver before the task at hand. On the other hand, what is my alternative? To just give up? To pack away the novel that is almost good enough and never give it the dignity of one last try? I have been writing for too long not to believe that with help I can write better. I have had too many books improve in the rewrite process. I have gone back to the drawing board too many times with good results. As much as my ego would love to claim that the novel was perfect as is, I know enough to know better and so I am willing, although I resent it, to try one more time.

A storm moves in from the west. Right on queue, Charlotte

The sight of the stars makes me dream.

Vincent van Gogh

Oh, one world at a time!

Henry David Thoreau

starts shaking. I queue up my novel and start rolling through the pages, making a tweak here and a tweak there. "Charlotte," I tell the little dog, "we will be fine."

And I believe it, whether Charlotte does or not. This round of changes will not kill me and if I am very lucky, I will edge ahead a little bit. My novel will get stronger and better. It will survive this round of surgery and grow stronger from it. In any case, I as an artist will grow stronger and better, having the self-respect that comes from being willing one more time to invest in my dreams.

We do not write as we want, but as we can.

W. SOMERSET MAUGHAM

Divining Rod

A life in the arts is not a life without detours and delays. Sometimes a project must be set to one side while another project—or projects—comes to the fore. Busy with our daily lives, we may let certain dreams go unattended. And yet, such dreams do not really die. They wait patiently, sometimes for many years, for us to one more time turn our focus their direction. Now is a time to excavate a "forgotten" dream. Expect your dreams to burn a little as they reawaken. We often feel a shock of pain as a dream reactivates.

Take pen in hand. Answer the following questions. Have you ever set aside a dream related to writing? Have you ever set aside a dream related to the visual arts? Have you ever set aside a dream related to music? Have you ever set aside a dream related to public speaking or theater? A dream related to film or television? Have you set aside a dream related to dance or movement? A dream related to the culinary arts? To a handicraft? To photography? These questions may spur you to remember a dream that is not covered by any of these topics.

Now ask yourself, what led you to set your dream aside? Are you ready to one more time pursue this dream? What gentle action could you take? If you once wrote many poems but for years have not written any, you might try your hand at a simple poem. Or you might attend an open mike and hear what other people are writing. You might buy yourself an anthology of new poets. You might go to hear an established poet read. Choose a first step for you that feels "doable." Be modest. In reentering an arena, do not set the jumps too high. You do not want to scare yourself. Allow yourself the grace of being an absolute beginner.

Company

Heavy clouds bank in the west. The sunset is a few stripes of cerise. It rained then cleared then rained again. More "weather" is moving toward us. The air smells of ozone. A pushy wind whips the trees. On the street people hurry home, eager to be "in" before the storm. It is a good night for reading.

Go oft to the house of thy friend, for weeds choke the unused path.

Ralph Waldo Emerson

The table by my bed is stacked high with books, many of them written by friends of mine. It gives me pleasure at night to curl up with a book written by someone I know. There they are on the page. It is almost like visiting with them. Lately, I have been rereading my friend Sonia Choquette. Her books brim with optimism. I long to brim with it myself. This morning, by e-mail, I heard from novelist Tim Farrington. Normally we write each other once a week, sometimes more. Recently, he has been radio silent for nearly six weeks. Now he has shown up with a good explanation. He writes:

"Hi there, my long-lost comrade, and please forgive my disappearance. I've been homestretching it on this novel and good for not much else. Two short anticlimactic chapters left, I should

Sooner or later you've heard all your best friends have to say. Then comes the tolerance of real love.

NED ROREM

be done by next week. Then I'll probably just cry for a week, and then take a good long look around and see what's left of my so-called life. I feel turned inside out, thrashed, and twisted like a wet shirt, but I'll be hung out to dry soon enough, God willing and the river don't rise. I'm looking forward to catching up with you. I've missed us."

The brief missive was good to get. I have missed Tim's company, too, although I did know where he was—"writing." My friend So-nia is just entering the tunnel known as "the next book." For the next several months her emotional weather will be determined by how it went during her day at the page. I am her "catcher's mitt." She calls me daily to check in on her progress. I cheer her on.

This morning, when I had my phone turned off, I got a mes-sage from another friend, another writer. "Ah, Julia. I am glad to hear you're not picking up. Mornings are sacred to us writers, I think . . ." She went on to propose a lengthy walk at midday to-morrow, a sortie to be sandwiched in between our writing schedules. I am eager to see her, eager for the easy intimacy of a longish walk. There is something comforting in spending a lit-tle time with another working writer. My friend has recently launched herself down the chute into another novel. On our walk, there will be four of us present: the writer and her novel, myself and my book in progress.

Our creations are like children. They can be pushy about what they want and what they need. If we neglect them, they neglect us. If we ignore them, they ignore us. Sometimes they sulk and pout and cry and squabble until they've got our atten-tion. In the end, we have to do what they want. It's the only way to make peace with them.

Making peace with our creations is an artist's primary task. We may be mothers. We may be wives or husbands. We may be colleagues and friends but we are first and foremost artists and we owe our creations our loyalty. If they don't get it, they rebel.

"I was a low-maintenance husband," recalls Tim Farrington. "All that was really required to keep me happy was a few undisturbed hours of writing time. If I could get up early and get my hours in, I was a happy camper. I didn't ask for much more than that."

I am divorced now for ten years and my daughter is grown. My days revolve around writing. I get in two sessions daily, one in the morning, one in the late afternoon. If I miss a session, I feel it. My creation throws a tantrum until attended to.

Last week I had lunch with a fellow writer. She was a writer of the political persuasion. She often serves on committees for worthy causes. We met at the Popover Café, named for its specialty. She arrived looking a bit the worse for wear. She had just come from a meeting.

"How do you do it?" I asked her. "All that you do?"

"I write in Connecticut," she told me. "I go there for long, green weekends. It's very quiet there." She rubbed wearily at her eyes.

"But you live in New York most of the time, don't you?"

"Yes, but if I don't get to the country on the weekend, I really miss it. I need to write." And for her writing in New York is difficult.

Anywhere that becomes too pell-mell can become the enemy. New York, which tends to the pell-mell, can be difficult on the artists in its midst. They must learn to live defensively. They need to learn to set a productive schedule amid the many attractions vying for their attention.

I need to set my own pace. And that pace is not this city's. I need to take long walks and have great bolts of quiet and solitude. I need to turn off the phone and turn down most of my invitations. It can be very seductive, the business of acting like an artist rather than actually being one.

Rain is pelting down. The bed beckons with its piles of pillows and comforting blankets. From the bedside table, I select *Your Heart's Desire,* a book by my friend Sonia. In Chicago, tonight, she is writing. In New York, tonight, I read what she has written. It is a dark and stormy night, but I spend it happily.

It's the friends you can call up at 4 a.m. that matter.

MARLENE DIETRICH

I am treating you as my friend, asking you to share my present minuses in the hope that I can ask you to share my future plusses.

KATHERINE MANSFIELD

Divining Rod

It does us good to keep the company of our friends. It does us good to have them present even when they are absent. By consciously cherishing our connections, we strengthen those bonds.

Purchase a small photo album or scrapbook. You are out to create a gallery of your friends and their projects. Start with photographs. (If you find that you do not have pictures of certain friends, ask for them.) Mount a photo and set aside additional pages for other images that speak to you of that friend.

Set aside a stack of magazines and search through them for images that remind you of your friends. Label these images with your friend's name, clip the image and mount it in your album. You may wish to include postcards or letters that you have received. You might include a playbill from a joint night at the theater. Or the pass that allowed the two of you to go backstage at a concert. What you are after is a mental snapshot of your relationship. You are aiming at rounding up "company" for yourself and your artist. Like a yearbook for grown-ups, it will remind you of the good times you have had and the dreams that you shared.

Your lost friends are not dead, but gone before, advanced a stage or two upon that road which you must travel in the steps they trod.

ARISTOPHANES

Staying Green

The park is green and verdant. Swans glide on the lake. Flotillas of ducks poke amid the reeds. An egret stands one-legged. In Turtle Pond, turtles are plentiful, large ones and smaller ones, poking their heads above the water's surface, nosing for tidbits. I stand at water's edge, talking with a distinguished writer. We are discussing the need for refreshment, for self-nurturing in the writer's day.

"It is fantastic that we have this park," the writer begins. "It's a window back onto the natural world and when we are in synch with nature, it is easier to write. Back at home, I go for bike rides. I glide out daily and pedal along the shore. I can go twenty miles along the bike path. Then I head home again and write."

The writer's novels are known for their meticulous research, for their deep grounding in facts. It is easy to see how, with her love of the natural world, she could have a fondness for specificity, a hunger for the small, telling detail.

"The last time I wrote, I had an interesting experience," she continues. "My inner writer said to me, 'No more research.' I was alarmed. I thought it meant I was being lazy. 'Are you sure?' I asked myself. 'Trust me,' the answer came back. 'I know far more than you give me credit for. Let me use a little bit of what I know.' And so, I wrote a book largely without research. I leaned into my imagination. I invented the kind of small facts I normally observed. It was challenging and it was fun. I had been looking for a way to put fun back into my work."

The distinguished writer's huge success has given a shape to her work life that occasionally feels onerous. Her books are contracted far ahead of time and eagerly awaited. Write them she must, not only to serve her public but also to serve her Muse. "I must write," she says. "When I am not writing, I am not happy. When I am writing well, everything else falls into place. I am a lot like a dog that turns around and around trying to get comfortable. I am like that until I settle into a writing routine. Once I do, I am fine."

Once a year, the writer produces a large novel. Her books typically debut at number one on *The New York Times* bestseller list. She is a cottage industry. There are numerous demands for her time and attention. She must battle to keep time and focus for her writing. She must keep the world at bay and live with her work.

"Right now I am at the beginning of a new book and my relationship with the book is rather formal. Every morning, I wake up and get properly dressed. I want to show the book I am

To be capable of steady friendship or lasting love are the two greatest proofs, not only of goodness of heart, but of strength of mind.

WILLIAM HAZLITT

respectful. Later on, once we know each other, I'll be able to tumble out of bed and write in pajamas, but not just yet."

The writer peers over the rail to see a flotilla of baby ducks cruise past. A butterfly flits close and lands on the back of my hand. "Will you look at that," the writer breathes, clearly delighted to take in whatever nature has to offer. Six times a week, the writer goes to a gym. There, solo, she works out for an hour, pushing her body through a grueling routine. As a result, the writer is lean and fit—just like her prose. "I found I needed the endorphins," she explains. She does not add that since the territory she writes about is dark, she may need endorphins more than most people. She must practice a gentle vigilance to keep positive energy around her. She does best, she has discovered, when she is able to keep the drama on the page.

"When I am not writing, I create chaos," she laughs ruefully. "I make all sorts of dramas to distract myself from the fact that I am not working. I buy and sell entire houses. I uproot myself—and it's all because I am not working well."

From under the surface of the pond, a dark bird suddenly bursts forth, a minnow clutched in its beak. The baby ducklings scatter. "Oooh," breathes the writer, "that is how it is in life, isn't it? Suddenly, from out of nowhere—" she breaks off and laughs. She has caught herself writing out loud.

"I think place is important," she volunteers suddenly. "Sometimes a book wants to be written in a certain place and nothing else will satisfy it. Take me last week. I was writing really well and I was holed up in a hotel room where I didn't care if the furniture was scratched." This week, she was in her posh New York apartment and she found herself circling again, just like a dog trying to make a bed.

"I want to learn to be comfortable here," she said firmly. "I want to learn to settle in. I don't want to keep it up anymore, this business of coming to New York and driving myself frantic so I just have to flee. This time, I need to set my own pace."

That pace will involve park time and gym time. It will involve steering clear of too many "boast and toast" high-powered

In our era, the road to holiness necessary passes through the world of action.

DAG HAMMARSKJÖLD

dinners. It will mean turning off the phone and turning down the volume. The writer recognizes this and is prepared.

"I can't do too many extroverted things. As a writer, I need to be alone—alone with my character. Lately, I have been saying to myself, instead of thinking of writing as something that you must do by yourself, why not think of it as time that you get to spend with your character? I love my character. Sometimes I wish she were real so that we could just hang out."

To the writer's many fans, her character is real. They send long personal letters wanting her professional advice and guidance. Sometimes at book signings, lips tremble and tears are shed—the character is so present and so real to people. The writer goes home drained.

"I am really determined to get it right," said the writer. "I think I have to find a way to find compassion for myself, for all my fears."

Meanwhile, to the casual eye, the writer is larger than life, jetting here and there, place to place, restlessly, always seeking out the right spot to write the next book, the place that her writer wants to stay in for a while.

"You know, New York is not a bad place, if you get to the park enough," I tell her.

Divining Rod

Our inner artist likes to be courted. Remember that no matter how mature our work may be, our artist is still like a youngster, vulnerable and easily discouraged. As our artist's adult trainer, we must be alert for any signs that our artist is feeling soured and out of sorts. It is up to us to coddle our artist when that is what's called for.

There should be less talk . . . Take a broom and clean someone's house. That says enough.

Mother Teresa

When I say artist, I don't mean in the narrow sense of the word—but the man who is building things—creating, molding the earth—whether it be the plains of the west—or the iron ore of Penn, it's all a big game of construction— some with the brush—some with the shovel—some choose a pen.

JACKSON POLLOCK

When our work feels difficult, it is sometimes good to feel a little spoiled. In a perfect world, our friends would spoil us and so would our family or significant other. Ours is not a perfect world but we can make it feel much better by taking small actions in our own behalf.

Take pen in hand. Number from one to ten. List ten small actions or purchases that you could make that would tell you in no uncertain terms that you were "seen" and cared about. Be specific. What precisely makes you feel spoiled? This list need not be expensive or extravagant, merely thoughtful. Most of my students find they are cheap with themselves about money or time or both. This exercise asks you to spend a little of both commodities on your own behalf. For example: I could buy good new stationery; I could take a really long hot bath; I could get a pint of raspberries; I could buy a fast-writing pen; I could take myself to the pet store and spend time with the birds; I could let myself call my friend Laura just to catch up . . .

Working

The day is silvery gray. Rain is one more time moving in from the west. I have spent the morning receiving Midwestern reports of all kinds. My friend Sonia is in the water on her new book, writing up a blue streak, two chapters in two days. My sister Libby is painting despite her sore arm, working on a new oil portrait with a new technique she doesn't feel she has totally mastered. Both of them report in that the weather they are experiencing is fine— particularly the emotional weather. There is nothing that makes an artist happier than a good day spent working.

"I am so relieved that I am finally writing," Sonia says. "This morning I had to spend an hour and a half in a waiting room, waiting for a doctor's appointment. Instead of being bored or angry, I just started to write. I wrote nearly twenty longhand pages, most of an entire new chapter and, I think, a good one. Then, after all that writing, the appointment went well, too. I am having an excellent day. I may just sit out on my front porch and write a little more."

"I got the glass yesterday for my trout table," Libby says. "With the glass in place, it really is like looking into a koi pond. Then, too, I said to myself that I really needed to get past my reticence regarding my new oil technique. I was sort of waiting for the day when it would be suddenly easy." She laughs at herself, a little embarrassed. "I decided to stop waiting for it to get easy and to just let myself do it. The minute I did that, of course it did all become easier. I hate to be the one to say it, but I really like the work I did today. I feel that I am really getting somewhere, and that feels great."

I would love to feel great, but I do not. Last night was another sleepless night, and so today I face my workday already fatigued. I prefer writing when I am fresh, but I have learned to write no matter what. And so, I head myself to the page and put in my time there. I scoop the barrel for images to use and I remind myself that it is time for me to take another Artist Date in order to keep the images fresh. On the phone with my opera singer friend Daisy, I am able to report in that work on *Magellan* is going well and that my piano time has now extended itself to include a half hour's practicing. I am still working in Level One books, but I am learning now to read bass clef, which is a triumph for me. I am ever so slowly and ever so slightly edging ahead. My Morning Pages are wan and fragmented these days, but not so wan that they fail to note my tiny scintilla of progress.

For artists, few things feel better than a sense of propulsion. The feeling of forward motion in our art brings us a deep and abiding happiness, carrying with it feelings of self-esteem. When we are procrastinating—"waiting for it to become easier"—we inevitably feel bad about ourselves. Nothing takes the place of actually doing the work, of being able to say at day's end, "I accomplished that."

Art is good when it springs from necessity.

NEAL CASSADY

Art is an absolute mistress; she will not be coquetted with or slighted; she requires the most entire self-devotion, and she repays with grand triumphs.

CHARLOTTE SAUNDERS
CUSHMAN

So much of being an artist boils down to: "Just do it." There is little point in analyzing our resistance, searching out deep reasons for why we cannot work. It is far better to face the resistance directly, to call a friend and say, "I need to work and I don't want to work, and I am going to work now for fifteen minutes." Signing up for a modest fifteen or twenty minutes usually gets us past our Inner Censor. It is such a slight amount of time that the Censor can be hoodwinked into thinking that it doesn't really matter. If we were to say to our Censor, "Now I am going to work for an hour or two," we would have a real fight on our hands. Because we say, "I'm just going to try a few minutes," our Censor can be gulled into letting us get to the page or the easel. A Censor has a great sense of self-importance. When we make our work small, humble, and doable, the Censor doesn't know how to fight us.

In order to be a good artist, I need to be willing to be a bad artist. Stalled on my book, I have to be willing finally to write anything—good, bad, or indifferent. The minute I am willing to write badly instead of well, then I am able to write freely. Libby at her easel, facing down her mastery of her new technique, was eye to eye with the same ogre. As soon as she was willing to paint badly, she was freed to paint very well. Humility was the door to mastery as it often is.

As artists we must remember that our work is about "the play of ideas." When we become too serious about our work, when we demand perfection, our work rebels. It is when we are able to play a little that our work takes on verve and elasticity.

"I think our artist is naughty," explains my friend the distinguished writer. "I think the part of us that creates is mischievous and defiant. When we put our artist on too tight a leash, it fights us like a spirited animal. When we allow it a little rope, it often cooperates with us nicely."

In other words, our artist can be tricked.

I think of my own arrangement with Daisy. We have made a deal with each other that we will both go to the keys and write a little bit of new music every day. I call her and say, "Daisy, I am on my way to the keys," and then I go to the keys. I am working on *Magellan,* filling in little gaps in the story line. I go to the keys and listen for melody. I am seldom at the keys for more than a few minutes before something, some tendril of music begins seeping through my resistance. Willing to settle for the tiniest scraps, I take down what I am hearing. There are many days when the small Something reveals itself to be a part of a much larger Something. *Magellan,* after all, is a grand story and its scope has room for large as well as small.

When I have finished with my time at the keys, I phone Daisy back. Usually, I get her service. "Daisy, I have just gone to the keys," I tell her. A little later, my phone will ring. "It's Daisy. I have written my two measures for the day." For the most part, our messages are snared by machines and we do not get to actually talk to each other and yet there is a delicious feeling of complicity. Daisy is setting fragments of poetry to music. She is building a scaffolding for her own soaring voice. It is wonderful to be a part of her architecture, and she tells me that it is thrilling to her to be a part of *Magellan.*

As artists, we make things out of nothing. We invent from the whole cloth of our imaginations. When I allow myself, I can feel the magic in this. When I allow myself, I can fall just a little bit in love with the artist that I am.

Rain moves in from the west. Charlotte, the little West Highland terrier, begins to shake at the approach of thunder and lightning. Tiger Lily, taking in the weather, gives an ominous growl. My plan at the moment is to use the storm for verisimilitude. I will go to the keys where Magellan is caught in a storm at sea. We will make music together.

If we are to change our world view, images have to change. The artist now has a very important job to do. He is not a little peripheral figure entertaining rich people, he is really needed.

DAVID HOCKNEY

Divining Rod

Very often our progress is made in such tiny increments that we fail to see and note it. Focused on what we "should" do and what we haven't done yet, we often turn a blind eye to our own ongoing accomplishments. It is a rare day that passes without our having done something right.

Take pen in hand. Number from one to five. Finish the phrase, "I am doing better at _____" five times. Your changes for the positive can be very slight. They will still make a large difference over time.

Take pen in hand again. Answer the following questions. Are you writing your Morning Pages? Taking your Artist Dates? Getting out for walks? Are you taking the time to check in with yourself? Are you doing better at contact with your friends? Has your comfort level with spiritual tools improved? Do you find yourself striving more consciously to be optimistic? Are you aware of having more choices? Do you find yourself playing the victim less often? Learn to give yourself credit where credit is due—and, in many cases, overdue.

The reward of art is not fame or success but intoxication.

CYRIL CONNOLLY

Consistency

At last, a warm, clear, and sunny day. The park is filled with casual strollers. Up by the reservoir, the runners make their rounds, nodding hello to one another. Many of them run at the same time each day and they know one another by sight. A number of runners have dogs in tow. Tiger Lily and Charlotte eye the running dogs with interest but no envy. They prefer the more leisurely pace that Emma and I set as we walk our slower circuit. Squirrels scamper near. Our dogs take the bait, skittering to the end of their long leashes. They cannot quite catch the squirrels who chatter busily from halfway up a tree trunk. Frustrated, the dogs leap at the tree's base. We walk on.

As artists, we do well to practice consistency. Our mad dashes after the squirrels of inspiration leave us frustrated and at our wits' end. There is much to be said for a slower and more leisurely pursuit of ideas. There is so much talk of creative "breakthroughs" that many of us expect our creativity to be dramatic. This is seldom the case. Very occasionally, we will have a flash of insight or intuition but more often we will experience a slow and steady course. Our creativity resembles sunlight more than lightning. Even in dark times, this is true.

My own dark time seems to be reaching an end. Despite my laundry list of fears, I am sleeping most nights. Despite my still turbulent emotions, my Morning Pages have more coherence. I am not yet optimistic, but my days do seem to be lit by a steadier lamp. One more time, the simple slogans of sobriety have done their good service. One day at a time, practicing "Easy does it," I have managed to muddle through. Now the light at the end of the tunnel is visible to me. I am on the mend. I am growing steadier. With every night's sleep and every day's writing, the abyss seems further and further removed. I am grateful. I focus on the light. "The key is consistency," my Guidance assures me. Every day when I listen for right action, the message is the same. "Be consistent. Stick to your grid." Obedient, I write, walk, and listen for further instructions.

Obedient, I try to write three pages a day. I listen for insight and write down what it is that I hear. The process is much more like taking dictation than it is like thinking something up. The directions are important here. When I take something *down,* it is an easy process. When I strain to think something *up,* I am striving for something that may be beyond my reach. And so it is that I write three pages daily. My job is less writing than listening. I keep an appointment with the Muse. We meet for an agreed upon time and quantity.

We work in the dark—we do what we can—we give what we have. Our doubt is our passion, and our passion is our task. The rest is the madness of art.

HENRY JAMES

I believe we are free, within limits, and yet there is an unseen hand, a guiding angel, that somehow, like a submerged propeller, drives us on.

RABINDRANATH TAGORE

When I teach creative writing, I urge my students to write Morning Pages, the daily three pages of longhand writing that primes the pump. Morning Pages miniaturize the Censor and train it to stand aside. When the Pages are completed, there is time for creative writing to step to the fore. The Censor is quiet. The Muse becomes talkative. We meet the Muse and take down what it has to say.

As a rule, I urge my students to try for three pages of new writing a day. It is not too daunting an amount. The key to its success is its gentle consistency. No mad gallops after elusive quarry, just a simple, doable routine.

"Julia, you make it so nondramatic," a student once complained. A poet, he had a long history of drama around his writing and he resisted the idea that writing could be consistent and even easy. Against his better judgment, he began the practice of Morning Pages and he quickly became hooked on them. From there, it was just a short step to trying his "real" writing. Imagine his surprise when good ideas began to come to him easily and daily. Where was his drama?

"I am writing on a regular basis now and I have to say that I cannot really tell the difference in caliber between one of the poems that was 'easy' to catch and one of the poems crafted my old way in a sudden fit of inspiration. To tell the truth, I think the new poems hold up very well. And it's sort of a relief not to have to 'act like' a poet in order to be a poet."

When we commit to creation on a consistent basis, we begin to dismantle some of our old ideas about artists. For one thing, regular work tends to improve the mood. We are less tortured and may even catch ourselves being sunny and optimistic. No longer restless, irritable, and discontent, we find ourselves suddenly user-friendly.

"Julia, you have wrecked my tantrums and tamed my temper," one writer, a recent convert to the Morning Pages, complains. "I used to be able to work myself up into a good fit when I wasn't writing. Now I am at least writing three pages daily and that seems to be enough to siphon off steam. I usually write three pages in the morning and then later, in early afternoon, I settle in and do my 'real' writing. In the interim, I no longer get on the phone and cause trouble. Some of my friends think I have had a spiritual awakening."

When artists are working regularly, they are spiritually centered. The act of making art is a spiritual act and our daily exposure to this realm does have an impact on our personality. It does not matter what language we use to describe it. Art puts us in touch with a power greater than ourselves. This conscious contact brings us a sense of optimism and grace. As we sense that there is a benevolent Something inclined toward helping us and our work, we begin to feel a sense of companionship. Higher forces are at our side. We are not alone.

There is a light evening wind. The runners around the reservoir lift their faces to the breeze. Fireflies glint in the undergrowth. The evening's light is turning golden. Skyscrapers are gilded by the setting sun. For the second time today, we have taken our dogs to the park. Tiger Lily is living up to her nickname, "Tiger." When a Jack Russell puppy makes its way toward us, Tiger Lily crouches, ready to spring. "No, girl," I tell her and give a tug at her leash. Reluctantly, she allows the puppy to pass, but not without a growl and a quick pirouette at the end of her lead.

Out of the crowd of joggers, a neighbor comes striding toward us. Her face is flushed and she is grinning. "I had the *best* run," she announces. I give her a grin of recognition. With a gay little wave, she is on her way. She runs daily, just as I write. In our own way, we are each athletes. For us both, a gentle consistency is key.

Nothing in the world can take the place of persistence. Persistence and determination are omnipotent.

Calvin Coolidge

Divining Rod

Over the period of time you have spent with this book, you have experimented with a variety of tools, some familiar to you already and some new. It is my hope that you have been able to experience a growing sense of your own creative power. This may manifest as excitement or restlessness, optimism, or irritability. You have freed up considerably more creative energy, and it is up to you to channel it productively. Choose now a selection of tools that you believe you will be able to work with consistently.

Take pen in hand. On paper, in writing, commit yourself to the tools that you will continue to use. "I commit myself to the continued use of Morning Pages," you might write. Or, "I commit myself to continued Artist Dates." Or, "I vow to continue my walks." Beyond the big tools, you may have benefited from some of the smaller and homelier ones. If so, pledge to continue their use. "I will continue to take quiet times in a sacred space." "I will make a regular practice of mending." "I will continue to call my friends for prayers and encouragement." "I will continue to call my friends and listen actively to their dreams and hopes."

When you have completed your list of choices for continued work, contact one of your "believing mirrors." Enlist your friend's support in what it is you plan to undertake. You might wish to inaugurate a further course of creative studies—perhaps in the company of your friend.

A little sleuthing will usually yield an Artist Way group in your area. A search on the Web will reveal communities working together on *The Artist's Way, The Vein of Gold, Walking in This World,* and *The Right to Write.* Any of these courses can be pursued through the combination of essays and tasks that you have just mastered. Additionally, you may find yourself devising your own creativity tasks.

When I go out to teach, I am frequently met by students who offer, "I used your tools and I made this _____." I have been presented with novels, children's books, gift cards,

What I did have, which others perhaps didn't, was a capacity for sticking at it, which really is the point, not the talent at all. You have to stick at it.

DORIS LESSING

DVD's, jewelry, and CD's. It is my delight that tools from my creativity kit have so often proved useful to others. It is my hope that you, in turn, will share these tools with still others. The Artist's Way is tribal and we all can contribute.

A classic is a book that has never finished saying all it has to say.

ITALO CALVINO

Just Do It

The day is back to cool and gray. Resolute runners make their way around the reservoir, pigeons flapping from their path. When breezes stir the trees, a shower of silvery drops fall to earth. It rained all night and in the early hours of the morning. Not to be deterred the runners are out in bright yellow slickers. They are ready to run in any weather and some of their best runs occur on days like today. It is a matter of grit. They do not ask to be coddled by sunshine.

As artists, we, too, need to work through many kinds of weather. It is lovely when we have a day of halcyon weather, when we wake up eager to work and have a day stretching out ahead of us filled with space and time. More often, we will feel resistant. We will move grudgingly and under half steam. Some of our best work is done under the least favorable conditions. We grab twenty minutes to write, telling ourselves it is barely worth the attempt and our sentences come flying to the page with winged feet. We go to the easel knowing we are going to be grabbing a few quick strokes before another interruption looms, but with those quick strokes we execute a tricky part of the portrait. It is done before we know it.

So much of being an artist involves that Nike slogan, "Just do it." So much good comes from our just showing up. Of course it is seductive, the idea that we will one day be in the mood, and we will work that day like a "real" artist. But a great deal of real art is made under the radar. We barely know we are working. We just suit up and show up and grab what moments we can, and it is only in cozy retrospect that we see the level of skill we were able to muster. It is humbling, the degree to which we are like automatons. Our art moves through us despite us.

So much of being an artist has to do with consistency and continuity. It isn't very glorious, the day-in-and-day-out labor of art. Books are made a page at a time which means a page at a time we must go to the typewriter. Symphonies are written measure by measure. "Just do it" works for all arts, lowbrow to highbrow. Right now, my friend the opera singer is learning to write music. I get a message on my machine, just checking in, "I wrote my two measures." Two measures doesn't seem like much but by the end of a month, the fragments will add up to a song cycle—glorious music that did not exist before my friend became humble enough to "try."

There is art in humility. There is art in the attempt to make art. Daily, I go to the keyboard and work on writing the saga of *Magellan*. Yesterday, I wrote a storm at sea. Waves crashed. Timbers groaned. The deck was slippery and the footing treacherous. I tried to convey all of this a note at a time. I could hear the music in my head. Whether I could get it to the page was the question. The task seemed daunting—but I could try and I did. When Emma, my collaborator, came in she could hear the storm I was striving for. "It just needs some of this," she said and laid down a few tumultuous chords. Magellan walked the decks.

The best, most beautiful things in the world cannot be seen, or even touched. They must be felt with the heart.

HELEN KELLER

As an artist, I write Morning Pages daily. After I have finished writing them, I sit quietly asking for Guidance. Again and again the Guidance comes back to me, "You need to stay steady as she goes." Again and again I am sent back to the page to try one more time to take down what I hear. There is no dramatic breakthrough where I say, "Ah hah! I have made it!" Instead, my work unfolds a page at a time, edging forward just a little. I listen, learn, and write.

"How are you doing?" my friend Natalie Goldberg, the famed writing teacher, often asks me. I tell her that I am soldiering on, putting in a day at a time, a page at a time at my craft. "The important part is not to get tossed away," Natalie tells me. "The important part is to just keep at the work, no matter how hard or how daunting the work may feel."

Out at the reservoir, the runners move with heads bent, arms and legs smoothly pumping. Some of them are running through stiffness. Some of them are recovering from injuries. Not all of them are running easily or freely, but run they do. As a result of their running, many of them are lean and fit. Fitness is the by-product of their commitment, just as art is the by-product of an artist's commitment. Our skills are honed by the doing. What is done is often excellent, but it is excellent in passing. We take care of the quantity, leaving it to the Great Creator to take care of the quality. When we labor so in humility, great art is often born. Very often the work that will later seem to be our best will be the most hard won.

My friend the distinguished writer works daily. She loves to write, but it is not always easy for her. She writes as the runners run, in all weather.

"I just work"—that is the ethic that serves us best as artists. Although we seldom talk about it, so much of an artistic career is the long hours of duty, the hours where we simply show up. In this regard, artists are very much like athletes. We must learn to work despite mood. We must learn to work despite conditions. We must learn to work day in and day out because that is our commitment. Just as the runners circle the reservoir daily, I go to the typewriter. It is a luxury to be in the mood to write. It is a good day's work to simply write.

I have been simply writing for nearly four decades. Writing is a habit for me and that habit has been my saving grace as I have fought with my depression and my alcoholism. One day at a time, I have managed to get to the page. I have written, not always well, but faithfully. In black periods, even my Morning Pages have been difficult, fragmented, and sad. I have written them anyway, trusting that if I just didn't drink, and I just kept writing, something good would come of it. And it has.

What has come of it is a writer's life, a productive life char-

The Infinite has written its name on the heavens in shining stars, and on Earth in tender flowers.

JEAN PAUL RICHTER

acterized by steady productivity despite my breakdowns, despite my stretches of fragility when the hospital has loomed close. There are the "real" breakdowns and then there are the shadow breakdowns, like this one, when I have felt myself to have been unhinged but have managed to avoid hospitalization.

"Just show up," I have learned and I have practiced this advice in all types of emotional weather. It is daunting, sometimes, to glance back through Morning Pages and see how close I have teetered to the abyss, only backing off with the greatest of difficulty. But back off I have, hewing to my gentle grid of Morning Pages, Artist Dates, and Weekly Walks, getting myself to the page and to the piano. Working daily, I have managed to have a life that works. I have come to know myself as very tough and very delicate. My friends know me the same way.

And so it goes. A day at a time, my friends and I egg one another on a little bit. We cannot make art by committee, but we can enlist one another's support. We may work alone, but we are in it together—"it" being the artist's life.

Divining Rod

The creation of a thousand forests is in one acorn.

RALPH WALDO EMERSON

On my right-hand third finger, I wear a silver ring. I bought it many years ago in New Mexico, and it was purchased to symbolize my commitment to the artist's life. "To thine own self be true," my ring signifies. It is a constant, subtle reminder to myself to always live by my own values.

Art is a language of symbols. Gift yourself with a symbolic something that speaks to you of your identity as an artist. Choose the symbol that suits you personally. It may be a ring, a pendant, or a bracelet. It may be something else entirely. The dragon is the Chinese symbol for creativity. You might want a dragon shirt or robe or paperweight. You might designate an acorn as a symbol of creativity or a satiny river rock or seashell. There are as many symbols of creativity as there are forms of creativity. Select the symbol that speaks most clearly to your heart.

CHECK-IN

1. **How many days this week did you do your Morning Pages?** If you skipped a day, why did you skip it? How was the experience of writing them for you? Are you experiencing more clarity? A wider range of emotions? A greater sense of detachment, purpose, and calm? Did anything surprise you? Is there a "repeating" issue asking to be dealt with?

2. **Did you do your Artist Date this week?** Did you note an improved sense of well-being? What did you do and how did it feel? Remember, Artist Dates can be difficult and you may need to coax yourself into taking them.

3. **Did you get out on your Weekly Walk?** How did that feel? What emotions or insights surfaced for you? Were you able to walk more than once? What did your walk do for your optimism and sense of perspective?

4. **Were there any other issues this week that felt significant to you in your self-discovery?** Describe them.

Glance at the sun. See the moon and stars. Gaze at the beauty of the green earth. Now think.

HILDEGARD OF BINGEN

EPILOGUE

AS WE REACH THE END of this collection of essays and tasks, it is clear that there is no real end to the creative path. It is a spiral path. You circle back through the same issues, over and over, just at slightly different altitudes. You now have a spiritual toolkit, which you can use in perpetuity. The simplest of tools—Morning Pages, Artist Dates, and Walks—will yield large, on-going benefits. The smaller tools, when repeated alone or in a cluster, will bring surprising new results.

I have long envisioned The Artist's Way as a movement more than a solitary journey. It is easy to found a group and easy to find one, as well. Groups proliferate in cyberspace, as well as in your very own neighborhood. Using this book or others I have written on the creative process, join together to support one another's unfolding. There are Artist's Way groups that have been meeting for more than a decade and a half. As their members flourish, it is like watching a great garden grow. As we find the spiritual water necessary to our growth, we are far more colorful than we know.

It's a great relief to me to know that I can actually be creative and be happy at the same time.

JAMES W. HALL

WHEN *THE ARTIST'S WAY* was first published, I expressed a wish for Artist's Way groups to spring into being. I envisioned them as peer-run circles—"creative clusters"—where people would serve one another as believing mirrors, uniting with the common aim of creative unblocking. It was my vision that such circles would be free of charge, that anyone could assemble one, using the book as a guide and a text. Many such peer-run circles did form and many more are forming still. Such artist-to-artist, heart-to-heart help and support are the heart of *The Artist's Way* movement.

Not surprisingly, many therapists, community colleges, wellness centers, universities, and teachers soon began running facilitated Artist's Way groups, for which they charged a fee. The Artist's Way groups were led rather than simply convened. To the degree to which they adhered to the spiritual principles of creative recovery and introduced people to the use of the tools, they were—and are—valuable. Any group that starts with such a leader should, however, rapidly become autonomous, "graduating" to a peer-run, nonprofit status.

There are no "accredited" Artist's Way teachers. I chose not to franchise *The Artist's Way* but to offer it as a gift, free of charge. It is my belief that creative recovery at its best is a nonhierarchical, peer-run, collective process. In this it differs from the academic and therapeutic modes. Any professional using *The Artist's Way* should realize that autonomous, peer-run creative clusters must remain the eventual goal. Facilitated groups can serve as a sort of bridge to this end.

In my years of teaching and traveling, I have frequently encountered excellent results from peer-group clusters. On occasion, I have encountered situations where *The Artist's Way* has been unduly modified. Whenever there is a misplaced emphasis on intellectual "analysis" or therapeutic "processing," there is the risk of undermining creative unfolding. Very often, what could be interpreted as "neurosis" or a deep-seated problem is simply creative resistance.

The Artist's Way and all my other "teaching" books are experiential books. They are intended to teach people to process and transform life through acts of creativity. Both books and *all* creative clusters should be practiced through creative action, not through theory. As an artist, I know this. *The Artist's Way* and other books are the distillate of thirty years of artistic practice.

It is my belief and my experience as a teacher that all of us are healthy enough to practice creativity. It is not a dangerous endeavor requiring trained facilitators. It is our human birthright and something we can do gently and collectively. Creativity is like breathing—pointers may help, but *we do the process ourselves.* Creative clusters, where we gather as peers to develop our strength, are best regarded as tribal gatherings, where creative beings raise, celebrate, and actualize the creative power which runs through us all.

GUIDELINES

1. *Use a Twelve-Week Process with a Weekly Gathering of Two to Three Hours.* The Morning Pages and Artist Dates are required of everyone in the group, including facilitators. The exercises are done in order in the group, with everyone, including the facilitator, answering the questions and then sharing the answers in clusters of four, one chapter per week. Do not share your Morning Pages with the group or anyone else. Do not reread your Morning Pages until later in the course, if you are required to do so by your facilitator or your own inner guidance.

2. *Avoid Self-Appointed Gurus.* If there is any emissary, it is the work itself, as a collective composed of all who take the

course, at home or otherwise. Each person is equally a part of the collective, no one more than another. While there may be "teachers," facilitators who are relied on during the twelve-week period to guide others down the path, such facilitators need to be prepared to share their own material and take their own creative risks. This is a dialectic rather than a monologue—an egalitarian group process rather than a hierarchical one.

3. *Listen.* We each get what we need from the group process by sharing our own material and by listening to others. We do not need to comment on another person's sharing in order to help that person. We must refrain from trying to "fix" someone else. Each group devises a cooperative creative "song" of artistic recovery. Each group's song is unique to that group—like that of a pod or family of whales, initiating and echoing to establish their position. When listening, go around the circle without commenting unduly on what is heard. The circle, as a shape, is very important. We are intended to witness, not control, one another. When sharing exercises, clusters of four within the larger groups are important: five tends to become unwieldy in terms of time constraints; three doesn't allow for enough contrasting experience. Obviously, not all groups can be divided into equal fours. Just try to do so whenever you can.

4. *Respect One Another.* Be certain that respect and compassion are afforded equally to every member. Each person must be able to speak his own wounds and dreams. No one is to be "fixed" by another member of the group. This is a deep and powerful internal process. There is no one right way to do this. Love is important. Be kind to yourself. Be kind to one another.

5. *Expect Change in the Group Makeup.* Many people will—some will not—fulfill the twelve-week process. There is often a rebellious or fallow period after the twelve weeks, with people returning to the disciplines later. When they do, they continue to find the process unfolding within them a year, a few

years, or many years later. Many groups have a tendency to drive apart at eight to ten weeks (creative U-turns) because of the feelings of loss associated with the group's ending. Face the truth as a group; it may help you stay together.

6. *Be Autonomous.* You cannot control your own process, let alone anyone else's. Know that you will feel rebellious occasionally—that you won't want to do all of your Morning Pages and exercises at times in the twelve weeks. Relapse is okay. You cannot do this process perfectly, so relax, be kind to yourself, and hold on to your hat. Even when you feel nothing is happening, you will be changing at great velocity. This change is a deepening into your own intuition, your own creative self. The structure of the course is about safely getting across the bridge into new realms of creative spiritual awareness.

7. *Be Self-Loving.* If the facilitator feels somehow "wrong" to you, change clusters or start your own. Continually seek your own inner guidance rather than outer guidance. You are seeking to form an artist-to-artist relationship with the Great Creator. Keep gurus at bay. You have your own answers within you.

A Word to Therapists, Teachers, Writing Instructors and Other Artist's Way Group Leaders. Thank you for the wonderful work you do. While I know that many of you are using *The Artist's Way* to run groups, I hope and expect that you will go on to explore your own interests using *The Artist's Way* for your process also. I encourage you to follow your own creative vision, to strive for your own True North. You will find that the facilitation process continues your own growth experience.

I cannot state emphatically enough that *The Artist's Way* fame and path should not be used in ways that differ substantially from the Artist's Way techniques as spelled out in the book. I have tested the tools for a decade and a half in order to find them roadworthy. I ask that you refrain from presenting yourselves publicly as Artist's Way "experts," though you may use the book within your practice. I ask that you remember that the wisdom of *The Artist's Way* is a collective, nonhierarchical experience. I have heard of abuses of this principle, such as a group leader's requiring the Morning Pages to be read in the group. This is not in the spirit of the book. Facilitated groups should "graduate" into free, peer-run clusters.

A Word to Therapeutic Clients. Please remember that the book itself remains the primary source of the Artist's Way teachings, and that it is your interpretation, and your work with the book and its tools, that are central to you in your recovery. I remind you that the work is your own, not just something done under the influence of a magic teacher. Please "own" your recovery as your recovery.

Thank you. I am delighted *The Artist's Way* is used in the many contexts in which it is (such as in colleges and universities, by therapists, and by peer-run clusters). I again offer the reminder that the Artist's Way is intended to be used in keeping with the spirit of the book, as written. There is always the book itself to refer to. This is an individual's journey that may be facilitated by the group process. If you cannot find or start a group, consider you and the book to constitute one!

Pass It On. To those forming a peer-run cluster, you do not need to make the Artist's Way a moneymaking venture, for me or for you. If you follow the spiritual practice of tithing, I recommend buying the book and passing it on.

SUGGESTED READING

My experience as a teacher tells me that those who read this book are better off doing something, rather than reading another book, but I have included many of my favorites just in case you feel compelled to research further. These books represent some of the very best in their fields. To keep it simple, try to finish Artist's Way work before adding this input.

Aftel, Mandy. *The Story of Your Live—Becoming the Author of Your Experience.* New York: Simon & Schuster, 1996. Persuasive and useful.

Ban Breathnach, Sarah. *Simple Abundance.* New York: Warner Books, 1995. Grounded in my own work and expanding on it, this is a profoundly touching book.

Berendt, Joachim-Ernst. *The World Is Sound: Nada Brahma.* Rochester, VT.: Destiny Books, 1991. Eloquent and persuasive book on sound theory.

Bolles, Richard Nelson. *What Color Is Your Parachute?* Berkeley: Ten Speed Press, 1970. Whimsical and pragmatic guide to goal-setting.

Bonny, Helen. *Music and Your Mind.* Barrytown, N.Y.: Helen A. Bonny and Louis M. Savary, 1973, 1970. An explicit guide to using music as an antidote for mental and emotional pain.

Bradley, Marion Zimmer. *The Mists of Avalon.* New York: Ballantine Books, 1982. A powerfully evocative novel of female spirituality in pre-Christian England. A mesmerizing novel of goddess worship in Arthurian times.

Brande, Dorothea. *Becoming a Writer.* 1934. Reprint. Los Angeles: Jeremy P. Tarcher, 1981. The best book on writing I've ever found.

Burnham, Sophy. *A Book of Angels.* New York: Ballantine Books, 1991. An elegant, deeply felt exploration of the spiritual powers and forces at play in our lives.

Bush, Carol A. *Healing Imagery and Music.* Portland, Oreg.: Rudra Press, 1995. A profoundly useful guide to listening for healing.

Came to Believe. New York: Alcoholics Anonymous World Series, 1973. Useful and touching book about embryonic faith.

Campbell, Don G. *The Roar of Silence.* Wheaton, Ill.: The Theosophical Publishing House, 1994. Seminal book on sound healing—clear, passionate and useful. All of Campbell's many books are important and persuasive, but this one remains a primer.

Cassou, Michelle, and Steward Cubley. *Life, Paint, and Passion: Reclaiming the Magic of Spontaneous Expression.* New York: Jeremy P. Tarcher/Putnam, 1996. Passionate and experienced into-the-water book for visual artists.

Chatwin, Bruce. *Songlines.* New York: Penguin Books, 1987. An exquisite, mysterious and powerful book.

Choquette, Sonia. *The Psychic Pathway.* New York: Random House. Crown Trade Paperbacks, 1994, 1995. Safe, grounded, practical guide to opening to spiritual gifts.

Choquette, Sonia. *Your Heart's Desire.* New York: Random House. Crown Trade Paperbacks, 1997. An extremely clear, step-by-step guide for manifesting dreams as working reality.

Eisler, Raine. *The Chalice and the Blade.* San Francisco: Harper & Row Publishers, 1987. Seminal book on the differences in masculine and feminine life approaches.

Fassel, Diane. *Working Ourselves to Death.* San Francisco: HarperCollins, 1990. A strong-minded intervention for workaholic personalities.

Fox, Matthew. *Original Blessing.* Santa Fe, N.M.: Bear & Company, 1983. An important corrective book on Christian tradition; brilliant, impassioned, compassionate.

Franck, Frederick. *Zen Seeing, Zen Drawing.* New York: Bantam Books, 1993. A fine treatise on the value of "attention" in the creative life.

Gawain, Shakti. *Creative Visualization.* Mill Valley, Cal.: Whatever Publishing, 1986. Helpful in learning to create and hold a vision.

Goldberg, Bonni. *Room to Write: Daily Invitations to a Writer's Life.* New York: Jeremy P. Tarcher/Putnam, 1996. A masterfully provocative and wise writer's tool.

Goldberg, Natalie. *Writing Down the Bones.* Boston, Mass.: Shambhala Publications, 1986. The best pen-to-paper writing book ever written.

Goldman, Jonathan. *Healing Sounds: The Power of Harmonics.* Rockport, Mass.: Element Books, Inc., 1992. Powerful and gentle teaching book on sound healing techniques.

Grof, Christina, and Stanislav Grof. *The Stormy Search for the Self.* Los Angeles: Jeremy P. Tarcher, 1990. A provocative book about the misunderstanding of spiritual experience in our culture.

Harmon, Willis, and Howard Rheingold. *Higher Creativity.* Los Angeles: Jeremy P. Tarcher, 1984. A valuable and often instructive book on creativity in frontline famous authors and others.

Hart, Mickey. *Drumming at the Edge of Magic.* San Francisco: HarperCollins, 1990. A great book on music as a spiritual experience.

Heywood, Rosalind. *ESP: A Personal Memoir.* New York: E. P. Dutton & Co., Inc., 1964. A delightful book of personal encounters with higher forces.

Holmes, Ernest. *Creative Ideas.* Los Angeles: Science of Mind Communications, 1973. A tiny, powerful and important book of spiritual law as applied to creative manifestation.

James, William. *The Varieties of Religious Experience.* Boston: Mentor Books, 1902. Seminal fountainhead describing different forms of spiritual awakening, much insight into creativity as a spiritual matter.

Jeffers, Susan. *Feel the Fear and Do It Anyway.* New York: Fawcett Columbine, 1987. An into-the-water book for getting past fear.

Leonard, Jim. *Your Fondest Dream.* Cincinnati: Vivation, 1989. Another into-the-water book; many brainstorming techniques.

Lewis, C. S. *Miracles.* New York: Macmillan, 1947. Inspirational, prickly, and provocative. A challenge in open-mindedness.

Lingerman, Hal A. *The Healing Energies of Music.* Wheaton, Ill.: The Theosophical Publishing House, 1983. Excellent book on music as medicine, learned yet friendly.

London, Peter. *No More Secondhand Art: Awakening the Artist Within.* Boston: Shambhala Publications, Inc., 1989. A manifesto for personal art as process, not product.

McClellan, Randall, Ph.D. *The Healing Sources of Music.* Rockport, Mass.: Element Books, Inc., 1994. A kindly yet wide-ranging source.

Maclean, Dorothy. *To Hear the Angels Sing.* Hudson, N.Y.: Lindisfarne Press, 1990. A lovely book, a fascinating spiritual autobiography by one of the founders of Findhorn.

Mathieu, W. A. *The Listening Book: Discovering Your Own Music.* Boston: Shambhala Publications, Inc., 1991. A companionable book that demystifies music as a life path.

Matthews, Caitlin. *Singing the Soul Back Home: Shamanism in Daily Life.* Rockport, Mass.: Element Books, Inc., 1995. A wonderfully rich book for grounded spiritual practice.

Miller, Alice. *The Drama of the Gifted Child.* New York: Basic Books, 1981. Seminal book on how toxic family dynamics dampen creativity.

Nachmanovitch, Stephen. *Free Play.* Los Angeles: Jeremy P. Tarcher, 1991. A wonderful book on creative freedom.

Noble, Vicki. *Motherpeace—A Way to the Goddess Through Myth, Art, and Tarot.* San Francisco: Harper & Row Publishers, 1983. Creativity through the lens of the goddess religion.

Norwood, Robin. *Women Who Love Too Much.* Los Angeles: Jeremy P. Tarcher, 1985. Seminal work on codependency.

Peck, M. Scott. *The Road Less Traveled.* New York: Simon & Schuster, 1978. A book for early spiritual skeptics.

Shaughnessy, Susan. *Walking on Alligators.* New York: HarperCollins, 1993. A companionable, savvy guide for anyone working to appreciate the worth of process as well as product.

Sher, Barbara, with Annie Gottleib. *Wishcraft: How to Get What You Really Want.* New York: Ballantine Books, 1979. A potent, catalytic book for creative living, similar to my own work and my current thinking.

Starhawk. *The Fifth Sacred Thing.* New York: Bantam Books, 1994. Mesmerizing novel of spiritual ecology.

Starhawk. *The Spiritual Dance.* New York: Harper and Row, 1979. Brilliant on creativity and god/goddess within.

Tame, David. *The Secret Power of Music.* New York: Destiny Books, 1984. A lucid introductory overview of the healing powers of music.

Ueland, Brenda. *If You Want to Write.* 1938. St. Paul, Minn.: Schubert, 1983. The care and maintenance of the writer as a creative artist. Shrewd, personal and pragmatic.

W., Bill. *Alcoholics Anonymous: The Story of How More Than One Hundred Men Have Recovered from Alcoholism.* Akron, Ohio: Carry the Message, 1985.

Wegscheider-Cruse, Sharon. *Choicemaking: For Co-dependents, Adult Children and Spirituality Seekers.* Pompano Beach, Fla.: Health Communications, 1985. Recommended for dismantling co-dependent workaholism.

Woititz, Janet. *Home Away from Home: The Art of Self-Sabotage.* Pompano Beach, Fla.: Health Communications, 1987. Important for arresting the mechanism of aborting success.

Wright, Machaelle Small. *Behaving As If the God in All Life Mattered.* Jeffersonton, Va: Perelandra. Ltd., 1987. A spiritual autobiography about work with "earth" and other energy forms.

Special Interest

These books are intended as special help on issues that frequently block creativity.

Alcoholics Anonymous. *The Big Book.* New York: Alcoholics Anonymous World Services. Care and maintenance of a sane and sober lifestyle for alcoholic and nonalcoholic alike. Inspirational guide.

Alcoholics Anonymous. *Came to Believe.* New York: Alcoholics Anonymous World Services, 1973. Useful and touching book about embryonic faith.

The Augustine Fellowship. *Sex and Love Addicts Anonymous.* Boston: The Augustine Fellowship, Sex and Love Addicts Anonymous Fellowship-Wide Services, 1986. One of the best books on addiction. The chapters on withdrawal and building partnership should be required reading.

Beattie, Meloy. *Codependent No More.* San Francisco: Harper & Row, 1987. Excellent for breaking the virtue trap.

Cameron, Julia, and Mark Bryan. *Money Dunk, Money Sober.* New York: Ballantine Books, 1992. A hands-on toolkit for financial freedom. This book creates new language and a new lens for money management. It grew out of *The Artist's Way* because money is the most often cited block.

Hallowell, Edward M., M.D., and John J. Ratey, M.D. *Driven to Distraction.* New York: Touchstone Books/Simon & Schuster, 1994; first Touchstone edition, 1995. Invaluable book on attention deficit disorder.

Louden, Jennifer. *The Women's Comfort Book (A Self-Nurturing Guide for Restoring Balance in Your Life).* San Francisco: HarperSanFrancisco, 1992. Applicable to either sex as a practical guide to self-nurturing.

Mundis, Jerrold. *How to Get Out of Debt, Stay Out of Debt, and Live Prosperously.* New York: Bantam Books, 1990.

Osborn, Carol. *Enough Is Enough: Exploding the Myth of Having It All.* New York: G. P. Putnam's Sons, 1986. Excellent for helping dismantle the heroic workaholic personality.

INDEX

ABOUT THE AUTHOR

Julia Cameron has been an active artist for more than thirty years. She is the author of twenty-five books, both fiction and nonfiction, including *The Artist's Way, Walking in This World, The Vein of Gold, The Right to Write,* and *The Sound of Paper,* her bestselling works on the creative process. A novelist, playwright, songwriter, and poet, she has multiple credits in theater, film, and television.

©Aloma

To order call 1-800-788-6262 or visit our website at www.penguin.com

The Artist's Way
ISBN   978-1-58542-147-3 (tenth anniversary hardcover edition)
ISBN   978-1-58542-146-6 (tenth anniversary trade paper edition)
ISBN   978-0-87477-852-6 (audio, cassettes)
ISBN   978-0-14-305825-0 (audio, CDs)

Walking in This World
ISBN   978-1-58542-261-6 (trade paper)

Finding Water
ISBN   978-1-58542-463-4 (hardcover)

The Vein of Gold
ISBN   978-0-87477-879-3 (trade paper)

The Right to Write
ISBN   978-1-58542-009-4 (trade paper)

The Sound of Paper
ISBN   978-1-58542-354-5 (trade paper)

Floor Sample: A Creative Memoir
ISBN   978-1-58542-494-8 (hardcover)

Answered Prayers
ISBN   978-1-58542-351-4 (trade paper)

Heart Steps
ISBN   978-0-87477-899-1 (trade paper)

Blessings
ISBN   978-0-87477-906-6 (trade paper)

Transitions
ISBN   978-0-87477-995-0 (trade paper)

Prayers from a Nonbeliever
ISBN   978-1-58542-213-5 (hardcover)

Letters to a Young Artist
ISBN   978-1-58542-409-2 (hardcover)

How to Avoid Making Art (or Anything Else You Enjoy)
Illustrated by Elizabeth Cameron
ISBN   978-1-58542-438-2 (trade paper)

The Artist's Way Workbook
ISBN   978-1-58542-533-4 (trade paper)

The Artist's Way Morning Pages Journal
ISBN   978-0-87477-886-1 (trade paper)

The Artist's Date Book
Illustrated by Elizabeth Cameron
ISBN   978-0-87477-653-9 (trade paper)

God Is No Laughing Matter
ISBN   978-1-58542-128-2 (trade paper)

Inspirations: Meditations from The Artist's Way
ISBN   978-1-58542-102-2 (trade paper)

The Writer's Life: Insights from The Right to Write
ISBN   978-1-58542-103-9 (trade paper)